VALUABLE & VISIBLE

VALUABLE & VISIBLE

Redefining Personal Branding
by Leading with
Impact Over Image

VANESSA ERRECARTE

WILEY

Copyright © 2026 by Vanessa Errecarte. All rights reserved.

Published by John Wiley & Sons, Inc., Hoboken, New Jersey.

No part of this publication may be reproduced, stored in a retrieval system, or transmitted in any form or by any means, electronic, mechanical, photocopying, recording, scanning, or otherwise, except as permitted under Section 107 or 108 of the 1976 United States Copyright Act, without either the prior written permission of the Publisher, or authorization through payment of the appropriate per-copy fee to the Copyright Clearance Center, Inc., 222 Rosewood Drive, Danvers, MA 01923, (978) 750-8400, fax (978) 750-4470, or on the web at www.copyright.com. Requests to the Publisher for permission should be addressed to the Permissions Department, John Wiley & Sons, Inc., 111 River Street, Hoboken, NJ 07030, (201) 748-6011, fax (201) 748-6008, or online at http://www.wiley.com/go/permission.

The manufacturer's authorized representative according to the EU General Product Safety Regulation is Wiley-VCH GmbH, Boschstr. 12, 69469 Weinheim, Germany, e-mail: Product_Safety@wiley.com.

Trademarks: Wiley and the Wiley logo are trademarks or registered trademarks of John Wiley & Sons, Inc. and/or its affiliates in the United States and other countries and may not be used without written permission. All other trademarks are the property of their respective owners. John Wiley & Sons, Inc. is not associated with any product or vendor mentioned in this book.

Limit of Liability/Disclaimer of Warranty: While the publisher and the authors have used their best efforts in preparing this work, including a review of the content of the work, neither the publisher nor the authors make any representations or warranties with respect to the accuracy or completeness of the contents of this work and specifically disclaim all warranties, including without limitation any implied warranties of merchantability or fitness for a particular purpose. Certain AI systems have been used in the creation of this work. No warranty may be created or extended by sales representatives, written sales materials or promotional statements for this work. The fact that an organization, website, or product is referred to in this work as a citation and/or potential source of further information does not mean that the publisher and authors endorse the information or services the organization, website, or product may provide or recommendations it may make. This work is sold with the understanding that the publisher is not engaged in rendering professional services. The advice and strategies contained herein may not be suitable for your situation. You should consult with a specialist where appropriate. Further, readers should be aware that websites listed in this work may have changed or disappeared between when this work was written and when it is read. Neither the publisher nor authors shall be liable for any loss of profit or any other commercial damages, including but not limited to special, incidental, consequential, or other damages.

For general information on our other products and services or for technical support, please contact our Customer Care Department within the United States at (800) 762-2974, outside the United States at (317) 572-3993 or fax (317) 572-4002.

Wiley also publishes its books in a variety of electronic formats. Some content that appears in print may not be available in electronic formats. For more information about Wiley products, visit our web site at www.wiley.com.

Library of Congress Cataloging-in-Publication Data is Available:

ISBN 9781394395002 (Cloth)
ISBN 9781394395019 (ePub)
ISBN 9781394395026 (ePDF)

Cover Design: Heather Olah
Cover Images: © MOHAMMAD JEFRY/Shutterstock,
© eka julian0/Shutterstock, © mattjeacock/Getty Images
Author Photo: © 2025 Julia Aue

Printed and bound by CPI Group (UK) Ltd, Croydon, CR0 4YY

C9781394395002_160326

*To all the immensely capable people who have ever felt unseen or unsure of their voice: this book is for you.
May you feel empowered by your expertise and value, and may your path forward be guided by purpose, contribution, and meaningful visibility.*

To my students: thank you for the honor of your trust and authenticity, and for the pleasure of watching you make an impact on the world.

To Ella and Jack: may you always know your worth, embrace your courage, and lead with the kindness that's always been yours.

Contents

Introduction		*ix*
AI Disclosure		*xv*
PART I	**ESTABLISH Your Brand Vision and Audience**	**1**
Chapter 1	Redefining Personal Branding	3
Chapter 2	Your Vision, Their Breakthrough	17
Chapter 3	Audience First, Always	33
Chapter 4	Tell the TRUTH to Stop Their Scroll	47
Chapter 5	Add Relatability to the TRUTH	59
PART II	**PACKAGE Your Insights and Frameworks**	**73**
Chapter 6	Name and Claim What You Stand For	75
Chapter 7	From Digital Renter to Digital Owner	89
Chapter 8	Frameworks and Your First Thought Leadership Piece	109

PART III	**INFORM Your Audience with Impactful Content**	**123**
Chapter 9	Your Simplified Digital Funnel	125
Chapter 10	The Words That Power Your Funnel	139
Chapter 11	The FaceTime Effect	157
PART IV	**CULTIVATE a Presence That Grows and Scales with You**	**175**
Chapter 12	Should I Charge for This?	177
Chapter 13	Surprising and Uncommon Marketing Strategies	191
Chapter 14	Your Working Brand Plan	203
Chapter 15	You'll Never Be Ready. Start Anyway	215

Appendix: Fifty-Two Power Prompts for Story Lead-Ins   *227*
Notes   *231*
Acknowledgments   *243*
Author Bio   *247*
Index   *249*

Introduction

At my core, I believe that everyone deserves to be seen, heard, and considered.

I went into marketing to promote others: other people, other companies, other causes, you name it. When someone is in front of me asking to be known, to be bigger, to be more visible, I am most passionate. After all, the best ideas and breakthroughs typically come from someone who dares to put themselves out there, even if they're terrified to do so.

Putting myself out there terrifies me, too. That's why I'm happiest teaching others and working my magic behind the scenes. I hate promoting myself.

If you picked up this book, I'm willing to bet you you're in the same boat. At the very least, you probably think you aren't any good at self-promotion, and you're not even sure you *want* to be any good at it. So much of what is typically considered personal branding feels like bragging. Or worse, it feels like influencer culture: the endless pursuit of virality, follower counts, and a carefully staged lifestyle.

That's not you. You don't want to be "famous for being famous." You don't want to feel fake, shallow, or self-promotional. You want to be recognized for your expertise. You want to share something real. You want your knowledge, the lessons you've worked hard for, to matter.

You want to be useful.

I work with countless students and professionals who feel just like you. To them, the idea of building an online persona makes them cringe. They want their work to speak for itself, but in a noisy, digital-first world, that rarely happens. Why? Because, at its core, branding isn't about *telling* people what you do, it's about helping people *feel* what you do for them. It's about building relationships.

Brands sell belonging, nostalgia, rebellion, comfort. People choose between extremely similar products, like Coke and Pepsi, for example, based on how the brands make them feel.

And yet, too often when we add the word "personal" in front of branding, we strip it of that relational meaning, as if it's all about polishing résumés, listing skills, or uploading a perfectly filtered headshot. It all feels so tedious, self-promoting, and, worst of all: fake.

No wonder people hate it.

But what if personal branding wasn't about self-promotion at all? What if it was about providing value instead? What if it was about using your unique expertise to make someone else's life easier, better, or more hopeful? What if your brand was about nothing more than forging relationships with others based on the transformation you can help them achieve?

That's what this book is about: expanding personal branding beyond celebrity influencers and elite thought leaders, and making it accessible to regular, brilliant, generous everyday professionals like you. This isn't another attention-at-all-costs book that will only make you feel uncomfortable and unqualified. Instead, it's a practical, service-first approach to personal branding where your value drives natural visibility, which leads to opportunity.

Personal Branding Isn't About You

I own a marketing consulting firm in Northern California, Marketing Simplified. I specialize in creating, recreating, and growing brands. I also teach classes on branding and marketing at the University of California (UC), Davis Graduate School of Management.

It was through my work at UC Davis that a student came to me with the same frustration I hear again and again. She told me how she hated self-promotion, but also how she desperately wanted to set herself up for career opportunities after business school.

"What if I told you that personal branding really isn't about you?" I asked. "Would that be easier?"

Her shoulders loosened, and I could see the stress leave her body. I gave her some tips, which led to something much bigger: She followed my recommendations and got the opportunity she wanted. And then she made a suggestion that was, in part, responsible for this book.

"You should make this a class," she said.

And just like that, the seed was planted. I couldn't get the idea out of my head. I shared my vision for a service-first personal branding class with my dean and associate dean, and they agreed that the idea had promise. As I created the course, I quickly realized that there was a gap in the current literature for people like you and me, people yearning for a more authentic approach. When the class opened for registration, I began teaching one of just three for-credit personal branding courses I could identify within MBA programs in the United States. While that may seem like a neat claim to make, personal branding has become such a critical topic in our digital-first world that I hope many more emerge.

Today, through both the classes I teach, and my work at my marketing firm, I've been fortunate to have taught thousands of students, executives, entrepreneurs, and researchers how to brand themselves in a way that feels authentic and valuable. And in turn, they've taught me something crucial: The people who have the most unique expertise—that is, the people who *should* build their personal brands—are the least likely to pursue it. Not because they shouldn't, but because impostor syndrome, doubt, and understandable misconception over what personal branding actually could be get the better of them.

These people come from all walks of life:

- **MBA students and graduate students** who want to stand out in competitive fields without relying on generic résumés.
- **Mid-career professionals** who want to move into leadership roles or shift industries.
- **Executives** who never took the time to brand themselves but now want to become visible thought leaders.
- **Researchers and academics** who want their work to reach real-world audiences.
- **Entrepreneurs and consultants** who want to attract clients and customers without chasing cold leads.

- **Professionals in specialized industries, fields, and trades** who want to share their unique approach.
- **Undergraduates and high school graduates** who want to get a head start on creating a pull marketing effect for their job searches.

The list goes on. If you, too, are sitting on knowledge that could make someone else's life better, but you've been too humble, too busy, or too skeptical of "branding" let alone "personal branding" to share it, then this book is for you.

In the following chapters, you will learn how to sidestep the trap of endless self-promotion, and package and share your ideas in a way that feels both useful and doable. You'll understand how to build a credible professional reputation as a generous person known for providing value to others.

Welcome to the World of Service-First Personal Branding

Most books about personal branding focus on visibility: growing followers, hacking algorithms, or curating a flawless image. Others emphasize value but assume you have to wait decades to earn the title of "thought leader." But that's ridiculous: Expertise doesn't come with an age minimum.

I wrote this book to show you a third option: Service-first personal branding.

Service-first personal branding redefines what it means to be valuable and visible. It starts with identifying the surprising, counterintuitive, or niche things you already know that could help someone else. Then it teaches you how to package those insights and share them consistently, which naturally grows your presence in a way that builds credibility, not just clicks.

The approach is simple, down-to-earth, and designed for busy people. Each chapter includes time estimates, so you'll know exactly how long the tasks should take. And once you've launched your service-first personal brand, you'll only need one to three hours per week to maintain it.

What's more, plenty of people, including most of the people whose journeys I share in this book, have implemented only *part* of this framework and still enjoyed benefits from it. So feel free to start slow and focus on the lessons that feel most relevant for your goals.

And if you decide to pick up this book in a few years and build your service-first personal brand out even more? No problem. Some of the specific technical tools I mention might change as the years go by, but the strategies and practices themselves are specifically designed to be timeless, practical, and universal.

Anchoring these practices is what I call the EPIC Method, my four-step framework for building a service-first personal brand. We'll explore the basics of each step of the EPIC Method in greater detail in Chapter 1, and then we'll spend the rest of the book learning how to put these steps into action.

I've also woven in a set of real-life stories to help bring the EPIC Method to life. These stories come from the experiences of more than a dozen students and professionals, from recent graduates to executives, who have launched service-first personal brands that have touched, improved, changed, or even saved lives. By following the EPIC Method, these people have gone on to become consultants, authors, leaders, and changemakers, all by leaning into what they *already* knew and who they *already* were.

And if they can do it, so can you.

A Love Letter to the Unassuming

This book is a love letter to the unassuming.

To the earnest, the modest, the diligent, the skeptical, the people who react negatively to the word "influencer" or even what the term personal branding has become.

To you and your knowledge. You may dismiss it as nothing special, but it could be life-changing for someone else.

It's exhilarating to watch both my students' and clients' brands grow and flourish, and sad to realize that there are so many ideas that remain yet unknown from those who never take the leap. While this book offers you a formula for creating an authentic, service-first personal brand, the bravery to execute that formula comes from you.

Believe me when I say this: The world is ready for you, and you're ready to guide them.

You don't need more time, more degrees, or more confidence before you begin. You are already valuable and visible to someone and have expertise in something. Now, through this framework, you can become more valuable and more visible to more people.

Personal branding doesn't have to be shallow or exhausting. It can be a calling. Imagine how much richer the world would be if we all shared our authentic knowledge to make meaningful impact instead of curating perfection through image only.

Just think of the possibilities:

- What if something you shared changed a person's career, health, or perspective—or even their life?
- What if the difference you made for others helped you avoid finding yourself in a digital stack of hundreds of résumés to be evaluated by AI because you were recruited for the position instead?
- What if you never had to apply for a job again?
- What if your visible knowledge lined you up for a promotion sooner than you thought possible?
- What if you became a pundit or industry expert, which in turn led to consulting opportunities?
- What if you were able to start your own business?
- What if you never had to worry about where your next client came from?
- What if you pursued a secret dream you never thought was possible?
- What if you advanced research, saved a life, or changed the world?

The possibilities are endless, but they all start with you and the expertise you already have.

That's the vision behind this book, and the journey I hope to start you all on.

I'll kick off that journey in Chapter 1, but before I do, I want to share the moment that shaped my conviction more than any marketing theory ever could. It didn't come from a classroom or a client meeting. It came from a hospital room, where I clung to my then three-year-old daughter before she was wheeled away for a life-changing procedure.

It was The Hug.

AI Disclosure

ChatGPT 5.0, 5.1 and 5.2 were used to find and analyze some of the research used in *Valuable & Visible*. All recommendations were thoroughly analyzed and validated before making content adjustments.

PART I
ESTABLISH Your Brand Vision and Audience

1 | Redefining Personal Branding

It all started with The Hug.

I remember it so clearly. I hugged my daughter so tight that I could feel her heartbeat. I knew it would be a long time before I felt her heart against mine again, and I so badly wanted to stop time.

Ella was groggy from a tranquilizer and about to be wheeled away. In a few minutes, she would be put under anesthesia and hung in traction so that her orthopedic surgeon could carefully apply a plaster body cast molded to counteract severe spinal curves that had resulted from a rare form of scoliosis. Her condition was so rare, in fact, that only one in 10,000 children are affected by it.

The sun was shining brightly outside the window, promising the hot Northern California summer that was only a few weeks away. There would be no baths, showers, or swimming pools for her to cool off in that year. What would life be like? How many casts would it take? We were warned to expect a year of casting at a minimum, but probably more, with only one-day breaks every three to four months. How could I put my toddler through this? How would it affect our family, her little brother, and selfishly, the career that I loved so much?

Infantile scoliosis. Early onset scoliosis. Such simple names for a problem with only this barbaric solution. But if we didn't put her in this series of casts, her own spine might suffocate her, collapse a lung, or move her heart. I never knew a person's own bones could lead to their demise, but here we were. At that age, chest cavities just aren't big enough for a spine dueling for space with vital organs.

The next time I saw Ella, six pounds of plaster covered her thirty-pound torso. Her little heartbeat and softness had been stolen from me for months. I was angry and sad, and there was nothing I could do to escape it.

In that moment, I decided to use my social media skills to share her diagnosis with everyone who would listen and support her. I asked them to call her cast her superhero shield. I wanted her to feel empowered. She wasn't sick; her spine was just squiggly. I had grown up with a twin sister who had cancer, and I wanted desperately to give my children the carefree childhood that had been taken from me. But I worried.

I wondered whether the business world would see my vulnerability as weakness. I had always actively downplayed my role as a mother in professional settings both in-person and online, concerned it would stymie my corporate image. The year prior, I didn't take maternity leave when my son, Jack, was born because my business was growing, and I didn't want clients to think I would lose momentum.

In fact, I'll never forget how I felt when Jack was just five days old. I had just arrived at an 8 a.m. client meeting, and everyone was asking about him. I gave short answers as I tried to get down to business, so short, in fact, that the client jokingly asked me if I even liked my own child. I chuckled, but internally I thought about how desperately I loved him and missed him, how tired I was from feeding him all night, and how selfish I felt for loving my career, too. But if I said all that out loud, would I seem like less of a professional?

I think about this meeting often. The client was clearly interested in me and my growing family. I had a chance to connect with this person, human to human, and yet I deflected every opportunity to do so because I was afraid. We're taught to leave the personal at home, when really, the personal is the most interesting part of our lives: It's what reality TV is made of; it's why social media can be so addictive.

But now, here I was. The Hug had forced me to come to a reckoning that was a longtime coming. I'd just broadcasted Ella's diagnosis all over social media to make sure she felt empowered. I could no longer continue to downplay the fact that I was a woman and a mother, and on top of that, there was a terrifying voice inside of me asking whether I was really accomplishing what I'd set out to do and whether I was who I wanted to be. Yes, my marketing consulting business was rapidly growing. I'd gained several big-time clients and even made some initial hires to expand my firm. But I didn't want to merely chase clients so I could exchange the skills of my staff and my time for money: wash, rinse, repeat. I wanted to make a bigger, lasting impact.

In addition to my marketing career, my true passion has always been teaching and service. When I was a little girl, I used to line up dolls on the couch and teach them things. When I was in college, I moonlit as a fitness instructor. I've always been on at least two boards at a time, sharing knowledge to strengthen and grow organizations. And those clients I just told you about? When I worked with them, I didn't keep my methods secret. I shared.

That sharing was the very reason I started my business. I knew my marketing methods were different, generating more visibility and digital conversions than more commonplace methods, and I wanted to teach those strategies in a digestible way and on a bigger scale to any organization or professional who wanted to learn them.

But was I ready? Wouldn't it be years down the line before I had the credibility to consider myself worthy of training masses of people?

That's what I thought over those first few years. But buried underneath all the heartbreak The Hug had caused me, I found a silver lining. After that moment, I understood that life was too short, moments were too fleeting, and feel-each-other's-heartbeat hugs were too precious for me to waste my time on anything other than what mattered to me most: the people I loved and the work I felt called to do.

We'll revisit the rest of Ella's story later in the book. (Don't worry, there's a happy ending!) For now, I'll simply say this: Many of us have experienced that kind of moment, that turning point that drives us to follow our truest dreams. This was mine, and I was determined to make it count.

Over the next few months, I was a flurry of action. I started sharing my counterintuitive approach to marketing both through advice online and in workshops. I changed my company name to Marketing Simplified to better describe who I wanted to be. I developed my first corporate and individual coaching and training programs.

I built my thought leadership without expectation. I didn't focus on fame or follower count, but rather on the people I helped. I also didn't shy away from the personal, from who I was. I was a collaborator, a mentor, a believer that all things are possible. I wasn't the buttoned-up, formal, afraid-to-show-any-softness person I thought I had to be. I stopped pretending, and it felt amazing.

After a few weeks, I started getting emails from strangers who had noticed me online or taken a workshop and had an "aha" moment based on what I shared. My approach was simple, and that's what made it different. I focused my workshops and early trainings only on the most important and timeless parts of the marketing process so that anyone, from sole proprietors to large corporations, could increase their visibility through valuable, intentional, and strategic thought leadership. I then layered logical but novel earned and paid marketing strategies on top of that initial funnel to help people accelerate the process once they started getting good results.

Those emails turned into bigger success stories months down the line. The more others succeeded in their goals, dreams, and businesses, the more motivated I became. It was truly infectious.

The feedback was both illuminating and validating. People weren't only telling me that my methods were getting them good results, they commented on my relatability too, noting that my personal stories alongside my professional advice made me seem more accessible. It turns out there are humans with real lives and emotions behind every business. And as the internet gets more crowded, it's those humans, the *personal*, who differentiate brands the most. I knew this to my very core, but it took The Hug for me to practice what I preached.

There is a pragmatic reason for all this, of course. I was and am very open about the fact that, just like the accountant who saves her taxes for last, I am the marketer who saves my own marketing for last. And just like other professionals, I don't have time to take a complex approach to my own marketing.

That's why I use the same simple and efficient method that I teach for my own marketing, too. It was born out of necessity because, like you, I am pulled in many different directions. Sure, streamlining and simplicity go against the grain of the marketing profession, where a complex and layered approach is often favored, but that's exactly why I share *my* approach: A more streamlined process gets results. And next steps are easier to implement when you can clearly deduce exactly what's working versus sifting through layers and layers of dashboards from expensive pay-per-click actions that are, in the end, hard to attribute results to.

Not long after The Hug, I had a waiting list of clients, numerous offers to do paid corporate trainings, and a world-class university recruiting me to teach. I realized that I had the career I dreamt about and was living the life I wanted but thought was still twenty years away. I am writing this book for you decades earlier than I thought I would—and I'm so glad I didn't wait.

While the security of a lead funnel based on pull marketing that my personal brand has brought to my business is nice, the best part is the fulfillment that comes from helping others. The kind of fulfillment and purpose that makes an impending Monday exciting.

My most important professional mission is now to teach you to do exactly what I did: how to build a personal brand that puts service first, creating a win-win by allowing you to better the world through helping and teaching others, which will naturally boost your credibility and unlock your dreams, much sooner than you, too, otherwise imagined. For the rest of this chapter, we're going to examine why this approach is so effective and how it relates to the EPIC Method, which is the backbone of my novel, stripped-down, simple-to-implement approach to personal branding.

Wait, What?

Fear and insecurity are exactly what you should feel when you're building your brand. They're proof you're stepping into something new and important, something the world actually needs. The only danger is letting that fear stop you. That's when it becomes unintentionally selfish, and that's not who you are. The world needs your knowledge now. Start with what you know, who you are, and the impact you can already make. Service-first personal branding isn't about waiting until you feel like an expert. It's about claiming the expertise you already have and growing from there.

The Value of Service-First Personal Branding

As I mentioned in the Introduction, through my work at the UC Davis Graduate School of Management I eventually began teaching one of the first formal, for-credit MBA-level personal branding classes in the country.

In some ways, I knew that a class called Personal Branding was a tough sell. Like me, the students, researchers, academics, clients, and professionals I interact with aren't motivated by get-rich-quick schemes or becoming internet famous. Even the idea of personal branding solely for the purpose of professional gain doesn't sound quite right to people like us. We're interested in what matters, in impact.

As these professionals and academics would soon come to learn, impact over image is precisely what real personal branding is all about. When they saw the opportunity to make an impact while also gaining credibility, they got excited and started thinking about all the different groups of people they could help.

Researcher Todd Rose has noted that on platforms like X (formerly Twitter), roughly 10 percent of users create about 80 percent of the content, and those few voices tend to be the most extreme. That means most people aren't actually being heard.[1] The 90-9-1 rule is similar to this. It states that on social media and in online communities, 90 percent of people just watch. Nine percent engage occasionally. Only 1 percent post consistently.[2] When you choose to speak up with honesty, kindness, and clarity, you're doing more than sharing your perspective, you're helping fill a massive gap with something the world is desperate for: authentic, useful, human connection.

If you're reading this book, then you're no different than the people I teach, coach, and consult. You, too, have knowledge that can help people and make a difference. If you fail to make the world aware of that, it's a tragic loss, not only for your own credibility, but for all those out there who you could be helping.

This is the "valuable" side of personal branding: expertise or thought leadership you can share. Unfortunately, many of the students and clients I've encountered tend to think, as I did, that thought leadership is reserved for the top-of-industry few with years of experience, degrees, and accolades. But that's not the case. If you understand something in a way that no one else does, or if you have a unique perspective, then you already have the raw knowledge to be a thought leader.

The "visible" part is the other side of personal branding. This is the part that makes you, me, my students, and my clients shudder, and it's not hard to understand why. In the mid-2010s, building an individual online presence had become a hot topic on many social media accounts, in books, on podcasts, and among pundits. Personal branding, these so-called experts said, was the secret to becoming rich and happy. All you needed to do was master a few image-based hacks to shortcut your way to thousands of followers and build fame.

Aside from a lucky few, most failed. Why? Because they learned the wrong lesson, that personal branding should be focused on self-promotion alone to build your likes, follower count, and credibility. But if your goal is to become famous for being famous and your followers aren't coming quickly, then what other metric do you have to base your worth upon? To me and the people I work with, that pursuit feels both superficial and undesirable.

These have become the two commonly known sides of internet fame. But in the space between top-of-industry, elite thought leaders with large platforms and influencers who trade their audiences for advertising dollars, there is room for a new, refreshing way to be successful online: service-first personal branding (see Figure 1.1).

Service-first personal branding redefines what it means to be valuable and visible.

- **Valuable.** You can become a thought leader much sooner, even at the start of your career, if you focus on teaching the novel, niche, and surprising things that you already know (and that I will help you formalize as we go). It also makes you naturally visible to the people who benefit from your advice because the success they achieve when they implement your lessons naturally proves your value to them.
- **Visible.** Your stories, shared experiences with your target audience, and authenticity enhance the valuable, which builds trust and connection with those who need you most. That, in turn, boosts your credibility and unlocks professional opportunity for you,

whether that's getting recruited for your dream job, achieving a promotion, never wanting for a client or customer, becoming a pundit or consultant, and the list goes on. Your visibility is also enhanced by the people who are moved by your value and share it with others, creating a ripple effect for your visibility.

A THIRD OPTION

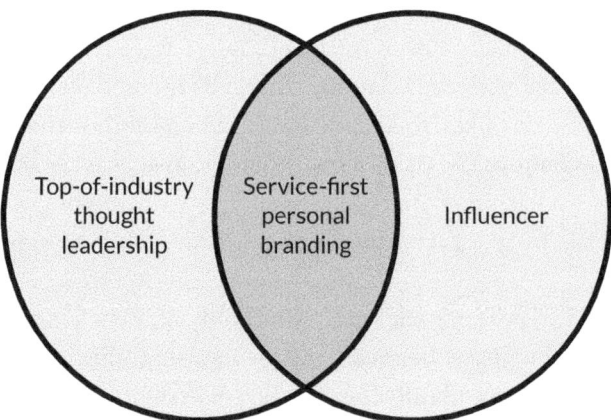

Figure 1.1 Service-first personal branding combines the importance of thought leadership and knowledge sharing with the human and relatable side of social media influencing.

In other words, you don't have to focus on viral trends or post your skincare routine on TikTok to have a successful personal brand, and you don't have to burn yourself out trying to measure your likes and follower counts. That's my promise to you.

Instead, through service-first personal branding, you get to focus on what matters to you most: the outcomes and impact you make for others, and the professional credibility and opportunity you gain along the way. Service-first personal branding combines the importance of thought leadership and knowledge sharing with the human and relatable side of social media influencing to create a space that feels right for *you*.

The EPIC Method

To teach you how to build a service-first personal brand, I've developed the four-step EPIC Method. EPIC stands for:

- **Establish.** Discover your brand purpose and clarify your vision and positioning.
- **Package.** Turn your ideas into a consistent, efficient, easily delivered virtual package.
- **Inform.** Define an insightful but uniquely personal approach to disseminating your messages to the people who need them.
- **Cultivate.** Grow your presence and manage it effectively, and possibly profitably, although that's optional.

More than a thousand professionals, university students, clients, researchers, marketers, consultants, entrepreneurs, and others with a dream have used these steps to make an impact. I have made them the backbone of this book so you can, too. Let's look at each step in more detail.

Establish

Establishing your brand is where the undoing starts. Think about your service-first personal brand not in terms of degrees or achievements, but as it relates to knowledge and points of view. What are you on a mission to enlighten others about so that they have easier lives or jobs? For instance, I wanted to liberate professionals from a complicated marketing approach and teach them how to be more successful by streamlining and doing less. What will you teach others that surprises them?

Speaking of "others": They are your ideal customers, your future audience. Brands, even the biggest corporate ones, can be surprisingly simple. At the very core of each brand is its transformational offer paired with the aspirations of its audience or ideal customer. After all, a brand without an audience or customer is just an idea. Brands that connect with those human aspirations in a credible and differentiated way gather the visibility needed to share their value.

In personal branding, this concept was lost somewhere along the way. "Personal brands" seemed to evolve into a showcase of the person behind the brand, rather than the connection to the audience and ideal customer.

The EPIC method restores the "branding" part of "personal branding" back to its roots and makes service-first personal branding about your audience instead of you. When you know your ideal customer or audience and their aspirations, you've taken an essential second step toward establishing your service-first personal brand.

Your third step is getting them to notice you. Researchers estimate that we consume over 34 gigabytes of information each day. This is equivalent to about 100,500 words every day, about the length of an average novel.[3] Talk about exhausting. No one wants to read something they've read before, our brains are too oversaturated already. To be noticed, you need a unique, scroll-stopping point of view instead. One way to accomplish this is by sharing a counterintuitive piece of knowledge or strategy, or by acknowledging a part of a problem that no one has discussed before.

By the end of Part I (Chapters 1–5), I will teach you the exact steps to follow to make sure your vision stops the scroll of your future audience. The goal is to surprise your audience in a helpful way with information they haven't heard about before, or points of view so contrary or new that they create "Wait, what?" moments (like the one I shared at the beginning of this chapter). Not only are these "Wait, what?" moments interesting and valuable, but they will also drive your brand visibility.

Package

Service-first personal brands are about sharing knowledge and ideas that your ideal customers need. The trick is to add structure and frameworks to those ideas so you're not bombarding your audience with an undifferentiated mess. Properly packaged ideas can become valuable intellectual property that can then be methodically consumed and retained.

This begs the question: Where do you store all that valuable intellectual property? Most people feel inclined to start with social media to launch their service-first personal brands, but social sites and apps are rented space. You do not own those platforms, which means that your brand depends on real estate and an audience you don't control. You need your own space online. Specifically, you need your own domain and website with an effective and easily noticed name and logo where your audience can opt in for more. Having that also adds to your credibility. In Part II (Chapters 6–8), I will walk you through all these steps in a simple and streamlined way.

Inform

Your ideal customers will typically use social media to discover your brand, but they won't pay much attention to you unless you've nailed your packaging and presentation. That's why it's so important to share your thought leadership frameworks at regular intervals. In Part III (Chapters 9–11), I will teach you a simple, consistent, and timeless social media system to inform your audience and boost visibility, from content creation to timing and everything in between.

Cultivate

Cultivating your brand is aspirational. Not everyone wants to monetize their brand or turn it into a business, but if you do, in Part IV (Chapters 12–15), I will show you how, with concentrated but impactful actions.

A Pep Talk for the Impostors

I know that you might be nervous. I know you might be counting yourself out. The thought of creating and posting with a deliberate online persona can feel scary. It's the number one objection I hear from students and clients (usually the ones with the best ideas to share).

The truth is, I'm an impostor. You're an impostor. We're all impostors. At least, we can all feel that way from time to time, especially when we share new ideas. In the following chapters, as I teach you how to create the scroll-stopping novel, counterintuitive, and surprising points of view I discussed earlier in this chapter, you will naturally feel nervous about being the "first" to say or claim something. You *should* expect to feel afraid, like an impostor, and doubtful, but that's exactly how you know you're onto something that's about to make an impact.

It's not you feeling like an impostor that's risky. It's that you might let it interfere with your responsibility to share your gifts with the world. Not to wax poetic, but what if Thomas Edison had kept his experiments with light bulbs to himself? How short would our days be? What if Erin Brockovich had kept her suspicions about cancer-causing chemicals to herself? Who else would have died a slow death of preventable cancer?

We often view knowledgeable people who hide their gifts as humble or unassuming. But what if, instead, we reframed the fear that keeps you from sharing your knowledge as something that withholds help, ideas, and opportunities from others? From that perspective, staying quiet isn't humility at all, it's unintentional selfishness, and that's definitely not you.

Instead of examining what you aren't, let's examine what you *are*. And then, let's package it and bring it to all the people who are waiting to learn from you.

Let's start today.

Here's the first thing I want you to do. Together we're going to look at the statement below and then fill in the blanks:

If only I _____ then I would _____.

In the first blank, state what you think you need to accomplish before you launch a service-first personal brand. In other words, why don't you think you're ready to start a service-first personal brand? Do you think you need another degree, another certification, or a few more years of experience?

Then, in the second blank, state the brand you ultimately want to launch.

When you're done completing the sentence, cross off the first half and focus on the second half. The first half is only holding you back from getting started, but the second half is your compass for defining your vision based on the knowledge and qualifications you already have.

Coca-Cola launched as a tonic. It didn't wait for Coke Zero. Disney launched with stories and imagination, not cruise ships, parks, and merchandise. Waiting for Coke Zero and Disney World would have been dream-killers for brands that *already* had value. That's why I encourage you to move past what you think you need in the first blank, so that you can focus on what you already have in the second blank.

Do you have something written down? Great. Now hold onto that statement. You'll need it as you begin to shape your brand in the next chapter.

Redefining Personal Branding, at a Glance

Main Idea
This chapter reclaims personal branding from being just the pursuit of fame or top-of-industry thought leadership and reframes it as a valuable, service-first tool that can be applied much earlier in your career to make a meaningful impact. It's a new approach to visibility and is anchored in purpose, credibility, empathy, and providing value to others, not merely self-promotion.

Key Takeaways
- A deeply personal story, *The Hug*, shows why our time, skills, and purpose shouldn't wait for "someday."
- Traditional personal branding models often chase followers or fame or focus only on top-of-industry thought leadership. This book offers an alternative path: *service-first personal branding*, where the measure of success is the transformation you create for others through knowledge, authenticity, and empathy.
- The EPIC Method provides a practical, four-step road map:
  - **Establish** your brand vision and audience.
  - **Package** your insights and frameworks.
  - **Inform** your audience with impactful content.
  - **Cultivate** a presence that grows and scales with you.

Your brand isn't about becoming someone else; it's about making your worth valuable to others by helping them, and in turn gaining visibility that boosts your credibility and professional opportunities.

(continued)

(*continued*)

Next Step

Identify your "second blank." What do you *really* want your service-first personal brand to be about? Start there. Leave the imposter behind. It needs to find a new friend, anyway.

How Long Will This Take?

Identifying that second blank is already in your head and heart. Take fifteen minutes to put it on paper, and we will refine it in Chapter 2.

2

Your Vision, Their Breakthrough

> It all feels so authentic because this has been my passion since the beginning. I've figured out how to scale myself, to infuse my passion into other practitioners and transform patient lives.
> —Dr. Lisa Hornick, the Dry Eye Guide

"I want to give people their lives back by improving the treatment of dry eye disease."

That's how optometrist Lisa Hornick introduced herself to my Personal Branding class. But I was puzzled.

"Don't we already have eye drops for that?" I asked.

"That's the problem," she said. Then, she proceeded to deliver a master class, in just a few sentences, regarding the nuances and misunderstandings surrounding this largely unknown medical problem.

Lisa has always wanted to make the world better. She joined the Navy, became an optometrist, and later settled at a clinic in California. But eventually, the routine of raising two boys and seeing patients day in and day out had begun to feel stifling, and it left her yearning for more. "There was only so much time in the day to be a doctor, wife, and mother, and I was filling every moment of it. Reaching my goals had never felt so. . .empty."

Sensing it was time to shake things up in her life, Lisa began attending a variety of medical conferences to learn about new treatments for dry eye disease, a condition she personally suffered from. At one such conference, surrounded by a mostly female audience, she noticed the panel on stage was all men.

A woman beside her whispered, "Why isn't there anyone on that panel who looks like us?"

Lisa thought, "Could I be the one up there? If I got up there, I could share what I know and show all the women in this field someone who actually looks like them." Once the idea entered her head, she knew there was no turning back.

Back to the moment in my class. After sharing her vision with us, Lisa went on to explain how serious dry eye disease can be, and why treating it with eye drops simply wouldn't cut it. As we learned, dry eye disease is often dismissed as minor, when in fact it can be linked to autoimmune diseases, diabetes, cancer, or even Botox.

"Would you treat diabetes or cancer with eye drops?" she asked. Some chuckled. Some didn't. Everyone listened. "Dry eye disease can get so bad that patients lose the ability to work or drive. It leads to anxiety and depression. They're passed from doctor to doctor, and no one connects the dots."

She continued: "We're on devices constantly, and as a result, even kids are getting dry eye disease."

One student nodded. "That might be happening to my kid."

At first, Lisa hesitated to build her brand around something seen as routine. "I didn't want to be the boring 'dry eye doctor.' But I knew what the disease felt like. I knew how much it was being overlooked. And I needed to speak up."

"I think I want to be the Dry Eye Guide," she told the class one day after thinking on the issue further.

No one laughed. We all smiled. "That's perfect," someone said.

I agreed. The distinction between "doctor" and "guide" may have been subtle at first glance, but it represented a complete shift of focus. Previously, Lisa had thought of her primary audience as patients with dry eye disease. However, the more she thought about it, the more she realized that the best way to reach more patients was to reach their *doctors*. By building her service-first personal brand as the Dry Eye Guide, she could do exactly that.

Reaching those doctors, however, turned out to be trickier than she thought. Lisa had already published more than a dozen articles in major journals like *Optometry Times* and *Modern Optometry*, appeared on podcasts like *Nerdy Optometrist*, been invited to speak at conferences, and contributed to the California Optometric Association. But she realized those channels weren't reaching everyday providers. Doing so could have a powerful network effect: The more doctors she could reach, the more patients she could reach as well. Even more, it allowed her to more effectively influence the followers she already had, a large portion of whom were other providers. "It really resonated with me that if I wanted to change the field, I had to break down these ideas and share them more casually online. I already had several other practitioners following me on Instagram and LinkedIn."

She began posting regularly on those platforms, not to millions, but to the right hundreds who needed her. "There was a ripple effect. The online work sped up the in-person work."

She shared personal stories too, like training for and running the Disneyland Half Marathon after fifteen years away from running. "I hope this post encourages someone to try something new," she wrote. "You'll always be better for it."

She even posted a video of herself undergoing intense pulsed light (IPL) therapy, a new and innovative dry eye disease treatment that she often spoke about at conferences and used on her own patients, for her own dry eye disease. "I don't love putting my makeup-free face on Instagram, but if it's in the name of science, I'll do it!"

She kept up the momentum, educating her followers about screen-time-related dry eyes, flagging risks tied to Botox and contact lenses, explaining three new Food and Drug Administration (FDA) approved drugs, and co-authoring a handbook on IPL therapy.

Then came the speech at UC Berkeley. "I thought the invitation was spam," she laughed. "It took me a day to click the link. Then I saw they were going to pay me a lot to speak. That was a defining moment. Berkeley, the gold standard, wanted to hear from me. *I* was the expert. Wow."

Now, speaking engagements make up over 30 percent of Lisa's income. And she only does paid appearances because she's so sought after. "It feels surreal to say that," she told me. "I could be speaking day and night."

What began with a yearning for more became a service-first personal brand. "I've figured out how to scale myself, to infuse my passion into other practitioners and transform patient lives. My goal is that no one suffers from dry eye disease without knowing there's more we can do."

Lisa had become valuable and visible at the same time.

Sometimes we take our own knowledge and strengths for granted, because they're already ours. But when you look at them through a different point of view, they become fresh and exciting, and exactly what *someone else* needs to thrive. In this chapter, I'll show you how to identify a clear, distinct service-first personal brand that not only resonates with you, but excites you, too.

> **Wait, What?**
>
> Your service-first personal brand isn't too simple, too boring, too general, or too. . . *fill in the blank*. It just needs clarity. When you frame your vision around the breakthrough it creates for others, everything changes. That's the heart of service-first personal branding.

Find Your Brand Clarity

Can you imagine if Lisa had chickened out and subscribed to the common view in her industry that dry eye disease was already solved, too boring, or too simple to focus on?

I find that students are often clouded by this kind of doubt when considering their brand vision. The fear always stems from two scenarios. One is Lisa's scenario, the fear that a concept isn't important or special enough to build a service-first personal brand around. If this is you, I can assure you that, like Lisa, some of the best brands are built around niche ideas.

Drybar, for example, started with hairstylist Alli Webb giving her friends inexpensive blowouts, driving from house to house while her kids were in school. Creating more happiness through confidence in beautiful hair at an affordable price, she said, would make the world a better place. She would sustain this, she thought, if she started a brick-and-mortar business offering just blowouts, filling a gap in the market, without the added cost and overhead of cuts and color. There are now 200 Drybar locations around the world making people happy every day.[1]

FIGS was founded by Heather Hasson and Trina Spear after Hasson noticed her nurse practitioner friend wearing uncomfortable, boxy scrubs and began prototyping a more modern, comfortable, stylish, and better-fitting alternative. When Spear joined, she left a successful private-equity career to help build the company, and together they bootstrapped the early years, personally delivering orders, meeting healthcare workers during shift changes, and operating out of their apartments while many investors dismissed the medical apparel market as too niche. Their direct-to-consumer approach, community-focused brand, and emphasis on comfort and dignity for healthcare workers fueled FIGS' rapid growth. In May 2021, FIGS became the first company led by two female co-founders to go public on the New York Stock Exchange, debuting at a valuation of approximately $4.4 billion.[2,3]

Keep going and be brave. Just like the people who were waiting to get a confidence boost from Drybar's blowouts, just like the medical professionals who were waiting go to work feeling comfortable and stylish in FIGS, and just as the optometry world was waiting for Lisa's insight to do better for dry eye disease patients, there are people out there waiting for your unique help, even if they don't know it yet. Niche ideas require bravery. Can you look past the inevitable fears that your idea isn't special or important enough for the benefit of the people waiting for you?

The second fear is that you might not have the right knowledge to build a service-first personal brand. This is also common and easily solved by what I call the Service-First Personal Brand Retreat. To help my students find brand clarity, I assign them to go on a day-long "retreat" with three distinct parts:

1. P/P self-interview for brand clarity
2. Interviews with trusted others
3. Synthesis

Most describe this experience as some combination of illuminating, difficult, fulfilling, and fun. Here's how to make the best use of your retreat time.

P/P Self-Interview for Brand Clarity

The first step is a self-interview. For this part of the process, I've designed a series of questions to make you think about your life in two domains: personal and professional.

Here's how the P/P (personal/professional) self-interview for brand clarity works:

Step 1: Answer the Following Questions as Quickly as Possible

1. How did a setback or unfortunate event turn out to be a positive learning experience for you?
2. What is one way that your life is better now than it was three to five years ago?
3. What is an experience of yours that few other people share?
4. What energizes you?
5. What exhausts you?
6. When is the last time you were deeply sad about something?
7. When is the last time you were truly happy?
8. What's one thing you wish people would ask you about? What would you tell them?
9. What's one thing you wish people would never ask you about again, and why?
10. What does Monday mean to you?
11. When is the last time you said yes when you really wished you had said no?
12. When is the last time you said no and wished you had said yes?
13. What would you do if you suddenly had an extra million dollars?
14. If you had one superpower, what would it be?
15. If you had a full month to learn something new, what would you learn?
16. What is something that you didn't learn or figure out for a very long time?
17. What is one of the worst decisions you've ever made?
18. What is one of the best, most brilliant decisions you've ever made?
19. When did you succeed at something because you Just. Never. Gave. Up?

20. What is something you would do differently if you had the chance to do it all over again?
21. When were you treated unfairly or cheated out of something?
22. Is there a time where you had to overcome a disadvantage that you were born with or into?
23. What's a way in which you just can't help but show off? Or are there a few ways you do this?
24. What is a big lifetime goal of yours that people close to you know about?
25. What secret or wild dream or ambition do you have that almost nobody knows about?
26. When did you back out of something or leave something? Why did you do it? Are you glad you did it?
27. Would you rather have 10 percent more income or four extra weeks off every year?
28. When did your life suddenly change in a big way? How did it change?
29. When did you try something for the first time? What was it?
30. In one sentence, how would your friends, family, or colleagues describe you?

Step 2: Review Your Answers Next to each of your responses, note which "domain" your answer falls into.

- The *personal* domain covers answers that revolve around family, friends, hobbies, or personal experiences.
- The *professional* domain covers answers related to work experiences or professional goals.

You may find that many answers cover both domains, and that's okay. Just label each question with both, and move on.

Step 3: Look for Overlaps Once you've answered these questions, draw a Venn diagram (as seen in Figure 2.1) with the two Ps, and note the places of overlap. Looking at your answers in a condensed, graphic form will help you get immediate clarity.

P/P OVERLAP

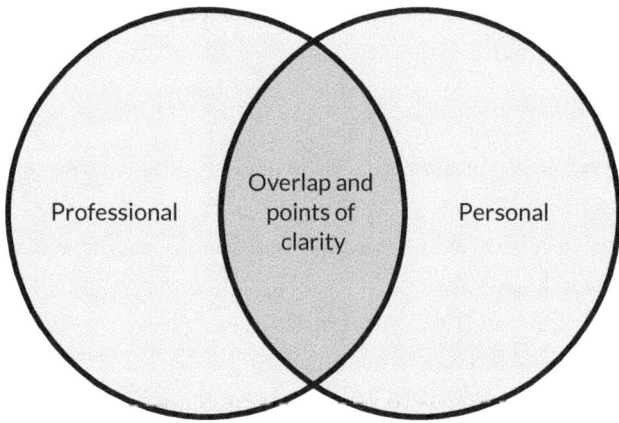

Figure 2.1 The overlap in your professional and personal endeavors often provides immediate brand clarity.

For example, Lisa found that her personal and professional domains overlapped in a few major areas. In either domain, she enjoyed educating others, holistic nutrition, and finding solutions for dry eye disease. While this may seem obvious after reading her story, this exercise was pivotal in helping Lisa realize how her personal experience with dry eye disease and her commitment to holistic health were connected to her brand clarity. "In optometry, there are several things that you can become an expert on, almost all of which are 'sexier' than dry eye disease, such as vision rehabilitation, glaucoma, or diabetic retinopathy," Lisa says. "Focusing on dry eye disease only seemed too boring or too simple before I realized how personally and professionally passionate I was about it."

After seeing the results of her self-interview, Lisa shared her epiphany with the class. "This exercise showed me the irony of my thinking," she said. "In my retreat, I had written about dry eye disease over and over again in both my personal and professional domains. That was the point where I confirmed to myself that it was anything but simple, and I owed it to my profession to talk about it."

Interviews with Trusted Others

After you find your brand clarity, the next part of your personal retreat is to reinforce that clarity. We all have blind spots about ourselves and our future service-first personal brands. The best way to get past those blind spots is to conduct interviews with "trusted others."

First, identify two close family members and two close colleagues with whom you currently work or have worked with in the past. These should be people you trust to give you honest feedback, even if some of what they say might make you uncomfortable. Then for each interview, ask them the following five questions:

1. In the time you've known me, what accomplishments or personal qualities stand out to you in a positive way? Which ones do you think I should be most proud of?
2. Are there any personal qualities or accomplishments of mine that you admire, but think that I might overlook or not give myself enough credit for?
3. What are personal growth areas you've seen me work on over time? How have you seen me improve?
4. Are there any habits, behaviors, or patterns that you think I might overlook but could benefit from recognizing?
5. Did this conversation bring up any insights that might expand or shift how I see myself?

Once you've completed your interviews, take a moment to review your participants' answers to identify common themes and observations. What about their feedback surprised you?

Synthesis: Bringing Your Self-Interview and Interviews with Trusted Others Together

After you speak to your four trusted others, you'll naturally find reinforcement between what they said and what you recorded about yourself. But not everything will align. For this last stage of your Service-First Personal Brand Retreat, I'd like you to reflect on the parts your trusted friends and colleagues told you that you *didn't* write in your self-interview.

For example, when Lisa spoke with others about her service-first personal brand, she realized through their feedback how much hope she gives to people. "My colleagues commented that by the time a patient finds me, they are usually really frustrated and fed up with their dry eye disease. Some of them have been gaslit about their condition and are really suffering. My colleagues tell me that I provide hope for those cases."

This feedback was reinforced by interviews Lisa did with close family members. "Apparently, I am a positive person who gives my family and friends hope and a confidence boost when they need it."

By conducting these interviews, not only did Lisa confirm that she was the right person to be the Dry Eye Guide, but she also learned that she should take an encouraging and hopeful point of view in the content she produces. "I always thought that the uniqueness in my approach to dry eye disease was the holistic way that I treat it and the collaboration I provide to primary care physicians about underlying conditions," Lisa says. "I hadn't thought of myself as the person who gives someone hope when they feel at the end of the road, but that's one of the parts of my brand that resonates with others the most."

Confirm Your Brand Clarity

Now that you've found both intrinsic and extrinsic clarity about your common brand themes through your P/P Self-Interview for Brand Clarity and your interviews with trusted others, I want you to think about the attributes that confirm your newfound brand clarity. There are three types of attributes that support your service-first personal brand: traditional certifications, credentials and qualifications, lived experience, and awards and accolades.

- **Traditional certifications, credentials and qualifications.** Lisa is an optometrist and has an MBA. She also has many specialty certifications in her field that qualify her to speak on dry eye disease. Her traditional credentials support her brand nicely. What are the traditional credentials that support your brand clarity?
- **Lived experience.** Lisa's lived experience also supports her brand. She is a woman looking to represent more women in her

professional field, and she also suffers from dry eye disease herself. She is generally a positive person who provides hope to patients and people in her personal life when they need it most. What is your lived experience and how does it support your brand clarity?
- **Awards and accolades.** Lisa has won several awards and is cited dozens of times in leading dry eye disease research. What are awards or accolades that support your brand clarity? If you don't have any official awards or publications, can you cite a track record of how many people you've helped, or collect testimonials?

Crafting Your Brand Statement

The final step of your Service-First Personal Brand Retreat is to turn the brand clarity that you've defined into a clear vision. In corporate branding, we use brand statements to achieve this, and I recommend it for your service-first personal brand, as well.[4] Your brand statement should be direct and clear. It's not a slogan, it's a simple, three-part internal vision statement that will serve as your brand's North Star, guiding your asset and content creation as you build your service-first personal brand.

Your brand statement might not be the same now as when you finish this book, but your first brand statement will give you a road map for refinement.

Here's the format I suggest you use for your brand statement:

> I do *[what]* for *[whom]* because *[why]*.

Lisa's brand statement could look like this:

> I provide education about dry eye disease for optometrists because I want to provide hope and treatment to more patients who are profoundly affected by a deceptive and debilitating disease.

As you write your brand statement, don't overthink it, and don't make it too long. Remember, the goal is clarity, not complexity. Follow the format above, and you should be able to contain your brand statement into a single, simple sentence.

Your Service-First Personal Brand Might Have More of One P Than the Other

Armaan Bhattal, whose story I explore in more detail in Chapter 12, looked different than my other students when he entered my Personal Branding class: He was wearing a turban, which I had rarely seen in person before.

I realized why that was the case when Armaan told me, "The Sikh culture is dying," he explained. "Young Sikh people, especially males, are embarrassed and targeted when they dress authentically. I can't imagine losing generations of cultural traditions because of this. I want to change the future through my brand." To make this vision reality, Armaan launched a Sikh clothing and lifestyle brand as a complement to his full-time job.

By trade, Armaan is a project manager; at first glance, his mission to revive and energize Sikh culture might appear completely unrelated to his work. But when Armaan sought brand clarity during his Service-First Personal Brand Retreat, he found many parallels that invigorated him.

Armaan worked at Union Pacific for three years. During that time, Armaan had been to nineteen US states, including some places he described as those that, "no one really has a reason to go to, unless you work for the railroad." In some of these places, he was racially targeted because of his cultural appearance. He was once even attacked on a plane. Armaan shared, "You might not think my personal brand is related to my profession, but through the work I do with my personal brand, I promote tolerance and diversity in the workplace. I also show my ability to motivate and lead others."

Armaan's example shows that it's okay if your brand isn't perfectly aligned professionally and personally. While Lisa Hornick hit the Venn diagram jackpot, not everyone will. In fact, your service-first personal brand might be the impetus for a business you want to launch someday. As Armaan said, "If my Sikh clothing brand grew to the point where it could be my full-time job, that would be my ultimate goal."

Which brings me to an important point: Passion is important when launching your service-first personal brand. When in doubt, go with the idea that brings you the most fulfillment, even if your Venn diagram isn't perfectly distributed between the personal and professional domains. Not only will you make a difference to those you care most about, but a service-first personal brand that isn't obviously aligned with your job will still give you a professional credibility boost.

As you embark on your personal retreat, remember that progress is more important than perfection. In fact, in Silicon Valley startups, there's an old saying, "Done is better than perfect."[5] I use this as a motivation tool for students and clients. After all, brands grow and change just as real people and relationships do. Brands, by their very definition, are the personalities of the companies they represent.[6] They make those companies relatable. If you look at any corporate brand that has been around for a long time, you will see that brand's evolution, just as you do in a human personality.

While your vision might not seem perfect right now, or you might worry that it will change in the future, it would be a shame if you let that hold you back. Armaan is trying to revive and continue an entire culture. That's important work, and I'm so glad he's willing to share his experiences along that journey.

When in Doubt, Quantify

When I asked Lisa Hornick to quantify everyone she's helped with her service-first personal brand, the ripple effect was incredible.

- She estimates that she has personally helped about 15,000 patients with dry eye disease.
- She has taught roughly 3,000 other doctors via conferences and has written in fourteen publications.
- Conservatively, she estimates that each of the articles in those publications has been read at least two hundred times.
- At time of publication, she has more than 2,800 LinkedIn followers and more than 2,000 on Instagram.
- Her YouTube videos have over a thousand views, and she's done eighteen different media and podcast interviews in the last few years. Through these efforts, she estimates that she has reached about 6,000 additional doctors.

Here's where it gets interesting. An average optometrist sees 4,000 patients per year, and based on Lisa's estimates, it's likely that 30 percent of those patients have dry eye disease. The math is simple: 6,000 doctors × 4,000 patients per doctor × 30 percent = 7.2 million dry eye patients helped *per year*.

If you ever doubt yourself or your vision, quantify who you could help. Raw estimates are a great place to start. If Lisa had abandoned her service-first personal brand vision over fears that it was too simple or too boring, as she had originally feared, she would have shortchanged millions of struggling patients per year and counting. That's the power of the service-first personal brand vision. When it's not about you but about those you can potentially help, the sense of urgency reveals itself.

It's your vision, but it's their breakthrough.

Your Vision, Their Breakthrough, at a Glance

Main Idea

This chapter explores how service-first personal brand clarity isn't about making yourself look important. Instead, it's about realizing how your expertise and lived experience can become a breakthrough for others. The story of Lisa Hornick illustrates how even a "boring" topic like dry eye disease can transform into a compelling, life-changing mission with the right clarity and commitment.

Key Takeaways
- Brand clarity begins with ownership of your unique perspective, especially when it's rooted in both personal and professional experience.
- Dr. Lisa Hornick overcame imposter syndrome and industry bias to become a nationally recognized thought leader in a niche many dismissed.
- To find brand clarity, take a guided Service-First Personal Brand Retreat, including the P/P self-interview and interviews with trusted others, to help you discover your brand's strongest themes.

- You don't need a massive following to make a massive impact. Lisa's influence spans millions of patients because of the ripple effect she creates by focusing on the right audience with the right message.
- Visibility follows value. Lisa didn't start with a viral strategy. She started with a clear mission and consistency, which earned her a platform.
- Your brand statement is your internal North Star. Use this structure to guide your clarity: I do *[what]* for *[whom]* because *[why]*.

Next Steps
Begin your Service-First Personal Brand Retreat with the P/P self-interview and the interviews with trusted others. Look for overlaps between personal passion and professional experience. Then draft your first brand statement using this prompt:

   I do [what] for [whom] because [why].

   Let this statement guide your focus as you move forward into packaging and sharing your brand.

How Long Will This Take?
P/P self-interview: Two hours
Interviews with trusted others: Three hours
P/P Venn diagram: Half hour
Brand statement: Half hour
Recommendation: Set aside one day for your self-interview and interviews with trusted others, and then set aside an hour the next day to make your P/P Venn diagram and create a brand statement.

3

Audience First, Always

> What people respond to is me being me. And if that means I don't get millions of followers, I'm okay with that. But ironically, that's what built my following anyway.
>
> —Kevin Leung

"Did we win?" Kevin asked his tribe, confused.

It was the first day of *Survivor 48*, and Kevin Leung was a member of the Vula tribe. He charged into the "marooning" challenge with determination, crawling through thick mud under a low-hanging net as his fellow tribe members raced to retrieve heavy supply chests. But just moments into the game, Kevin caught his hand awkwardly, slipped, and dislocated his shoulder, "right out of the socket," as he later recalled, with such force that he blacked out in the mud.

The producers paused the challenge as paramedics rushed in. Kevin was handed a "green whistle" (a fast-acting pain reliever), and the paramedics set his shoulder on the spot. The portion of that moment that was aired showed millions of viewers exactly who Kevin is: a tenacious, enthusiastic team player who refused to leave the show despite feeling a massive amount of pain from the injury and vomiting continuously from the pain relievers.

He was a fan favorite because of his tenacity and dedication to his team, and I saw why.

When I met Kevin in my class a couple years before his *Survivor* appearance, I noticed right away that he had an incredibly friendly and welcoming personality. He was also accomplished but completely humble, and in his own way, downright inspiring. But he hadn't always been that way.

"My life was so different growing up," Kevin says. "My parents worked so hard to finish their college degrees, work multiple jobs, and give me every chance at success. I always felt a weight to pay it back, but I was a quiet kid, shy about everything. I often wondered what other people's lives were like, so I got really into watching reality TV." When he saw an Asian American contestant win *Survivor*, Kevin made it his dream to do the same. "Ever since then, I was obsessed with getting onto *Survivor*. I just had no idea how."

Kevin eventually came out of his shell: "Through high school and college, I realized I was actually quite outgoing." He excelled as an engineering student at UC Davis, and, after graduating, Kevin eventually leveraged that degree into a promising finance career at Meta. While at Meta, he decided to continue his education, enrolling in the MBA program at UC Davis. "I was building a career at one of the world's most influential companies and excelling at a top MBA program," Kevin says. "But I still had that yearning. I love social media. I still loved reality TV."

While juggling work and graduate school, Kevin applied to and quickly was cast on the reality show *I Survived Bear Grylls*. There was just one catch: The show wanted a "fitness transformation" story. "They asked, 'Are you into fitness?' and I said, 'Absolutely!'" he recalls. It felt like it was meant to be. When they went on to ask if he had a fitness account on social media, "I said yes, even though I didn't." That night, he created the Instagram handle @KevFitness. It was spontaneous, strategic, and the beginning of his service-first personal brand.

As Kevin populated his Instagram account, he realized that his brand wasn't just about fitness, and, in fact, it never totally had been. "People didn't care about my bench routine," he says. "They cared about my energy. They cared about the joy I showed. They liked the way I talked to the camera, or the way I shared my day." His early posts, filled with Barry's Bootcamp selfies and runs for boba tea, became a way for followers to see themselves in him, especially the young Asian American men who made up a big segment of his following.

When Kevin eventually made it onto *Survivor*, it was a purpose-driven decision. "I applied to *Survivor* because I didn't see Asian American men represented on TV in a way that felt like me," he says. "We're always portrayed as the quiet, smart guy in tech. Never social, never strong, never funny. And I thought, what if I can be all of those things?"

Kevin's Instagram following surged. But for him, the numbers were never the goal. "If I really wanted to be famous, I would have played the algorithm game. I work at Instagram. I know exactly what performs," he says. "But I've always been about authenticity. I didn't want to be someone I'm not, just to go viral."

Instead, he focused on a "FaceTime approach," posting stories and videos as if he were talking directly to a friend. "What people respond to is me being me. And if that means I don't get millions of followers, I'm okay with that. But ironically, that's what built my following anyway."

What Kevin didn't expect, though, was the responsibility that would come with visibility. "Some people messaged me and said, 'You keep saying you're small and not fit, but that's not how you look.' I realized that in trying to tell my own story, I might be projecting unrealistic expectations. Becoming strong didn't happen to me overnight. That feedback really hit me," he recalls. "I stopped thinking about my brand as just Asian representation in fitness. It's about anyone who has ever felt unseen or forgotten."

Kevin now enjoys some partnerships with a few fitness brands, but more than brand deals or sponsorships, he wants to make an impact. "If someone takes the time to message me, to say they felt inspired by a post, that matters. It's not just content. It's connection."

Kevin finished his MBA at the top of his class, winning one of UC Davis's most prestigious leadership awards. As of this writing, he is still thriving in his double life: working hard at Meta and chasing his dreams. "You can have both," Kevin says. "You can fulfill your primary dreams and your ultimate dreams. And you don't have to wait to start on your ultimate dreams. You can start now."

This is the message Kevin wants to be remembered for—to break molds, just as he did. And even though he's already sharing that message far and wide through his social media presence and reality TV appearances, Kevin has no intention of stopping there. For his next act, he hopes to bring his message to young adults through speaking, coaching, and mentorship opportunities. "Whether it's a kid who's five feet tall and wants to join the wrestling team, or a college student who thinks they don't belong on a reality show, I want to be for them the person I didn't have whispering in my ear. The one who says: You can," Kevin says. "Even if I help one person feel empowered to be who they are, all of this, every post, every DM, every late night I spend editing videos is worth it."

A brand without a customer is just an idea. That's why service-first personal branding actually works. When you focus on serving an audience, you automatically build in a theme to your content and brand, rather than just posting a bunch of disjointed content. I'd like you to think about your audience as your *ideal customers*. In corporate branding, we use the term "ideal customer" to refer to the segment or segments of people we want in our brand's audience. And defining the attributes of that ideal customer is essential to your brand's success.

Why? Because as I mentioned in Chapter 1, at its core, a brand is about serving customers. Personal branding should be no different. In this chapter, I will build on why identifying your ideal customers is an essential step to building a service-first personal brand. When you maintain a relentless focus on your ideal customers' wants, needs, and desires, you will naturally cut through the online noise and become more visible by being more valuable to the people who need you.

> **Wait, What?**
>
> A brand without a customer is just an idea. A service-first personal brand isn't vague, it's focused. When you commit to serving one audience clearly, others will find their way to you, too. Impact doesn't scale by trying to appeal to everyone. It scales by deeply connecting with someone and giving them a breakthrough.

Audit Your Audience

The first step to defining your ideal customer is to audit your audience. Kevin did this organically by paying attention to the feedback he was getting from his posts. He noticed that whenever he posted "a day in the life" content, it made more of an impact than talking specifically about how he gets fit. He could tell by the direct messages (DM)s he received. "People would message me and say that my "a day in the life" content made them relate to me more as a regular person and feel like they could do it, too." This led him to reflect further on why people were following him in the first place. In his words, "People felt like they could follow their crazy dreams, too, by seeing how I was following mine." This was a big *aha* moment for Kevin, causing him to dramatically rethink the value he brought to his followers.

Kevin had the advantage of having fans from *I Survived Bear Grylls* and family and friends who already followed him as he built his Instagram account. But you can figure your audience out from scratch, reality TV bona fides not required. At the end of Chapter 2, in your brand statement, you filled in "for whom." For instance, Dr. Lisa Hornick's "for whom" answer was optometrists:

> I provide education about dry eye disease for *optometrists* because I want to provide hope and treatment to more patients who are profoundly affected by a deceptive and debilitating disease.

You might recall that Lisa took a little time to understand her audience. At first, she thought it was dry eye patients. After more reflection, though (which I will discuss later in this chapter) she made a distinction: While she ultimately wanted to help dry eye patients through her advocacy, they weren't her audience: Optometrists were.

Even if Lisa's first guess wasn't exactly right, it was close, and then her instincts got her the rest of the way there. If Lisa and Kevin can do it, so can you. Instinctively, you already know your ideal customer, or, at the very least, you have a good idea. Whatever you wrote in your "for whom" blank is probably pretty close. Now, all you need to do is validate it.

But how? In marketing, we use numerous methods to gain insight into ideal customers, including surveys, focus groups, customer immersions, sales trends, and market analysis. But my favorite way to define the ideal customer is much simpler: Call them.

According to my colleague, and entrepreneurship and innovation expert Andrew Hargadon, "You can overcomplicate consumer research, or just call a customer."[1] In his Managing Innovation course, Andrew even devotes an hour of live class time to customer calls. The result? Rich, firsthand data about what ideal customers need from your product, invention, or in your case, your service-first personal brand. This concept forever changed my mind about market research. To this day, I regularly make customer calls to make sure I am hitting the mark with the content I produce.

Customer Call Interview Script

To start, pick a person who represents the ideal customer that you described in your brand statement. The key to getting to know your ideal customer isn't just to ask them about your brand. It's to ask them about who they are, too. That's when you uncover insights, as Kevin did, that will help you to decide what kind of content your audience wants. My call script, which I can run through in an hour or less per interviewee, has twenty questions and is divided into three parts.

Part I: Basic Questions   Basic questions warm up your interviewee and give some perspective about your ideal customers' interests outside of your brand.

1. What is your family like? (Are they married/single? How many kids?)
2. What is your occupation?
3. What are your three all-time favorite books?
4. What type of music do you like/who are your favorite musicians?
5. What is your all-time favorite movie?
6. What are your favorite podcasts or blogs?
7. What are your hobbies and/or a daily/weekly ritual that makes you happy?
8. Where is your favorite vacation spot?
9. What are your favorite social media sites? How often are you on them?
10. What sites do you regularly visit on the internet?

Part II: Personal Questions Personal questions help you form content for your ideal customers that includes empathy and relatability.

1. What do you hope to be known for?
2. What are your ultimate goals for your family?
3. What is your ultimate career goal?
4. What are your biggest fears and stressors?
5. What is your biggest source of happiness?

Part III: Questions About Your Brand Questions about your brand help you figure out the specific components of your brand that your ideal customers relate to the most. Read your brand statement to your interviewee. Then, ask:

1. Why do you believe a brand like this would help you?
2. Why do you believe a brand like this wouldn't help you?
3. What is your biggest struggle related to [insert brand topic]?
4. What do you wish someone would teach you about [insert brand topic]?
5. Who do you know who might be interested in my brand? Why?

Ideal Customer Interview Reflection

Once you complete the interview, reflect on whether this person represents the ideal customer. Sometimes interviews reveal that your ideal customer isn't actually who you thought they were, and that's a great insight. It's what led Kevin to lean in on inspirational content rather than just fitness-oriented posts.

Any clarity you gain is useful, even if you learn your aim was a little off the mark. Keep talking to customers until something clicks. Through this process, you might even realize that you have two or three segments of ideal customers, like Kevin. By engaging his audience and listening to their feedback, Kevin now knows his ideal customers segment into two overlapping groups: anyone who wants to achieve an ultimate goal, and Asian men who feel boxed into stereotypes and want a different kind of example.

Your Ideal Customer Avatar

Just as your service-first personal brand statement keeps your vision and mission on track, an ideal customer avatar (ICA) can help you define your audience. In branding, a well-built ICA helps you understand your customers' needs and can help guide product, service, or content strategies.[2] ICAs are typically presented as detailed, semifictional representations of your most aligned customer, the person who benefits most from your brand and is most likely to become a loyal advocate. A strong avatar includes surface-level traits like age, gender, or income, then goes beyond that with details such as goals, frustrations, motivations, lifestyle, personality traits, and specific challenges. The goal is to understand this person so clearly that you can craft messages that speak directly to them, as if you're having a one-on-one conversation. Just like Kevin does.

Let's imagine a hypothetical ICA for Kevin's service-first personal brand.

> Eric is a 26-year-old Asian American law student about to graduate from a top-tier program. On paper, he's everything he was raised to be: disciplined, dependable, driven. He's fielded offers from respected firms, and everyone around him, including his family, professors, and peers assume he's on his way to a prestigious legal career. But what Eric really wants is to use his knowledge of the legal system to be an investigative journalist. He's not naive about how hard it will be, but the alternative, staying safe, feels even harder. On the side, Eric trains at a CrossFit studio near campus. It's the one space where he doesn't overthink everything. He follows Kevin on social media, because Kevin makes him feel like the impossible is actually possible, and as a bonus, he doesn't mind some occasional fitness inspiration.

I've included a template for you to design your own avatar once you've finished your ideal customer interviews (see Figure 3.1).

IDEAL CUSTOMER AVATAR TEMPLATE

Goals:

Name:
Gender:
Location:
Education level:
Occupation:
Annual income level:
Marital status:
Language:
Family info:

Pain points/problems:

Favorite brands, books, movies, hobbies, etc.

Sources of information:

Additional background info:

Figure 3.1 An Ideal Customer Avatar template brings your ideal customer to life and helps you think about your service-first personal brand in terms of their wants, needs, and desires.

Your Product Is Not Your Offer

Imagine you'd like to hang a canvas of a family picture. When you buy a hammer, nails, and level, what are you really buying? In marketing, we often mistake the product with the offer. Nails, hammers, and levels are *products,* and they are, frankly, boring. But a living room that feels homey because it's decorated with a sentimental picture is an *offer*. Offers represent an exciting transformation that your ideal customers and audience want. The product is simply a means to get there. When marketers focus on the product, they lose visibility. When they focus on the offer, they maximize it.

To help clarify this concept, picture a proverbial tightrope (see Figure 3.2). When your ideal customer is trying to decide which brand to follow, the promise of your offer (the transformation they receive) gives your ideal customer the courage to step out onto that tightrope and spend time researching you versus someone else. The safety net underneath is your product (your advice, credentials, etc.), which supports your offer and gives your ideal customer reason to believe that you can help them achieve their desired transformation.

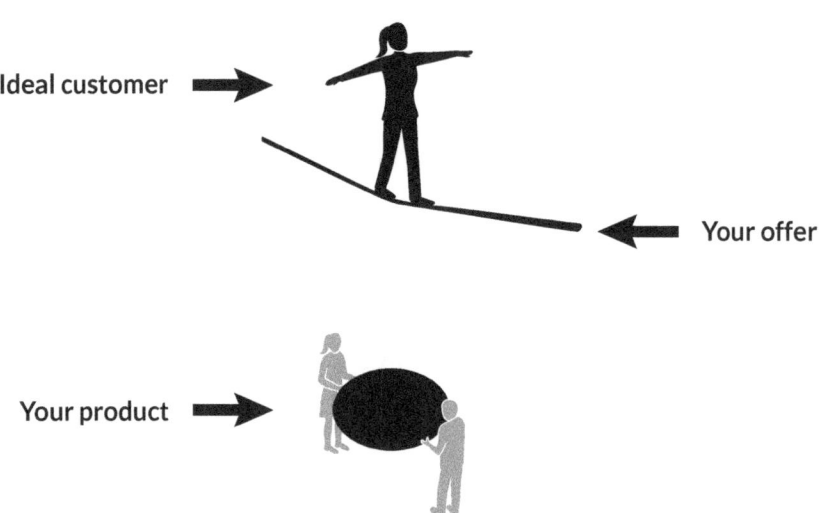

Figure 3.2   Your offer is the transformation your ideal customer seeks. Your product is the information that makes them believe your service-first personal brand can help them achieve that transformation.

I call this *information* versus *transformation*. If you focus too much on how-tos or product features, your content gets boring and information-heavy. If you balance that by talking about the ideal customer's life after they have accomplished their goal, your brand is noticed with ease.

Take Eric, for example, Kevin's ICA. Eric is trying to get the courage to follow a non-traditional career path. Kevin's offer is to provide the inspiration and bravery, through his content, that Eric needs to take next steps. That offer will help Eric notice Kevin and learn more about what he has to say. Once Eric has noticed Kevin, he might do some research and realize that Kevin not only has the right offer, but the right product. In other words, the right lived experience and qualifications to back up his offer. However, that understanding only comes after Eric first notices Kevin for the transformation he believes Kevin can help him make. In short, when you have a transformational offer, ideal customers will naturally notice and validate your product (credentials, qualifications, and lived experience), which means you get to focus on purpose instead of self-promotion. A win-win.

Dr. Lisa Hornick Realized She Had the Wrong Ideal Customer Avatar

When Lisa Hornick, the optometrist from the last chapter, set out to launch her brand, she identified her ideal customer as "dry eye disease patients." But as she did her ideal customer interviews, she realized that they didn't fit quite right. When she asked her patients about her approach of helping them integrate their care with their primary care doctors and encouraged them to seek out new treatments with their optometrists, like intense pulsed light therapy, it didn't click. It sounded either new and intimidating to them, or "been there, done that." What's more, she realized that patients weren't really following her online.

This mismatch led her to interview a second type of ideal customer: other optometrists. Lisa realized quickly that not only were other optometrists more likely to already be following her, but they also were discovering things about the topic during her ideal customer interviews. Comments like, "I had no idea," or, "Wow, this is complex," came up over and over.

Don't be afraid to search for the right ideal customer until you have the right fit. In some cases, when you change your ideal customer, you might have to change your brand statement as well. Lisa had to change the "do what" section of her brand statement from "educate about dry eye care," an objective appropriate for patients, to "educate about dry eye *treatments*," a statement that made more sense for optometrists. The shift was subtle, but important.

Understanding your ideal customer isn't just a marketing tactic, it's an act of service. When you take the time to learn who you are best positioned to help, you don't just sharpen your message, you deepen your impact. Kevin and Lisa's journeys remind us that clarity comes through action and listening, not just planning. Whether you're inspiring people who feel boxed in like Kevin, or educating peers like Lisa, your service-first personal brand becomes truly powerful when it's built around the transformation your audience seeks. Don't be afraid to adjust your path or refine your avatar. Keep listening, keep learning, and keep serving. I teach an audience-first approach because when you know who you're showing up for, everything else falls into place. After all, a brand without a customer is just an idea.

Audience First, Always, at a Glance

Main Idea
This chapter reinforces one of the most powerful truths in service-first personal branding: Your brand isn't about you, it's about who you serve. Through Kevin Leung's journey from shy kid to reality TV star and confident content creator, this chapter illustrates how visibility, impact, and momentum grow when you focus on your audience's transformation. That's what turns a service-first personal brand into movement.

Key Takeaways
- A brand without a customer is just an idea. To matter, your brand must connect with a specific, real audience: your ideal customer.

- Kevin Leung changed his brand perspective because he listened to his ideal customer's desires.
- Conducting ideal customer interviews (as Kevin did) helps you sharpen your message and adjust your focus.
- Your offer is not your product. Your product is what gives people confidence in your offer, *which is the transformation (value)* you promise to them. Your offer is what gives you visibility.
- Your ICA should be as real and specific as possible. Think: Who are they? What do they dream of? What's in their way?
- Revisit your brand statement and make sure it reflects not just your "what" and "why," but the exact person you are here to help: I do *[what]* for *[whom]* because *[why]*.

Next Step
Define your ICA using the questions from the ideal customer interview.

How Long Does This Take?
Set aside three hours to interview three ideal customers who closely align with your ICA. Then, if needed, spend a half hour analyzing how their responses reshape the *who*, and subsequently, the *what* or *why* of your brand statement.

4

Tell the TRUTH to Stop Their Scroll

> Each time I made a post, I challenged a norm. I wanted parents to realize that despite all the conflicting advice and philosophies, there are ways to succeed in feeding and raising healthy children.
> —Jennifer Anderson

"I've totally failed my child."

Dietitian Jennifer Anderson was sitting in the pediatrician's office when the doctor told her that her nine-month-old son wasn't gaining weight as expected. "Can you imagine how I felt? Here I was a dietitian, and my son was having eating problems," Jennifer says. "That moment set me on a journey researching child nutrition."

Jennifer didn't know it at the time, but this moment would be the catalyst for what would become Kids Eat in Color, a brand that's helped millions of parents find more success feeding their children. "I come from a deeply personal place when I say that I wanted to make parents feel capable again," she says.

The real problem, Jennifer explains, is that parents are given all the "right" information but none of the context to apply it. "We have all this research and all this knowledge that tells us the 'right' way to do things," she says. "And that really sets people up for failure." As parents struggle to reconcile the advice they receive with the practical realities of their lives, they worry constantly that they are messing up their kids.

"There's a tension between physical health and mental health when it comes to food. Families have a kid who weighs a lot and a kid who doesn't weigh enough. A kid they're worried might develop an eating disorder, and another who already has diabetes," Jennifer says. "So, how do you feed your kid when the food options aren't great, but you also don't want to give them a complex?"

Jennifer placed her flag right at the heart of this mismatch, building her brand on a counterintuitive insight: less perfection, more nuance. Less shame, more strategy. Less, "Here's what you're doing wrong" and more, "Here's how you can make it work."

One of the clearest examples, which I still use in my Personal Branding class slides, came from a simple Instagram post (see Figure 4.1). In it, Jennifer displays the same photo twice with two different captions: "Is your child overweight?" and "Is your child underweight?" Other than the captions, the images and the words were identical, and it stopped my scroll immediately. At the time, my kids were young and always seemed to have different eating preferences and qualms. For the first time, Jennifer's post helped me realize I could think about my kids and their eating habits at the same time and in the same way. As she had for so many other parents, Jennifer had made me feel *seen*.

How did Jennifer land on this highly effective, scroll-stopping approach?

One day she was in her kitchen, tired from food prep, thinking, "I can't be the only one who struggles with feeding children." All the research she'd done and strategies she'd tried to feed her children had consumed so many waking hours outside of her full-time job. Reflecting on this challenge, she thought, "Why not share a bit with others who may be struggling but don't have the resources I do to figure all this out?"

She began by posting photos on Instagram of her son's preschool lunchbox with short notes about exposure and food modeling. "I'd write things like, 'I introduced salad at breakfast and dinner, and now I'm putting it in his lunch. That increases the likelihood he'll eat it.'" The captions were evidence-based, but accessible.

All this work started as a hobby. Jennifer didn't set out to be an online educator. But after a year and a half of sharing, she realized that her small,

Tell the TRUTH to Stop Their Scroll

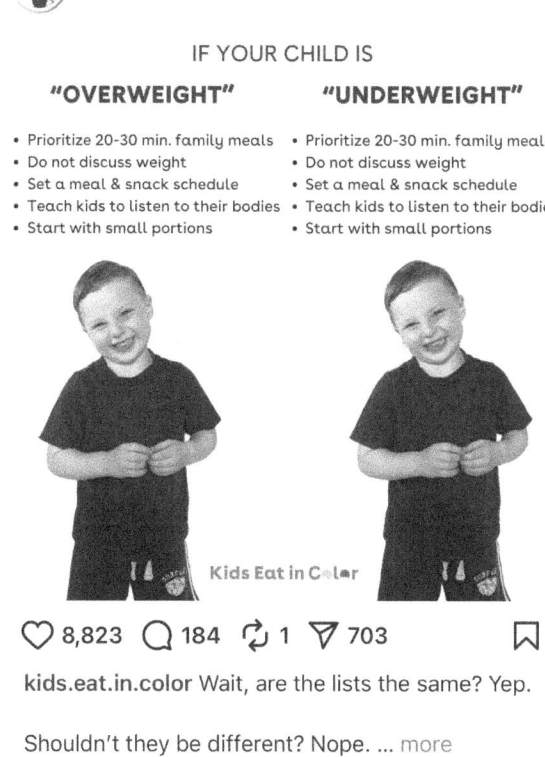

Figure 4.1 Jennifer Anderson's counterintuitive approach to her educational social media posts makes them scroll stopping.
Source: Kids Eat in Color.

actionable educational posts received the best engagement from her audience. So she started turning most of her posts into educational content with visually engaging takeaways. Her follower count jumped from 10,000 to 30,000 in a matter of months, and more importantly, her audience engagement metrics improved as well. "Each time I made a post, I challenged a norm," Jennifer says. "I wanted parents to realize that despite all the conflicting advice and philosophies, there are ways to succeed in feeding and raising healthy children."

When she asked her audience what they wanted to see more of, they overwhelmingly responded with a desire to see a meal plan. "I had a visceral reaction," Jennifer said. "I immediately thought, 'I would never make a meal plan.'"

Shortly after, though, with her son entering first grade and life getting more chaotic, she built one for herself just to stay sane. She swallowed hard and posted a poll to see if anyone else might want it. The answer, again, was a resounding yes.

Jennifer's meal plan, born of necessity, was so successful as a product that it matched her income at her full-time job for three consecutive months. With some well-deserved savings tucked away, Jennifer now had the confidence to leave her job and pursue Kids Eat in Color full-time.

From there, Jennifer launched her now-famous BetterBites® picky eating program. Eventually she developed it into a line of home-based therapeutic feeding programs to support families waiting for or looking for alternatives to clinical help, especially for conditions like avoidant/restrictive food intake disorder (ARFID) and extreme picky eating.

ARFID is a complex disorder that rarely goes into remission without clinical help. It can stem from a range of underlying factors, like a child who refuses most foods due to extreme sensory sensitivities, a child who loses her appetite entirely after a choking incident, or a child whose anxiety around vomiting leads him to avoid eating altogether, making it deeply rooted not just in behavior, but in fear, trauma, and biology.

"Kids with ARFID have true phobias about food and there is a specific way to help them achieve positive outcomes. Parents are baffled because they think they should be able to do it themselves and have often been told that their kids will grow out of it. But with true ARFID, that's nearly impossible," Jennifer says. "One mom told me after my program that her daughter, who has ARFID, ate a full meal and said, 'Mommy, I'm full,'" Jennifer recalls. "To most parents, that sounds like nothing. But for her, it was life changing. It meant her daughter was in touch with her body and feelings of both hunger and subsequent fullness. It meant healing had begun." Her work wasn't just practical. It was transformative.

What keeps Jennifer going are the messages she receives almost daily from grateful parents. "You changed my life," they write. "You helped me feed my kid without crying. You helped me undo years of guilt." One of her favorites? "You're the only parenting expert I follow because you don't make me feel bad."

That kind of feedback reminds Jennifer why she started: not to be famous, not to build a business empire, but to empower parents. "I'm not here to just give you tools," she says. "I'm here to remind you that you *can* change things. That you have power. And that feeding your child doesn't have to feel impossible. You can even feel joy at the dinner table."

Having expertise is different from being an expert. Experts are traditionally thought of in a generalist way, at the top of an entire industry. Expertise is a counterintuitive approach, different point of view, or a new idea. It doesn't have to be all-encompassing of a subject matter. If you're waiting to launch your service-first brand until you become an expert, then the audience who needs your expertise right now is missing out. In this chapter, you'll learn how to unlock that expertise by standing in your TRUTH.

> **Wait, What?**
> Your audience isn't looking for more noise and hype; they're looking for help. When you can articulately challenge a flawed belief and replace it with clarity and hope, people listen. The TRUTH framework isn't just for social media, it's for shaping powerful, persuasive communication in everything you do.

Know Your TRUTH

We rarely stop our scrolls for information we already know. Remember, we already encounter the equivalent of 100,500 words a day. No one reading a 300-page novel a day has the time or energy to be reminded of things they already know. They want the information they *need*.

It's just biology. The Reticular Activating System (RAS) is the brain's filtering system that prioritizes information aligned with our goals, emotions, or identity, explaining why we instinctively stop scrolling for content that feels personally relevant, while ignoring the rest.[1] It's a protective mechanism, designed to prevent us from getting overwhelmed and paying attention to the wrong things. It's what helps a mother ignore a blasting television commercial right in front of her but tune into cries from her baby all the way down the hall.

To gain an audience of ideal customers for your service-first personal brand, you must get past their RAS. This happens naturally when you challenge a commonly held view with a different point of view, show a counterintuitive approach, or teach a new way of doing things. Not only do such behaviors make your ideal customers stop their scroll and listen to you online, but they also make you a more powerful communicator in real life.

Many of my students don't think they have a counterintuitive point of view or a new approach. It's one of their most common objections to building a service-first personal brand. It might be yours, too. I don't want this to be what holds you back from sharing things that other people need. Listen up: If you know things and do things, you have a counterintuitive approach. You just need a strategy to tease it out. For this reason, I've developed the TRUTH framework.

T Is for Tropes

A *trope* is a commonly used theme or concept. What tropes do your ideal customers think or believe? For example:

- Most parents think or are told that picky eaters will just "grow out of it."
- Most parents think or are told that telling their child they "can't have that" will give them an eating complex forever.
- Most parents think or are told that their children falling off or rising above the growth charts means they are failures.

These are some of the many commonly held tropes about feeding children that Jennifer Anderson challenged in her Instagram content. In short, Jennifer knows that parents are told over and over again that feeding their kids is complex, conflicting, and nearly impossible.

To establish a counterintuitive point of view for your brand, you must first establish the underlying, commonly held belief—the trope—that inspired your brand. For example, Dr. Lisa Hornick challenged the common trope in her industry that dry eye disease is a simple condition with a simple solution. Kevin Leung challenged the commonly held trope that Asian men are small, studious, and quiet.

What is the commonly held trope in your industry or personal life that inspired the "I do *[what]*" section of your brand statement?

R Is for Real Problem

Despite what I just told you about commonly held beliefs, people don't respond well to being told that their beliefs are wrong.[2] The key to changing minds isn't to tell people that they're wrong for following a commonly held belief. It's to make them *come to that conclusion on their own*. If you achieve that with your ideal customers, they establish agency, or ownership, over the decision that you'd eventually like them to make: to learn more from you or to follow you.

The first step to helping your ideal customer establish this agency is to offer them the underlying or misunderstood problem inherent in the commonly held belief. Show them the *real problem*. In Jennifer's case, the real problem is that parents were inundated with information about feeding their children, but there was no actionable advice on how to implement that information in bite-sized pieces. Or as Jennifer said, "Less perfection, more nuance. Less shame, more strategy."

In Lisa's case, the real problem was that common approaches to dry eye disease only treated the symptoms of dry eye disease and not the cause. In Kevin's case, the real problem was that Asian men, or anyone who believes they can't do something, were waiting too long to realize they could be different and break out of the molds they thought they had to fit into.

What is the real or misunderstood problem underlying the commonly held belief you identified?

U Is for Understanding

After you present the real problem to your ideal customer, next present your understanding of a better approach. This goes hand-in-hand with the real problem. In fact, sometimes it's natural to state the understanding in the same sentence as the real problem. In Jennifer's case, the understanding would be that parents don't just need knowledge, they need bite-sized instruction and strategy for effectively feeding their children. Combine that with the real problem, and you get, "The real problem is that parents are inundated with conflicting and vague information about feeding their children, when they really need bite-sized instruction and strategy to succeed."

In Lisa's case, the understanding combined with the real problem was that dry eye disease is most often driven by an underlying condition that eye drops don't treat. Inadvertently ignoring that condition in favor of first-line treatments that only treat symptoms causes the disease to progress until it's debilitating. In Kevin's case, the understanding combined with the real problem is that there aren't enough role models out there representing people and telling them that they can do it, too.

How would you address the real or misunderstood problem your audience faces by presenting a better understanding or perspective?

T Is for Tested Reasoning

Once you explain the real problem and present an understanding of a better solution or perspective, then you need to back it up with tested reasoning. Is there supporting logic, data, or evidence to support your claim? For Jennifer, her own experience initially acted as evidence to support her claim, as often happens with service-first personal branding. Years later, she also has hundreds of testimonials and success stories. She also supported her information with industry-backed evidence and research that she had access to as a dietitian.

For Lisa, her personal experience, her own research, and industry evidence also backed her assertions. For Kevin, his personal experience also played the biggest role.

What tested reasoning supports your better understanding?

H Is for How to Act

After you've highlighted your counterintuitive point of view, take the opportunity to tell your ideal customers what to do next. Jennifer could say to start simple, as she did in the post I highlighted at the beginning of the chapter. One of her suggestions was, "Prioritize twenty- to thirty-minute meals." Offering a to-do for your ideal customers, especially if they try it and it works, creates trust between you and your audience. This is called reciprocity theory, a widely cited and effective persuasion strategy.[3]

You can also use a call to action (CTA) here. I will explain more about how and when to use calls to action in Chapter 9.

Lisa might ask an optometrist to rethink their perception about the complexity of dry eye disease and alert a patient's primary care physician about it. Kevin asks his ideal customers to break through barriers and stereotypes so they can start achieving their goals and dreams sooner.

How will you ask your ideal customers to act on what you inspire?

Bringing the TRUTH All Together

Let's take a look at the TRUTH framework in context. The first part of the caption accompanying the social media post Jennifer Anderson made about feeding overweight and underweight kids that I shared earlier in this chapter identifies a common trope:

> Wait, are the lists the same? Yep. Shouldn't they be different? Nope. Any child can have medical needs that will require a more individualized set of recommendations. But this is where I recommend starting with any child.[4]

It's explained simply and elegantly, and parents like me will instantly identify and stop our scrolls.

Next, Jennifer goes on to explain the real problem:

> I know how hard it can be to be concerned about a child's weight. I've been there in the doctor's office having them tell me my child had an issue. I know how easy it is to want to make my child eat or not eat something.
> Forcing kids to eat or not eat is not going to give anyone the solutions they are looking for.

Notice how Jennifer did not tell the ideal customer what to do and not to do, she simply highlighted a problem in a relatable way.

After that, she added her understanding of a better solution:

> Instead, they need to be able to decide on what they are eating,

And then she added tested reasoning by applying commonly established logic:

> but as parents we are responsible for creating a healthy mealtime environment.

Jennifer ends her caption with a CTA when she tells her audience how to act:

> If you are struggling with picky eating issues or any other eating issues, the free picky eater guide is a good place to start. DM or comment GUIDE25 and I'll send it to you.

Once you memorize the TRUTH framework, you'll be able to start inserting it into your messaging so that you'll be, literally and figuratively, scroll stopping.

Shannon McPartland's Aha Moment

When Shannon McPartland (who I'll tell you more about in Chapter 14) walked into my Personal Branding class, she wasn't sure what to expect. "I heard it was a good class," she said, "and I was intrigued by the topic." Shannon, a senior coroner technician for Sacramento County, was mystified at first by what she should choose as her service-first personal brand. Then when she considered the "real problem" component of the TRUTH framework, she had her *aha* moment.

"I assisted in identifying 18 bodies at the site of a California wildfire in 2018. As a result, all but one of those families had closure. It was one of the most fulfilling moments of my life to know that I had helped in that way." But it's not always this way; often families never get this kind of closure when a loved one goes missing.

Shannon says that people in her field often become exhausted by their jobs, perhaps for obvious reasons. This exhaustion leads to a common trope. In search of renewed satisfaction and career fulfillment, coroners and their staffs often turn to cold cases, or as she calls them, "*Dateline* cases." Part of this motivation is practical: More funding is available for coroners interested in solving cold cases, which can interfere with solving the current ones. This understanding led Shannon to identify the real problem: Exhausted coroners need the satisfaction that can come from investigating both cold cases and more recent lost body cases, *and* they need to have the funding to do both.

I share this part of Shannon's story with you because when students struggle to find brand clarity, I ask them about the real problem underlying the trope. This often leads to the *aha* moment that Shannon had with the TRUTH framework and tightens up the "I do *[what]*" portion of your brand statement.

Let's get you *your* aha moment. Take a look at the sentence below. Can you fill in the blanks?

The real problem is _____ not _____.

Now let the TRUTH flow from there.

Tell the TRUTH to Stop Their Scroll, at a Glance

Main Idea

In a world where we scroll past the equivalent of 100,500 words a day, your service-first personal brand needs to offer new information that your ideal customer has never heard before. That's what generates the perception of expertise. This chapter introduced the TRUTH framework, a tool for crafting scroll-stopping content that challenges common beliefs, builds trust, and provides transformation. Using the case study of Jennifer Anderson's journey building Kids Eat in Color, we see how powerful counterintuitive insight can be when it's rooted in tested reasoning.

Key Takeaways
- People don't stop scrolling to read the familiar; they stop for a new perspective that's transformational to them. Jennifer's breakthrough came when she voiced what millions of parents were silently feeling.
- Effective service-first personal brands often emerge from a *counterintuitive insight* or a new way to frame a common problem.

(continued)

(continued)
- The TRUTH framework helps you turn your expertise into compelling content:
  - **T**: The trope your audience believes
  - **R**: Your recognition of the real problem
  - **U**: Your understanding of a better approach
  - **T**: Your tested reasoning behind it
  - **H**: How to act on what you've shared
- Jennifer's TRUTH-driven content made parents feel seen, not shamed or overwhelmed. That emotional resonance is what sparked community, credibility, and growth.

Next Steps
Use the TRUTH framework to map out your own counterintuitive message. Start with this sentence:

> The real problem is _____, not _____.

Then revisit your service-first personal brand statement and ask yourself:

- Does it speak to a belief that needs to be challenged?
- Does it point toward a transformation people are longing for?

Refine your statement so it reflects what you stand for and who it's meant to help.

> I do [what] for [whom] because [why].

How Long Does This Take?
Set one hour aside and get specific with your TRUTH framework. Then, if needed, spend an extra fifteen to thirty minutes revising your brand statement (especially the *what*).

5

Add Relatability to the TRUTH

> I was speaking to a real pain point no one else wanted to acknowledge.
>
> —Desiree Garcia-Solano

"I want to make sure that at the most vulnerable time in someone's life, there's someone standing next to them who actually cares."

I couldn't argue with this pearl of wisdom from one of my students, especially after I learned about her life's work.

Desiree Garcia-Solano is a former embryologist with nearly a decade of lab experience. However, she got weary of living behind the scenes. "I thought I'd get to see the babies, be a part of these journeys," she says. "But we were in the background. It was sperm and eggs and transfer, and then we never saw the patient again." This transactional experience left her yearning for more. "I wanted to see the stories and not just track the data points."

Desiree has always been curious. She grew up watching her single mother struggle. "As a child, I didn't want to be a burden. I was always thinking of things I could do to help. I remember selling candy and frozen water balloons to neighbors in the summer to afford my favorite snacks without having to ask my mom for money," she says. "I've always been scrappy. And probably a little too curious."

That same curiosity led her to spot a dangerous and unnoticed pattern in the in vitro fertilization (IVF) world: When patients transfer between clinics, their embryos are often shipped as though they're just packages. "Transport companies would literally send them by FedEx," she recalls. "Embryos are incredibly fragile. Tiny shifts in temperature can destroy them."

Once Desiree was aware of this troubling blind spot, she couldn't ignore it. "I became an embryologist to give hopeful parents their ultimate gift," she says. "It really frustrated me that there were all these hidden risks patients didn't even know about."

One day, she said something in class that stopped me in my tracks. "You would never ship a baby via FedEx. But that's essentially what patients do when they transport their embryos to new clinics." Following the TRUTH model, Desiree had identified the *trope* in a powerful way. Next, she zeroed in on the *real problem,* which eventually became the impetus for her service-first personal brand. "Patients think the biggest hurdle during IVF is whether or not the pregnancy will take, but what if the embryo was damaged on a shipping journey and it affects their chances of success, and they don't even realize it?"

A conversation with her mom, who also worked at the clinic, changed everything. "She said, 'There's got to be a better way,' and I realized I knew how to create one," Desiree says. The idea became an obsession. "I know this science. I know the weak points. I knew I could create a process that would actually protect these embryos."

Desiree's business, BioMat Transport, was born out of both scientific authority and moral urgency. Rather than shipping embryo tanks through impersonal logistics systems, she personally hand-carried each embryo tank, a practice that remains in place in her company to this day. "It never leaves our sight," she explains. "We use a special logger that tracks the temperature down to negative 196 degrees Celsius, and we give the family a full report card when the embryos arrive, just as you'd want if your child went to daycare."

Taken in this context, BioMat Transport's value makes immediate sense. However, as Desiree notes, patients were unaware of the problem her service solved. "I had to find a way to educate them without terrifying them," she says. Her solution? Honesty and metaphor. "I would tell them, 'I know this is a vulnerable time, and I also know you don't realize your embryos are about to go on an uncertain journey.' And when I said, 'You would never leave your baby alone on a plane,' it always clicked. People paid attention. They felt appreciative to receive information that they would never have thought about."

That ability to see what others miss is at the core of Desiree's brand. BioMat Transport earned traction quickly through personal trust, clinical referrals, and word of mouth. "I was speaking to a real pain point no one else wanted to acknowledge," she says.

Her work, though, wasn't finished. "Even with BioMat, I didn't get the connection I craved with families. The interaction was still short." This led her to simultaneously take a job at a surrogacy agency after scaling BioMat Transport with a team. Again, her innate curiosity led her to finding more problems. "The agency I worked at was run by people who didn't treat patients or employees with any humanity. There were no systems, no empathy, no transparency. It was just about money." When a situation arose involving a surrogate's failed drug test, Desiree raised concerns about how it was being handled.

The response from her supervisor? "When you own your own company, you can make the decisions."

"Fine, I will," she thought to herself.

That push led to her next brand: Babymoon Surrogacy. "The name came from the idea that this is the couple's last calm journey before parenthood. I wanted it to feel personal and meaningful." It also encompassed a new kind of surrogacy experience that included the transparency, ethical leadership, and compassionate design she couldn't find in the existing industry. "I built the CRM system. I created every form. I designed the logo. I didn't have outside funding. It was just me and my savings," she says. "I know what's broken in this industry. I've lived it, and I want to fix it."

What needed fixing? The parent experience, the surrogate experience, and the lack of trust that plagued both. "I was the person who had to explain to a surrogate why the parents were nervous. And then explain to the parents why the surrogate hadn't texted back yet. I was the bridge."

And she didn't just build a better bridge. She began turning it into a movement. First, she created quarterly wellness webinars for surrogates. Then, she began piloting a journal for the expecting parents so they could track the pregnancy week by week. Through it all, she's trained her team to act not as gatekeepers, but as guides. "I want our parents to feel secure. I want our surrogates to feel respected. It's not about collecting a paycheck. It's about delivering a family."

What qualifies Desiree to lead in this space isn't just her technical expertise. It's her lived experience. "I grew up without money. I've watched women be overlooked. I've worked at companies where nobody listened. That's why this matters so much to me," she says. "I don't want this to be just another transaction for anyone involved."

"I look at the corners while everyone else is staring at the center of the process," she explains. "They look directly at the clinic, the embryo transfer, the baby. I'm looking at all the loose ends: the surrogate who's confused, the parent who's desperate, the missing notary, the dangerous shipping process no one should be using. That's where things fall apart. That's where I step in."

Desiree also refuses to stay still. "I'll finalize a system and already be thinking of ways to improve it," she says. "The world keeps changing. Why wouldn't we?"

That mindset powers her long-term vision. "I want to hit three hundred cases a year. I want to give parents a money-back guarantee if they don't get a baby. I want to lead the way in accountability. I want to deliver ten thousand babies and start a nonprofit because, to me, this vision is all about giving back first and foremost."

What does she hope people say about her brand? "That I advocated for them. That I believed in them. That I left them better than I found them."

Empathy and relatability are two of the most powerful ways brands connect with their audiences. However, while corporate brands struggle to create empathy and relatability because they aren't human, service-first personal brands cultivate these traits into two of their most essential superpowers. No doubt, you've experienced the power of empathy and relatability firsthand. You know right away whether you relate to someone or not. You know right away if an experience like a new restaurant is going to be good, or just okay. You may not know how to articulate it, but you just *like it better*.

Desiree never shies away from her passion for helping people become parents, a passion driven by years of witnessing their heartbreak. And yet, too many experts play down their superpowers when they should be playing them up, like I when I tried to hide my own personal journey and passion points from my clients. You might be doing the same. In this chapter, you will learn how to make your TRUTH more relatable with a little help from your AEIOUs.

> **Wait, What?**
>
> Your ideal customer isn't just looking for someone who's smart, they're looking for someone who gets it. When your story overlaps with theirs, your visibility comes naturally through relatability. That's the superpower of a service-first personal brand that corporate brands work hard to manufacture. Desiree didn't start a brand to sound impressive. She did it to right a wrong. In the process, she earned both trust and traction. If she can do it, so can you.

Adding Relatability to Expertise

In both of Desiree's business endeavors, she did a fantastic job identifying the trope, isolating the real problem, and applying it to the TRUTH framework I outlined in Chapter 4. To Desiree, the real problem in both the IVF and surrogacy industries lays on the periphery, the unseen edges. But Desiree had something else that made her customers pay top dollar for her services over her competitors: deep empathy and relatability.

Jonah Berger, a renowned persuasion theorist, argues that the ability to give someone inside information, or "social currency" is a major reason why people share information with others. Relatable emotion is another.[1] This emphasizes what I noted earlier: corporate brands work hard to create empathy and relatability for these reasons with founder's stories, symbols, and spokespeople, but it's a built-in superpower of the service-first personal brand because you already have those qualities.

My Fab Four question set is designed to help remind you of the transformation your ideal customer seeks, while pairing it with your counterintuitive, contrary, novel, or unique approach. Answer these four questions:

1. Who is your ideal customer, and what pain points or frustration are they feeling right now?

2. What transformation does your ideal customer seek to overcome those pain points?
3. What counterintuitive, novel, or surprising idea can you present to give your ideal customer that transformation?
4. How will your ideal customer feel when they complete the transformation?

If Desiree were to answer these questions, it would probably look something like this:

1. *Who is your ideal customer, and what pain points or frustration are they feeling right now?*
   Patients who are desperate to have children. They are feeling hopeless because they are experiencing infertility.
2. *What transformation does your ideal customer seek to overcome those pain points?*
   To become parents either through a successful biological pregnancy or pregnancy through a surrogate.
3. *What counterintuitive, contrary, novel, or surprising idea can you present to give your ideal customer that transformation?*
   Control what you can. There are two possible types of heartbreak during the IVF or surrogacy journey to become parents: avoidable ones and unavoidable ones. Don't let the avoidable heartbreaks of embryo transport or poorly managed surrogacy processes interfere with becoming a parent.
4. *How will your ideal customer feel when they complete the transformation?*
   Couples will know they did everything they could to keep their embryos safe at all points of their journey, even if they don't achieve pregnancy.

The answers to questions 1, 2, and 4 are the keys to empathy and relatability. Question 3 weaves in your expertise by calling out your understanding of a better solution. I created these questions because, together, they ensure that your service-first personal brand is on point and customer-focused.

Desiree has done a fantastic job of positioning her embryo transport business and surrogacy because she can answer these four questions. When she began sharing more knowledge online, this was essential to her gaining traction as a service-first personal brand.

To Be Noticed, Don't Forget Your Vowels

In corporate branding, positioning is a key component of brand success. To find a winning position in the market, brands must find a value position that no one else has, which is usually a combination of offer and price.[2] In service-first personal branding, you may not be selling a product, which means you need to establish unique positioning through offer and empathy. My AEIOUs of service-first personal branding ensure that you find the right blend. When your brand content reflects these five vowels, it stops being noise and starts becoming necessary.

A Is for Authority

Robert Cialdini, known in marketing circles as the father of persuasion theory, challenges readers of his book, *Influence,* to figure out why they look twice at a product with the sticker that reads, "As seen on TV."[3] That phrase is meaningless but generates immediate authority because in general, a person or a product has to be pretty special (or pay a lot of money) to get on TV.

Not convinced? Let me put it another way: Do you trust your doctor more when she is wearing a white coat or street clothes?

See? Symbols or statements of authority matter. Your ideal customers need to know that you are who you say you are. Use statements of authority to gain visibility.

For example, if you read the inside flap of this book or looked me up online, you know that my experience and degrees qualify me to write this book.

The key to establishing this authority is that it needs to be done immediately, upfront, and visibly.[4] This means you need to be sure to add visible credentials to your social media bios and include qualifications on social media and blog posts whenever possible.

Here's how that might read for Desiree:

> "As a qualified embryologist. . .," or
> "More than a decade of practicing embryology has taught me. . ."

Meanwhile, Jennifer Anderson, founder of Kids Eat in Color (Chapter 4), makes sure to state that she is a dietitian and a mom on all her social media bios and frequently in her content. She also leads many of her posts by saying, "As a mom and dietitian. . ."

It's not hard to do. Just focus on a few identifying words and then use them to build your authority, post after post.

E Is for Expertise

Expertise comes from presenting a counterintuitive or novel viewpoint, or a new way of doing things, just as we discussed with the TRUTH framework in Chapter 4.

If Desiree told her ideal customers that the most dangerous part of IVF is the implantation itself, or that surrogacy is a transparent and well-vetted process, she would be easy to overlook. Those are common tropes.

Instead, she warned about the peripheral risks that no one thinks about, and that only she sees through over a decade of industry experience, namely that transporting embryos safely is an overlooked yet essential part of the implantation and surrogacy process.

As I said in Chapter 4, when someone tells you something you've heard before, you simply validate your own knowledge and move on. When someone (with proper authority) tells you something you have not heard before, you regard them as an expert, which creates the scroll-stopping quality that I want your content to achieve. When Jennifer Anderson shared that parents could succeed with the same tactics to help kids with opposite types of eating issues, she showed the unique expertise that only years as a dietitian and a mom could give her.

I Is for Involvement

In Chapter 1, we defined thought leadership as an intellectual pursuit that does not need a personal element. When you add personal authenticity, you reach your sweet spot as a service-first personal brand. Part of that authenticity comes from living the struggle or repeatedly observing the struggle of your ideal customer. Through hundreds of interviews and coded personal narratives to identify recurring emotional patterns, renowned social scientist Brené Brown has proven that empathic storytelling communicates credibility and sincerity, which are building blocks to trust.[5]

In Desiree's case, she observed her own patients' struggle. She saw the heartbreak from pregnancies that didn't take. She saw how desperate couples were to find a surrogate at the end of the road. She saw how easy it was for them to miss things or get taken advantage of because they were in such a vulnerable position. Through these repeated observations, she formed a deep empathy and connection with her patients and wanted to make them feel seen, heard, and empowered.

In Jennifer Anderson's case, her involvement came from living the same struggle that her ideal customers do. Remember, she got her start because she had an underweight child, which led to her brainstorming ideas to get him to eat a better variety of healthy foods. She attained visibility and trust when she started sharing those ideas *and her own struggle* in blog-style social media posts.

O Is for Offer

Recall from Chapter 3 that your offer is distinct from your product. Your offer is where the magic happens. It's a description of how you can help your ideal customer achieve the transformation they seek. To stop an ideal customer's scroll, stay tightly focused on the offer.

Patients don't stop and take notice of what Desiree has to say just because she tells them all the details of what happens when she hand-carries embryos from clinic to clinic (her product). They notice because she tells them that she wants them to be informed of the peripheral and often invisible risks in the process so that they can get their ultimate wish: a child (her offer).

As I mentioned in the last chapter, I didn't notice Jennifer Anderson online because she shared every detail of her meal plans or recipes with me (her product). She gained visibility with me because she dared to tell me that mealtimes with my kids could be simple and enjoyable, even though my children are two different types of eaters (her offer).

U Is for Understanding

Not only do ideal customers need to hear your offer, they need to understand it. This is perhaps our greatest challenge as marketers: getting our ideal customers to think what we want them to think.

Many thought leaders and marketers try to establish this by having their ideal consumers imagine something in the future, but that's risky. For instance, if Desiree tells her ideal customers to imagine how heartbreaking it would feel not to achieve a pregnancy due to factors in the transport process that they could have changed, that may not register because her patients haven't been in that position before. But if she asks them to remember how empowering it felt the last time they took control of something in their lives, then they have something concrete to recall. From that point, she can explain the peripheral parts of the IVF process that they can control, like embryo transport, knowing she has guided her customers toward the right mindset to truly understand her offer.

I can't tell you how many times I've seen brands ask me to, "imagine being healthier than ever," or to, "imagine having more money than you ever thought possible." As a consumer, I can't really imagine those things because I've never experienced them. As a marketer, I lose a lot of control over how my ideal customers interpret my message when I ask them to imagine the abstract. Instead, always have your ideal customer reference concrete feelings to orient them to the point of view you want them to have.

An example of how Jennifer does this is when she captions an Instagram reel[6]:

> POV (point of view) inside your head: Listening to someone tell you their child was never a picky eater like yours because they did baby-led weaning and never fed their child a special meal. LIKE this post if you've ever felt judged by other parents. Complex picky eating and complex feeding are HARD. I recognize how hard you are working and how much of a drain it is on you. As a professional in this area, I'd also like to let you know it's not your fault. There are a lot of things that go into complex picky eating. If you want your picky child to get on the road to eating more foods, I'd love for you to get my free 14-page picky eater guide. It's so helpful. DM or comment GUIDE25 and I'll DM it to you. If you have a complex picky eater, it won't fix your problem overnight, but it can get you started with some best practices!

For purposes of explanation, baby-led weaning is a feeding concept where parents feed a baby small amounts of whatever they themselves are eating. If you have a picky eater like I did, your child may starve before they adapt to this method. When Jennifer called this out, I imagined what I felt like when my daughter was a toddler and all the other parents were talking about their kids eating bites of salmon while mine was (maybe) accepting a few slurps of baby food from a pouch. I felt like a failure in those conversations, and I knew Jennifer understood that because she asked me to imagine that concrete moment I had already experienced. Her understanding established my emotional connection with her and helped me trust her.

> **Making the AEIOUs Work for You**
>
> Think of my Fab Four question set as a must-do to position your brand, and the AEIOU question set as the cherry on top. If you can answer the five questions below about your service-first personal brand, you will have all the ingredients to make your value visible and relatable:
>
> 1. What qualifies you to help your ideal customer overcome their pain points? *(Authority)*
> 2. How is your solution to their pain points different from everyone else's? *(Expertise)*
> 3. In what ways can you relate to your ideal customer through lived experience or observation? *(Involvement)*
> 4. What transformation will your expertise provide to your ideal customer? *(Offer)*
> 5. How will your ideal customer's life or situation change when they make that transformation? *(Understanding)*

Outcomes

Until this point, you may not have thought of yourself as a valuable expert, but now that you've established your edge, don't turn back. Great positioning can make your subsequent marketing easier and more powerful.

But another reason it's one of my favorite parts of service-first personal branding is because it's where you inevitably realize that you have something to share that nobody else does. It's impossible to copy authenticity. That value is a gift to the world that's tough to hold back.

Just think of how many patients may have faced further disappointment had Desiree held her knowledge back. What about all the parents who would still dread mealtime had Jennifer held back?

Don't hoard your value. Make it visible to the people who need you. Pair your offer with the empathy and relatability that helps them trust you.

Add Relatability to the TRUTH, at a Glance

Main Idea
You can't build trust with credentials alone. This chapter explores how *relatability*, combined with expertise, turns a good service-first personal brand into a transformational one. Through the story of Desiree Garcia-Solano, we see how lived experience, emotional clarity, and deep empathy allow a brand to stand out, solve overlooked problems, and serve people powerfully at their most vulnerable.

Key Takeaways
- Desiree's authority as an embryologist gave her credibility, but her visibility came from addressing hidden pain points and her shared struggle with patients that no one else was talking about.
- Relatability + Expertise = Trust.
- Two tools for standout positioning:
  - The Fab Four questions define your offer and relatability and reinforce your expertise.
  - The AEIOUs of service-first personal branding (Authority, Expertise, Involvement, Offer, Understanding) strengthen trust and resonance with your ideal customers.

Next Steps

Use the Fab Four question set to refine your message and shape your brand statement.

Ask yourself:

1. Who do I serve and what pain are they feeling?
2. What transformation do they want?
3. What surprising insight or method can I offer to help them?
4. What *specific feeling* will they experience when they reach the transformation?

Then run it through the AEIOUs to enhance your offer and content.

How Long Does This Take?

Set a half hour aside to go through the Fab Four question set to ensure relatability to your ideal customer. Take an extra hour to solidify that relatability with the AEIOUs.

PART II
PACKAGE Your Insights and Frameworks

6 | Name and Claim What You Stand For

> In my head I always thought logo creation was this big thing, where you involve a big marketing team and all this stuff. But as you showed me, just get started, mess around with it. See what happens.
>
> —Eddie Ramirez

"There was a specific moment in third grade when I realized others saw me as different for being Mexican," Eddie Ramirez says.

Like many first-generation American kids, Eddie Ramirez always felt like he lived a life split down the middle. "Once, kids at school made me go through a bunch of 'tests' to be in their friend group. The last one was a race. And I actually won." Just as Eddie believed he'd made it in, one boy turned to him and said, "You can't be in our group. You're Mexican."

Eddie spent the next several years rejecting his heritage in order to fit in. When he was a young adult, the death of his grandmother reset his path. "I realized that my culture is something I should appreciate more," he says. "I knew I had to learn more about it and become more involved."

This shift in perspective became especially apparent through one of Eddie's great passions: photography. From portraits, to landscapes, to traditional Mexican food, Eddie uses photography to tell rich, nuanced stories that always leave the viewer intrigued. And yet, despite his talent, Eddie came to my class frustrated by his inability to build a compelling photography brand. "I found myself drowning in a sea of Instagram reels and TikTok dances," Eddie says. "There had to be another way."

As we explored Eddie's brand, I was instantly moved by its breadth. Eddie wasn't just a photographer, he was an aggregator, a platform builder, a creator of community. "Could you lean into that?" I asked him.

"That was a realization," Eddie says. "My goal through storytelling could be to build people in my community up, and to do the same for anyone who is straddling cultures, moving to a new city, or trying to hang onto who they are while stepping into something new."

Precisely.

We often think of naming brands as an exercise in brainstorming and analysis. For Eddie, it was more like soul work. "I started by thinking, what's a blend of both Spanish and English, but still something that most people could relate to?"

As Eddie narrowed his focus and thought about what he was really offering, the idea became clear: "I'm someone who's now getting more and more into cooking and being comfortable with cooking. Cooking and eating are symbolic ways that people come together across cultures and enjoy each other. I thought it would be a good thing to reference in my business name because I wanted cooking to also become a big part of my platform."

Out of all the words he brainstormed, *sabor* stuck with him for the way it could take on multiple meanings. In Spanish, *sabor* means *flavor* or *taste*, while in English, it sounds an awful lot like *savor*. "All of those associations felt right to me," Eddie says.

To balance out the Spanish *sabor*, Eddie says, "I needed an English word. *Soul* came to me immediately because it describes something that we all have. Something that ties us all together is that soul. And it's very powerful. I think it's something we need to tap into a little bit more."

When he put the two words together, he got Sabor y Soul. It fit his offer perfectly, not just in terms of food and photos, but in terms of the voice, perspective, stories, and pride that had taken him decades to fully own. To Eddie, the name wasn't about being catchy. "It was about being authentic and true, but it did end up pretty catchy in my opinion," Eddie says.

Next, Eddie set out to symbolize the name with a logo. Like most people starting a service-first personal brand who haven't spent years in the marketing field, Eddie didn't have a design background, but he used what skills he had along with curiosity and simple tools. "In my head, I always thought logo creation was this big thing, where you involve a big marketing team and all this stuff," Eddie says. "But as you showed me, just get started, mess around with it. See what happens."

Eddie used templates in Canva to experiment and iterate. "I ended up having, I don't know, maybe fifteen different drafts before I actually ended up picking the one I felt was good."

The final logo is a blend of simplicity and symbolism. "I've always liked things that are fairly simple, but I knew I needed some imagery beyond just the fonts. I ended up adding a camera and a pot into the logo to represent two things that are both very important to me but also powerful for everyone in the way they tell stories and bring us all together."

Sabor y Soul formalized the concept that Eddie has been exploring for years. Finally, his service-first personal brand was born, creating, as Eddie says, "a place for people to feel seen and empowered for who they are."

Eddie's service-first personal brand has also helped him in his day job in admissions at UC Davis. "I'm not just trying to sell them [prospective students] a university. I talk about the experience they're going to get. I connect with students on a whole other level by sharing my story. Their families are less afraid about whether or not their kids will be happy here. Sabor y Soul shows us that we are all different, but we are all the same, regardless of where we come from."

What do you want your name and logo to represent about you? How do you want people to feel when they encounter your service-first personal brand? Your brand name and logo represent the genesis of your service-first personal brand. As the saying goes, when you name it, you claim it. A good name and logo build credibility and authority for your service-first personal brand. In this chapter, you'll learn how to get the clarity and ownership necessary to make these important decisions so you can move forward and launch with confidence.

> **Wait, What?**
>
> Trying to design, wait for, or find the "perfect" name or logo for your brand is only hurting you and the audience waiting for you to share your expertise with them and make their lives better. It will slow or stop your launch for as long as you chase it. I know the stakes feel high because your service-first personal brand feels very personal. But what if I told you that your need for perfection is damaging your brand?

Naming Your Brand Isn't as Daunting as You Think

It's really not, and I don't want it to be a hang-up for you. I've noticed many people struggle through the process of picking a name for their service-first personal brands because the stakes feel so high. After all, it's personal. What's more, before this moment, your brand was simply an exciting idea, but now it's getting real.

For all these reasons, you'll want to make your brand name and logo perfect the first time. But perfection is impossible to achieve, and the pursuit of perfection can actually be damaging to your brand.

In corporate branding, when a company updates major parts of its identity like its name, logo, or overall look and feel to reflect how it has grown or changed, it's called a rebrand. Studies in leading marketing and finance journals show that when companies rebrand thoughtfully, the move often pays off. Investors tend to respond positively to rebranding announcements, and companies that make strategic identity changes frequently see stronger long-term stock performance.[1,2,3] Research also shows that rebrands can refresh how customers see a company, strengthen loyalty, and attract new audiences, especially when the new identity feels like a natural evolution of what people already trust.[4]

Of course, this upside isn't automatic. A rebrand that feels confusing, cosmetic, or out of step with what customers value can fall flat.[5] But the larger point is this: brands are meant to evolve. Treating your name or logo as permanent can keep you from adapting, signaling progress, and reinvesting in the trust you've built.[6] Look at the logo history of almost any major

APPLE LOGO EVOLUTION

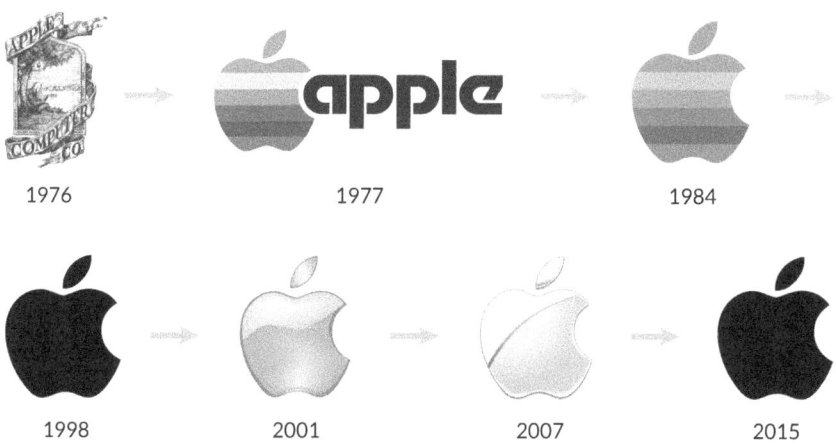

Figure 6.1 Apple has rebranded its logo multiple times since its initial launch.[7]

company, like Apple, and you'll see a timeline of refinements (Figure 6.1). Each shift is an opportunity to reintroduce the brand and strengthen its connection with the people it serves.

Don't let the quest for perfection paralyze you. It will not only be a fruitless pursuit, but it will delay you in getting your service-first brand into the world. Methodically name and launch your brand step-by-step instead.

Three Types of Brand Names

I recommend three options to name your service-first personal brand: descriptive, connotative, or surname-based. Let's take a closer look at all three.

Descriptive

A *descriptive name* implies brand function in the actual brand name. If Eddie had called himself something like Soul Photography, for example, that would have been a descriptive name. It might not be the flashiest choice (and it might have already been taken, based on a quick web search), but it does have some distinct advantages. As I've noted a few times throughout the book, we're inundated with the equivalent of 100,500 words a day. In a world that noisy, many people won't sit around and contemplate what a brand means. Worse, they might hastily make the wrong interpretation. A descriptive name solves that risk by spelling things out. It also helps with search engine optimization (SEO) and solves some marketing problems right out of the gate. You don't have to spend time and resources educating your audience on what you do; it's right there in the name.

The downside? It can be limiting. If Eddie had named his brand Soul Photography, he might have been boxed into a narrow category, skipping over the broader sense of platform, perspective, and shared experience that's so central to his service-first personal brand's identity.

Connotative

In contrast to a descriptive name, a *connotative name* works through implication and emotional resonance rather than literal description. It doesn't tell you what the brand is; it hints at what the brand feels like. Sabor y Soul is a connotative name. It doesn't describe Eddie's services, but rather evokes the culture, depth, and story behind them.

Connotative names can be powerful because they leave room for evolution. They allow your brand to grow with you, rather than locking you into a single product or service. They're often more emotionally compelling, which makes them especially useful for lifestyle products or mission-driven work.

But that freedom comes with a trade-off: Connotative names can be misunderstood. If the meaning isn't immediately clear, or if the associations don't land the way you want them to among your ideal customers, you may have to work harder to educate your audience. When the name implies part of the story but leaves it up to the consumer to identify the rest, your marketing has to carry more weight.[8]

Surname

A surname-based brand is a third option for naming a service-first personal brand. If you have a unique surname, then adapting it for your brand name would help you stand out and be difficult to replicate. It also puts your expertise, your story, and your reputation at the center of the brand, which is especially powerful because service-first personal brands are built on trust, thought leadership, and authenticity. People don't need to decode meaning, they just need to remember what you stand for.

A surname can also be an alias, pen name, or a "doing business as" (DBA) name if you want a layer of anonymity. For example, as a teenager, Eddie Ramirez felt self-conscious about his last name because it symbolized his Mexican American heritage, which he felt often drew unwanted assumptions and biases. Looking for a fresh identity, he adopted "Monix" from a character in the film *Semi-Pro*, which felt neutral and distinct, and did business with this name until he rebranded to Sabor y Soul.

As with descriptive and connotative names, surnames also come with trade-offs. If your name is very common, you risk blending in. If your name is unusually complex, it might be hard for others to remember it. And like connotative names, surname brands require more storytelling and marketing to make the meaning of your brand clear to your audience.

Now that you know the types of brand names and their pros and cons, decide which appeals most to you, and "WIP up your brand name."

WIP Up Your Brand Name

If you've chosen a surname for your service-first personal brand and don't want any other words to go with it—for instance, if I just named my business "Errecarte" instead of "Marketing Simplified—then you can skip this section. Otherwise, you'll need to create your brand name by focusing on *words*, *integration*, and *practicality* (WIP).

Words

The first step is all about finding *words,* descriptive or connotative. This is the raw material you'll build your brand name from, so think of it as workshopping ideas, not nailing things down. Start this step by brainstorming everything that describes what you do, how you do it, who you serve, and what makes your work different. Include emotional words, industry terms, metaphors, and even colors or cultural references. You can also explore other languages, as Eddie did. AI tools are helpful for generating ideas at this stage, as are sites like Thesaurus.com or WordHippo.

I recommend generating an initial list of words so long that you are sick of your own ideas. Specifically, list at least forty words. The point right now is quantity over quality because it gets the emotion out of the process and forces you to look deeper than your obvious first instincts. Once you have your longer-than-you-ever-thought-possible list, narrow it down to your favorite ten words. Did your choices surprise you?

Integration

Next, it's time for *integration*. This is where the naming magic happens. Take your ten words from step one and start pairing them with words needed to make the brand name complete. For example, once Eddie landed on the word *sabor*, he knew he needed something that reflected depth, commonality, and identity, so he added *soul*. Together, "Sabor y Soul" had a cultural rhythm that matched his brand.

As in the *words* phase, feel free to lean on AI and creative naming resources here. Try to generate five brand names for each of your favorite ten words so that you have fifty names to choose from. I want you to have so many that you get sick of these ideas, too. The more emotion you take out, the more clarity you invite in.

Practicality

Finally, we get to *practicality*. From your long list, narrow it down to your top three name options, and then check whether they're viable through the following steps:

1. Do a domain search to see if the URL is available. (I use GoDaddy.com or Namecheap.com.)
2. Perform a web search with the full name in quotes (e.g., "Sabor y Soul") to make sure there aren't other brands using it already. Check social media handles, too.
3. Search to see if someone has trademarked your name in the category where you intend to use it. If so, cross that name off the list.

Throughout this process, you may need to go back and add to your shortlist (yes, many people building service-first personal brands have found that all three of their top options were taken in some way), which is why it's handy to have forty emotion-free ideas to choose from in the first place.

Once you've confirmed a few names that are available to use, you're ready to commit to one of them. Send the names you're considering to those ideal customers you interviewed back in Chapter 3, and get their opinions. Their perspective might surprise you, and now is the time to find that out. Talking to others will also help you get rid of doubt in your choice. When I asked Eddie if he could lean into all his interests instead of just photography, this validated his inclination to shift from naming his brand descriptively for photography to a more connotative route. Your ideal customers will help you find your path, too.

It's Time to Make a Logo

Having a logo for your service-first personal brand immediately adds to your credibility and authority. It's also a fun step that many people skip, so you automatically stand out if you have one.

Research in the *Journal of Marketing* shows that visual designs with clear structure, like symmetry and balance, lead people to view a brand as more capable and high-performing.[9] Research in the *Journal of Marketing Research* also finds that logos that visually represent what a brand does are perceived as more authentic and generate more positive brand evaluations.[10] To create symmetrical, representative logos, I recommend using Canva or an AI tool like Looka. Canva is a do-it-yourself graphic design tool (with a free option) that laypeople can use to make professional-looking graphics with templates, icons, and built-in styles. Looka is an AI tool that asks you several questions about your business and generates several logo mock-ups for you to choose from. I recommend using both, especially in the initial brainstorming phase.

By the time you read this, there may be newer, even more exciting tools available to you, especially on the AI front. The key is to find a program that gets you started with logo templates. In Canva, you can find thousands of templates by searching for "logo templates" in the search bar. From there, you can "mess around," as Eddie put it, or experiment with different templates by simply deleting the example brand names used in the templates and typing in your own. Simple, font-based logos work well, especially for

SABOR Y SOUL LOGO

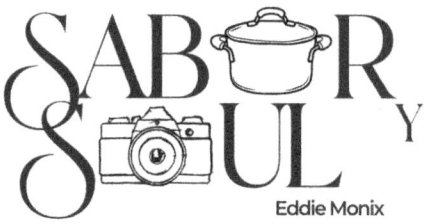

Eddie Monix

EST. 2025
California

Figure 6.2 Eddie Ramirez created a logo to blend his photography skill with his passion for food and culture. (Obtained with permission.)

descriptive brand names or surname-based brand names. For connotative brand names, you might want to add icons, but be sure to keep them simple and symmetrical.

I've included the logo Eddie created in Canva and ultimately used to launch his service-first personal brand (see Figure 6.2). You can see that he added icons to his logo to enforce his brand meaning of community-based storytelling through food and photography, but he kept it symmetrical by putting a cooking pot at the end of the first word and a camera at the beginning of the second. He also used simple line-art icons that don't overwhelm the eye.

Adding Color to Your Logo

Color can add meaning, emotion, and energy to your logo, but because logos will inevitably be printed without color from time to time, a strong logo should work just as well in black-and-white. Eddie's logo, for example, is powerful without any color at all, but when color is added, it deepens the story. He chose an earthy orange that evokes clay pots, sunbaked walls, and the Southwestern US landscapes that connect to his heritage. That color choice was intentional and rooted in meaning.

If you're choosing two colors, they should be complementary (opposite each other on the color wheel, like orange and blue) or analogous (next to each other, like orange and red). These combinations create harmony and contrast that feel intentional rather than chaotic. Canva even has a color wheel calculator tool to help you find a winning color combination.[11] Since you're using premade templates or AI to create your logos, the tools will automatically choose complementary or analogous colors, but it never hurts to double-check.

One quick caution: be careful with blue. While blue is widely associated with trust and calm, it's used by approximately 33 percent of top global brands in their logos, making it the most common logo color.[12]

It also blends into the background on platforms like Facebook, LinkedIn, and Zoom, making your brand less visible online. If you do choose blue, choose a unique and striking shade, or better yet, pair it with something warmer or bolder to give it contrast. Green also conveys trust as an alternative to blue.

I recommend creating your logo in black-and-white first to avoid overreliance on color. Color should support your brand identity but not define it. To help you choose your colors, or stick with black-and-white, I've listed some common meanings of color here, adapted from psychologist Jill Morton's well-known global color survey. Not all colors are included, but you can always consult Morton's many books and resources that expand on the basics if you're interested.[13]

- Red: energy, warmth, strength, passion, excitement, courage, dominance, aggression
- Blue: trust, tranquility, contentment, security, passivity, melancholy
- Green: nature, growth, renewal, youth, health, envy, serenity
- Yellow: cheer, hope, vitality, optimism, communication, enlightenment
- Orange: energy, cheer, warmth, excitement, activity, sociability
- Brown: reliability, durability, warmth, comfort, realism, homeyness
- Black: power, sophistication, mystery, strength, sexuality, elegance
- White: purity, cleanliness, truth, innocence, spiritual clarity
- Gray: neutrality, intelligence, futurism, modesty, indifference, sophistication

Put the Pencil Down

Remember Desiree from Chapter 5? You might recall that her classmates and I were intrigued by her niche in the fertility industry and her unique knowledge about hidden risks. After class one day, she surprised me when she said, "I know it sounds weird, but I can't name my brand. And if I can't name my brand, I can't launch it. I'm really stuck." She'd gone through all the steps. She had her lists of names. But still, none of the contenders felt right.

Trying to help, I asked her what job she wants her brand name to do for her. Since Desiree was using her service-first personal brand as an embryologist to launch an actual business, her answer was clear, "I want it to get me leads and customers," she said.

I asked her to tell me, as precisely as possible, what was most important to convey in her brand name. "I want people to understand that I transport fragile embryos, but I want to give families privacy, so I can't have the word 'embryo' in my name," she told me. I saw her point. As we discussed it, we agreed that by the time someone hears about her business, they probably already know it's for embryo transport. I asked her how else she could describe an embryo. She said, "biological material."

I asked, "Is BioMat Transport too obvious?" It was descriptive enough to be searchable, and it enabled her to add emotional marketing to a factual name if she wanted.

"That's it," she said, and she was ready to launch.

I highlight Desiree's experience here because while the steps I gave you to name your brand usually simplify the process and take the emotion out of it, sometimes they can have the opposite effect. You might end up with a long list where none of the names seem familiar or right anymore. If that happens to you, put the pencil down and talk to someone, but this time, don't talk to an ideal customer. Talk to someone who needs a bit of an education about your brand. Tell that person, in a sentence, what you will teach your ideal customers (you could even read them your brand statement), then ask them what your brand should be called. When that person answers your question, they might take you in a direction that you hadn't thought of or had abandoned.

In Desiree's case, she realized she needed a descriptive name instead of the connotative names she had on her list. She wanted quick leads from already-aware customers, so it made sense that the connotative names were feeling too abstract and ineffective.

When in doubt, reach out.

Now, a final word of caution. Once you've settled on a brand name, you will be tempted to change your mind, maybe several times. You did a lot of great work to get to this point, and it doesn't have to be permanent.

But put your pencil down. Move on. Done is better than perfect. You're ready to launch now.

Name and Claim What You Stand For, at a Glance

Main Idea
This chapter offers a practical brand-naming framework and explains how you can create your own logo without a design background.

Key Takeaways
- A great brand name doesn't need to be perfect. It needs to be intentional, meaningful, and flexible enough to grow with you.
- There are three common types of service-first personal brand names: descriptive (clear, but sometimes limiting), connotative (emotional, but requires storytelling), and surname-based (memorable, but often needs extra explanation).
- The WIP method (words, integration, practicality) guides you through brainstorming, combining, and testing your name options.
- Your logo doesn't need to be professionally designed for it to be credible. Simplicity, symmetry, and descriptive elements go a long way. Canva and AI tools are great for DIY logos.
- Color can add emotional resonance to your logo, but it should never carry the entire brand. Always create a black-and-white version first.
- When naming feels overwhelming, reach out to someone else and go back to the purpose you need your name to serve.

(continued)

(continued)

Next Steps
1. Use the WIP method to create your brand name.
2. Create your logo.

How Long Does This Take?
As an estimate, I recommend blocking off a five- to seven-hour session or splitting the naming and logo-creation process into shorter sessions over two days.

    Word brainstorming: forty-five to sixty minutes
    Name combinations: one to two hours
    Practicality testing: one hour
    Customer feedback and final decision: one hour
    Logo design and iterations: two to three hours

7

From Digital Renter to Digital Owner

> Social media platforms were helpful for getting discovered, but I realized that stopping there was holding back deeper relationships with my audience.
> —Carrie Prince

"I'm a dating coach, but I have a different approach. I teach people how to care less." When Carrie Prince first introduced herself this way, I was intrigued. I'd never met a dating coach before, let alone one who had just told her classmates they should "care less."

Unlike other dating coaches who focused purely on romantic strategy, Carrie brought a business mindset to dating apps. "When you get on an app, remember that they [the people who created the app] want to please you as the customer," she tells her clients. "If nobody found each other through a dating app, then dating apps would fail. Leave reviews. Push them to give you more matches. Don't give up until you are satisfied." Treating dating apps like the businesses they are, rather than mysterious forces working against you, became her signature insight.

Then came her advice to "care less" while on the apps, which resonated deeply with her audience. "You should not care about anyone until you get to the date in person," she says. This isn't callous, she explains, but a strategic detachment that helped her clients avoid emotional investment before meeting someone face-to-face, a mistake she feels is rampant in the online dating world. "Don't get connected to words in direct messages. It takes objectivity away when you actually meet the real human."

Carrie's journey to service-first personal branding began before she stepped into my classroom. Back in 2012, she was hosting a local radio show about dating in Los Angeles when she decided to challenge herself to go on ten online dates and write about the experience. "I loved writing about it, and I felt like I was really good at it," she told me. But despite her confidence in the content, she never published those stories. "It felt super scary."

As the years went on, Carrie eventually went public with her experiences. First she started blogging on Medium, and eventually she landed a part-time job as a matchmaker at Tawkify. She also created advice-based content and posted it on social media. "My audience was growing, and people were discovering me, but I felt like I wasn't making lasting relationships with my audience. People would stop in and look at my content, but I knew I needed to find a way to keep in touch."

When we talked about "rented" versus "owned" space online, Carrie understood the concept right away. "Social media platforms were helpful for getting discovered, but I realized that stopping there was holding back deeper relationships with my audience." She also pointed out other hurdles. "You're always at the mercy of algorithm changes and platform policies that you can't control on social media."

To balance out her reliance on social media, Carrie focused on creating her own website and email list, where she could connect directly and deepen relationships with people who genuinely wanted her help. She also found comfort in owning her leads rather than relying on social media platforms to keep them. "I really thought about the concept of owning my audience. That's why I started funneling people into my email newsletter whenever I could."

Carrie focused on solving her audience's common problems with educational content on social media to build trust. Those small wins would then help her drive interest to her website and newsletter subscription. "I put longer-form content and freebies on my website and in my newsletter to entice people to sign up and subscribe. It's been one of the stronger ways to make really big announcements to the core group that cares."

As her snippets gained traction, her website got more hits and her newsletter grew. "This was an intentional step," Carrie explains. Every video, every piece of advice, every social media post was designed to funnel people into her owned audience.

More importantly, her website and email subscription list became the foundation for expanding the focus of her business. Then when Carrie added leadership coaching to her services (more on this in Chapter 9), she didn't have to start building an audience from scratch. She already had a group of people who trusted her insights and knew she could help them, or their referrals, solve their problems. "So much of the same stuff applies to leadership as it does to dating when we talk about giving people the benefit of the doubt or having space and grace for people on a team because they're different from you. Having that owned audience gave me a big head start."

Today, Carrie Prince is enjoying the great variety of coaching work that comes her way through carrieprincecoaching.com. "It all started with ten dates, but it continued with massive intentionality around my brand," Carrie says.

This intentionality begins with the one bit of digital real estate you can own where you're not subject to the whims of another platform's algorithms and filters: your website. Believe it or not, your website matters *more* than your social media presence, which is why I've placed this chapter on website creation and owned audiences *ahead* of the chapter on social media strategy.

Without your own piece of digital real estate, the bulk of your social media efforts essentially go toward growing another company's bottom line. Every post, every video, every piece of content you share on Instagram, LinkedIn, or TikTok just makes these platforms more valuable while leaving you vulnerable to their many algorithm changes, policy updates, and platform failures, not to mention the risk of getting kicked off the platform outright.

Most service-first personal brands get their start on social media as Carrie did with hers, but when you think of owned versus rented space online, it's easy to see how this is backward. Building a digital home is essential for your service-first personal brand. Your website is your brand's hub, your very own corner of the internet. Here, you can develop your most important brand asset—your audience—who will become regular visitors to your site, seeking your expertise and, eventually, maybe even your products and services.

We rent social media to get discovered, but we own our websites to get data, form deeper relationships with our audience, and convert leads into customers. And yet, so many of my students and clients are often hesitant to make their own website for fear that it will be too hard, or out of concern that the site needs to be complex, but the opposite is true. So, whether you've already started your brand on social media or are currently starting from scratch, make a website as soon as possible. In this chapter, you'll get a no-frills lesson in how to make a simple website that not only looks good but that also will become a cornerstone of your service-first personal brand.

> **Wait, What?**
>
> Social media algorithms change, and platforms disappear. When you own your audience through your website and email and text list, you control the relationship. This safeguards your brand's success from external platforms and changes that you don't control.

Complex Websites Ruin Marketing

"I'm so excited to compile all the information I need to make a website," said no one, ever. Most of my students and clients *hate* the idea of making or updating a website, and I get it. People seem to think that websites need to provide massive amounts of information, have amazing graphics, and include all kinds of functionality. They don't.

In fact, the opposite is true: Simple websites convert. Complex websites kill your marketing.

It's a well-established principle of marketing theory that less is better. Research indicates that offering *less* information helps consumers make quicker decisions and purchases, while information overload (whether image- or text-based) is bad for conversions.[1] For example, Google's user experience team worked with university researchers to study what makes websites functional, and when participants were presented with websites of varying complexity, they rated visually complex websites or websites that deviated from "design prototypicality" of their industry as "less beautiful" and "less trustworthy" compared to the simpler sites they were shown.[2] In the classic book *The Paradox of Choice*, psychologist Barry Schwartz reaffirms this principle, explaining that when options increase, people become overwhelmed by the mental cost of comparing them. This can lead to *analysis paralysis*, where decisions are postponed indefinitely.[3]

Even more compelling is a study published in *Harvard Business Review*, where researchers surveyed more than 7,000 consumers and interviewed more than 200 marketing executives with 125 brands to find what drives "stickiness," which is the likelihood that a consumer will purchase from a brand again, recommend the brand to others, or remain loyal over time. Ease of decision-making was the top driver of stickiness. Consumers rated more information as overwhelming and a source of decision friction, even as marketers assumed that more information empowered their customers.[4]

Websites are daunting because everyone thinks they need to be complex. Everyone is wrong. When we make complex websites, we lose our audiences, we lose engagement, and ultimately we lose conversions. From this day forward, you have permission to make simple websites.

A Simple Website Architecture for Your Brand

Your website will serve as the central aggregating place for your audience. Its job: to get visitors to opt in to your email list, text list, or both, so that you can build a database of your audience, a database that *you* own. You can drive these opt-ins with four simple pages: Homepage, About, Blog, and Contact.

The Homepage

Websites almost always start off with a logo on the top left and a navigation menu on the top right (mobile) or expanded across the top (desktop). You already have your logo ready to go from the last chapter and I've just given you your menu items, so let's move on.

Right below the logo and navigation menu, there is usually a horizontal graphic image, a header. Your header should immediately establish who you are with your name or your business name, followed by a short, compelling description of what you do. Refer to your brand statement for inspiration. To see examples, here are the headers that Carrie Prince has on both her dating coaching and leadership coaching websites (see Figures 7.1 and 7.2). In both cases, there is no doubt about who she is and what she does.

If you'd like to really stand out in the header, fill out each sentence of the TRUTH framework (as discussed in Chapter 4), and ask your AI platform of choice to write you a differentiating power sentence for your website header.

1. **T**: The trope your audience believes. Prompt: Everybody thinks [insert common trope].
2. **R**: Your recognition of the real problem. Prompt: The risk in thinking that is [fill in what you miss out on when making common assumptions].

YOU CAN DATE BETTER WEBSITE HEADER

Figure 7.1 The You Can Date Better website header clearly describes what Carrie Prince offers to her dating coaching clients.

(*Source:* You Can Date Better; obtained with permission.)

CARRIE PRINCE COACHING WEBSITE HEADER

Figure 7.2 The Carrie Prince Coaching website header clearly describes the company's offerings.
(*Source:* Carrie Prince Coaching; obtained with permission.)

3. **U:** Your understanding of a better approach. Prompt: I approach things/think about this differently by [fill in your unique or counter-intuitive approach].
4. **T**: Your tested reasoning behind it. Prompt: I know this works because [add evidence].
5. **H**: How to act based on what you've shared. Tell your users how you want them to act by asking them to opt in.

Here's a hypothetical example, using Carrie's coaching brand:

> Everybody thinks leadership coaching is about vision. The risk in thinking this is that most leaders forget about the nuanced relationships that they need to capitalize on to achieve their vision. I approach leadership coaching with an emphasis on supporting and

> communicating with different types of people who have different goals first, because most leaders inherit the staff who will be key in implementing their most important priorities. I know this works because I've successfully coached hundreds of clients in dating relationships, which are the most complex kind. Opt in to get more information about how you can improve communication with your team so that your vision effortlessly comes to life.

Now that you have that example, prompt your AI platform of choice in the following way: "Please create a powerful sentence or two for the header of my website that earns email and text opt-ins, using the paragraph below." Then paste your TRUTH paragraph.

Here are two powerful and differentiated options that my prompting yielded:

1. "Most leadership coaches talk about vision. I help you communicate with the people who make it real."
2. "I've helped hundreds master the hardest communication of all—dating—and I can help you lead your team just as powerfully."

The more detailed you can make your TRUTH statement, the more powerful and differentiating this output will be. Get specific and try again until you find something you like. This sentence is the most important part of your website.

The Opt-In Your homepage should immediately offer a way for members of your audience to opt in to your email list, text list, or both. Owning your audience is the primary job of your website, so don't wait to convert visitors into email and/or text subscribers. Ask immediately.

A great service-first way to do this is through what's called a "lead magnet" or "gated content." A lead magnet can be a discount or, for service-first personal brands especially, a PDF that gives free information in exchange for your email address and/or phone number. This strategy works because of reciprocity theory: When you give something valuable first, people feel compelled to reciprocate. For instance:

- Jennifer Anderson put a "start here" opt-in button in the Kids Eat in Color website header (see Figure 7.3), which leads consumers to choose which age- and eating-problem appropriate feeding guide they want, and then enter their email address to get it.
- Carrie Prince, when she was an active dating coach, offered a document called "Benefit of the Date: A Single's Guide to Thriving in the Digital Dating World."
- I use a weekly newsletter as a lead magnet on my website.

In Chapters 8 and 9, I will teach you how to create and send weekly thought leadership pieces to your audience that double as opt-in tools.

You might wonder whether you should put your own picture in the header or not. If your service-first personal brand is mainly a thought leadership or consulting brand, like Carrie's leadership coaching and my marketing consulting work, then include a photo of yourself (see Figure 7.4). If you're selling products, either put a picture of yourself or one that symbolizes what you are selling, as Jennifer Anderson did when she used a picture of a child to represent her meal plans.

KIDS EAT IN COLOR WEBSITE HEADER

Figure 7.3 Kids Eat in Color includes an opt-in button with a lead magnet in the header of its website.

(*Source:* Kids Eat in Color; obtained with permission.)

MARKETING SIMPLIFIED WEBSITE HEADER

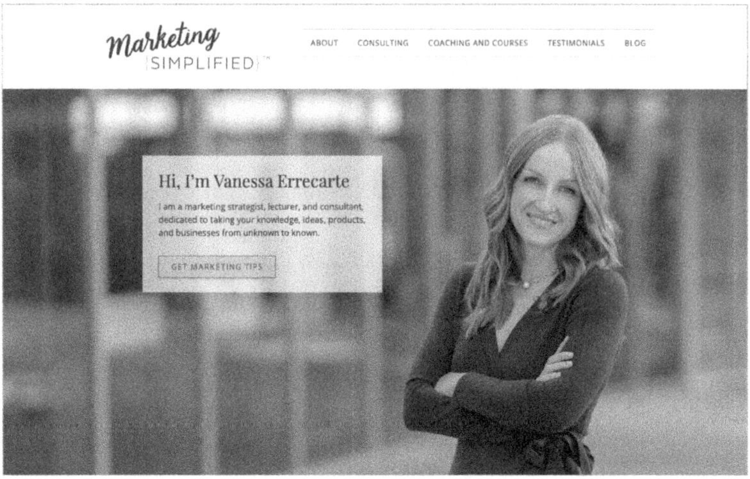

Figure 7.4   I include an opt-in button on the Marketing Simplified website header, using my newsletter as a lead magnet on the homepage.

The Informational Snippet   Beneath the header, brands often take the opportunity to say a little more about themselves, an informational "snippet." For instance, Carrie takes the opportunity beneath the header on her leadership coaching website to list the type of coaching she does (see Figure 7.5). You could do the same, or if you're not offering services, you can use this real estate for your TRUTH statement, which you already wrote as a prompt for the power sentence in your header. You'll want to take out the "How to Act" step, though, since you already covered that in your opt-in.

Sneak Peeks   After that additional snippet, I recommend you show a bio preview, linking to a full bio on your About page. I will share more about how to write and format your bio in Chapter 10. Figure 7.6 shows how it appears on Carrie's website.

After the bio preview, I recommend a blog preview, followed by a testimonial scroll if you have testimonials. Testimonials are a great way to add

CARRIE PRINCE COACHING INFORMATIONAL SNIPPET

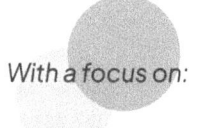

Figure 7.5 Below the header of her Carrie Prince Coaching website, Carrie highlights her services.

(*Source:* Carrie Prince Coaching; obtained with permission.)

CARRIE PRINCE COACHING BIOGRAPHY PREVIEW

Figure 7.6 Carrie's biography appears below an additional informational snippet about her service offerings.

(*Source:* Carrie Prince Coaching; obtained with permission.)

social proof to your brand. Don't just leave recommendations on your LinkedIn profile, repeat them on your website. Figure 7.7 gives a preview of how this section looks on my website.

Finally, at the bottom of your homepage, I recommend one additional email opt-in opportunity for your audience. Remember, gathering leads is the primary goal of your website. Keep it simple and obvious. Figure 7.8 shows how Carrie does that on her coaching website in a clean and simple way.

Media Icons or Scrolls We've now gotten all the way to the bottom of the homepage. At this point you might be thinking, "What about social media icons?" And to this, I'd like to give a warning. Remember: Your primary goal is getting people to your website and then opting in to your audience. If we use online real estate and real-life real estate as a parallel concept, putting social icons on your website is like putting a sign on the

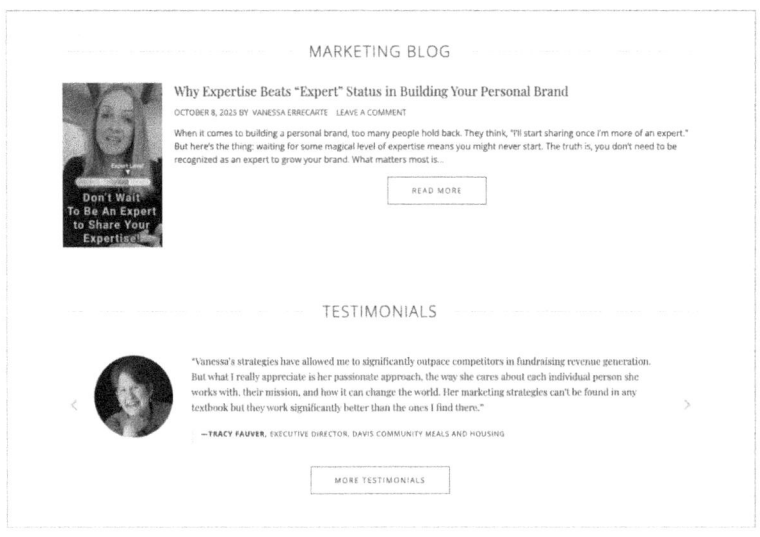

Figure 7.7   Under my bio preview, I include a preview of my blog and testimonials.

(*Source:* Marketing Simplified.)

CARRIE PRINCE COACHING ADDITIONAL OPT-IN

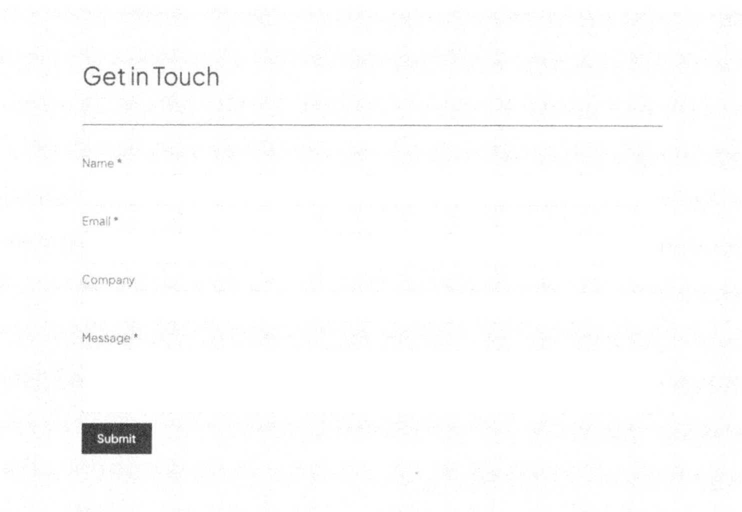

Get in Touch

Name *

Email *

Company

Message *

Submit

Figure 7.8 At the bottom of her homepage, Carrie Prince gives her visitors another chance to opt in with their information.

(*Source:* Carrie Prince Coaching; obtained with permission.)

front door of your storefront displaying instructions on how to get your direct competitors' storefronts. Remember, social media is where people discover you, and your website is where they opt in to your audience. If you are going to put directions to a competing online storefront on your website, please put them at the very bottom.

Another option you can consider is adding a social media scroll to the bottom, instead. Many website design platforms (e.g., WordPress, Shopify, and Squarespace) offer plug-ins that can facilitate this. Visitors will see that you are on social media and get to explore your content without clicking away from your site. That's the best of all worlds.

The About Page

For many service-first personal brands, the About page will simply be your bio. If you grow from a service-first personal brand into a business, this is a good place to talk about your team, board, and company history as well. You can also include a description of services you provide on this page, but I recommend that if you sell products or services, you add additional pages to your navigation menu for them. On Carrie's leadership coaching website, she added an individual coaching page and a peer coaching page to describe those services in detail.

The Blog Page

Your blog will build itself as you populate it with thought leadership posts. As you build your website, the important thing to remember is to make sure that feature is enabled. I recommend having a handful of blog posts finished before you launch your website. In Chapter 8, I'll explain exactly how to create those posts.

The Contact Page

Your Contact page should be a simple opt-in form that has the following cells: name, email, phone number, and message. Carrie's contact page is identical to her additional opt-in on the bottom of her homepage. That's great. Remember, you might want your website to be fancy, but your users want it to be simple.

In addition to the contact form, you can also put a disclaimer about how long your response time is on that page, but if you do that, be sure to stick to it. When you first launch your brand, it might be easy to deliver a response time of two business days, but what happens when your brand grows and succeeds?

Your Site Map

Marketing professionals often create a site map as a guide for designing their website (a tool for the site designer, not for visitors). Figure 7.9 provides a site map that summarizes the website format I've described above. Start here. Draw a simple site map for yourself and plan out how your website will look.

WEBSITE MAP TEMPLATE	
HOMEPAGE	
• Logo and navigation menu • Header with opt-in • Informational snippet • Bio preview	• Blog preview • Testimonial scroll • Additional opt-in • Social media scroll or icons

ABOUT	CONTACT	BLOG
• Bio • Team bios • Company stories • Note: Add pages for products or services	• Name • Email • Phone number • Message • Response time (optional)	• Thought leadership posts

Figure 7.9 A website map template is a vision board for your owned real estate on the internet.

Email and Text Marketing: Your Conversion Engine

While email may seem like an outdated form of marketing, it's still one of the best ways to own your audience. Email marketing may not feel as flashy as social media, but as of this writing at least, it still outperforms it where it counts: engagement, conversion, and ownership. Remember, social media is rented space, subject to shifting algorithms and changing trends, but you own your email list. That's why service-first marketers like Carrie use their newsletter to form deeper relationships with their customers and make big announcements.

According to Campaign Monitor's recent benchmark report, the average open rate for marketing emails is 21.5 percent, a stark contrast to the far lower reach you get on social media.[5] LinkedIn company pages, for example, now reach just 1–2 percent of their followers organically, a decline that mirrors what marketers have long experienced on Facebook, where average organic reach is around 1–1.6 percent, and Instagram, where it hovers around 3.5 percent.[6] Even posts that do reach people often disappear quickly in crowded feeds.

Conversions also show a real difference when email and social media are compared. A Monetate study found that email converts at more than double the rate of social media: 4.29 percent compared to just 1.81 percent.[7]

Marketing texts are also having a moment. They used to be seen as obtrusive but are rapidly becoming tolerated, and the statistics speak for themselves. Marketing text messages currently have open rates of 98 percent within the first three minutes of delivery.[8,9] And people don't just open them, they act. A recent survey by SimpleTexting found that 71 percent of consumers opted in to receive texts from brands, and 45 percent of those people made a purchase as a result.[10]

The shift to mass texting for marketing is happening quickly. Brands often make the mistake of failing to collect phone numbers on their opt-in forms. Even if brands aren't using text marketing yet, they should be preparing by collecting both phone numbers in addition to emails. Don't forget to ask for phone numbers on your opt-in forms and contact page, as well.

As consumers, our preferences for how we receive marketing messages will continue to evolve. Right now, we receive most of our information online through email, text messaging, or social media. You may not own your social media channels, but you do own your database of phone numbers and emails. As long as outreach through these channels is shown to be effective, use them. That said, pay attention to long-term trends. As consumers, we will all continue to change the way we consume info. As marketers, our job is to be aware of these changes and ask, "If [fill in the blank] platform goes away tomorrow, will I have a way to get back in touch with my audience?"

Choosing and Integrating Software

There are dozens of website design, email marketing, and text marketing software solutions. My current recommendations are to use either WordPress or, if you plan to sell products soon, Shopify. Both have do-it-yourself templates, many of which now include AI assistive technology to help make the creation process easier. Those platforms also integrate well with other software, like email and text marketing software. Of course, if you are using another website development platform that you like and are comfortable with, stay the course.

To decide which email and text marketing software to integrate into your website, do some quick internet research. Free (Mailchimp) or inexpensive (Constant Contact) options are always good places to start, and an increasing number of programs have both email and texting services built in or available as add-ons (including both Mailchimp and Constant Contact). All of these programs have an integration section where you can copy automatically generated HTML code and paste it on the pages of your website where you'd like to include opt-in buttons. There are plenty of YouTube videos that will take you through both website setup and email and text marketing integration.

As you go on your website creation journey, remember: Simple is best. You might even consider outsourcing the website work if you're a busy professional and willing to invest a few thousand dollars into getting it done quickly.

Your URL Is Your Online Identity

You need a landing place for your website, and that is your URL. Your primary URL will be your brand name, but I also recommend purchasing your own name as a URL and pointing that to your brand name (if they aren't already the same). Your service-first personal brand will become highly associated with your name to your audience, which means some people might search for your service-first personal brand using your name. Having your name as a URL also ensures that you own your identity online. Don't wait to buy URLs for your full name *and* your brand name (if they are different); stake your online claim as soon as possible.

Business Websites Are Also Simple

Ryan Wilson, who I'll describe in more detail in Chapter 13, originally built his service-first personal brand around his time in the military and as a veteran. A couple of years later, he launched a fleet maintenance business with his brother called WilsonTech Fleet Services. "I promoted my new business through the veterans' organizations I was associated with personally, and it started to really take off." In fact, the business itself took off before the website was even in place, so he had to act quickly to make a website.

One day, Ryan showed me a very simple website he had designed and seemed shocked when I told him to keep it like that.

"Even for a business brand?" he asked.

"Especially for a business brand," I assured him. I then reminded him about the same information I shared with you earlier in this chapter: People make decisions quicker when they aren't overloaded with information.

With this reassurance, Ryan launched his simple website. The site's homepage gets straight to the point: There are no flashy animations, no overwhelming navigation menus, and no confusion about what the company does. Instead, visitors immediately see WilsonTech Fleet Services' core message about fleet and commercial vehicle service, with a prominent phone number and opt-in in the header that's impossible to miss. There are no additional choices. It's simple, and it worked.

Within seven months of launching WilsonTech Fleet Services, Ryan was fielding expansion opportunities that typically take established businesses years to achieve. "We would not be even looking at an expansion opportunity at seven months in without that website. I attribute all of it to the storytelling, the branding, and then on the backend, the website."

When an executive needing services for many of his fleets discovered Ryan through his LinkedIn posts and then went to the company website, he reached Ryan within minutes. "He said it was the fastest decision he's ever made because he didn't have all kinds of extra information and flashing windows to sift through," Ryan explained. "I have to admit that I always secretly worried our website wasn't enough, but I trusted the process and the evidence, and it worked."

If your brand started as a service-first personal brand and you are now monetizing it or launching a separate business, please resist the temptation to complicate your website simply because you are now a moneymaking business. I see this mistake often, and it's nothing but a time suck and conversion killer. Just add a services or products page to the site map. Keep it simple, visually clean, and concise.

From Digital Renter to Digital Owner, at a Glance

Main Idea
This chapter explores why building your own website and owning your audience is an important component to service-first personal branding, because it creates the foundation for lasting relationships and business growth.

Key Takeaways
- Own, don't rent: Social media platforms are great discovery tools, but your website and email list are where you build real relationships with your audience.
- Simple websites convert better: Research shows that visually complex websites are rated as less trustworthy.
- Your homepage has one primary job: to convert visitors into subscribers through clear opt-ins and lead magnets.
- Your website architecture should include: Homepage (with header, opt-in, bio preview), About, Blog, and Contact. Keep navigation simple and focused.

Next Step
Create your website site map using the simple four-page structure: Homepage, About, Blog, Contact. Focus on one clear call-to-action throughout: opt-ins. Remember that less information helps consumers make quicker decisions.

(continued)

(continued)

How Long Does This Take?

Start by designing a simple site map, then building or outsourcing your website. Launch it with basic functionality and improve it over time. Here are time estimates for each step.

    Website mapping: one hour

    Basic website setup: four to eight hours (or outsource)

    Email and text platform integration: two hours

    Remember: Done is better than perfect.

8

Frameworks and Your First Thought Leadership Piece

> I wanted to make sure what I was saying actually helped people. The conversations that came out of those posts made me realize I was onto something.
>
> —Carter Delaney

Seventy-four strikeouts in one season. That was enough to get the attention of the scouts who recruited Carter Delaney to play Division I baseball at UC Davis as an undergraduate. But Carter wasn't just focused on baseball. He eventually went on to simultaneously pursue his Master of Management degree, which meant he needed to balance the demands of Division 1 athletics with graduate-level coursework.

When he walked into my class, he shared a familiar frustration. He knew he had valuable experiences as a student and athlete, but he wasn't sure that was enough to support a service-first personal brand. "I am not even sure how I would define a personal brand anymore," Carter shared with me. "And I'm also not the type of person to post a lot of day-in-the-life stuff and self-promotion on social media. It doesn't feel right." I sympathized, but I also knew Carter was in the right place. I secretly couldn't wait to see the ideas he came up with. You don't have a seventy-four-strikeout season as a college pitcher without strategies and insights to back it up.

In the halls, Carter told me about a breakthrough moment in class: teaching with frameworks. "I didn't expect a tools-based approach, and I'm getting a lot of ideas now." Creating frameworks resonated with Carter, and he started formatting his knowledge so that it would be easier for others to understand and use.

Carter's first attempt at organizing his insights into a teachable framework yielded the PITCH framework. It emerged from his observation of the five principles that he believed made him successful in both Division I baseball and business school. He wanted to create an easy-to-remember acronym that represented the lessons he learned in both worlds:

P: Prepare like a professional.
I: Instincts come from repetition.
T: Teamwork makes the difference.
C: Compete with purpose.
H: Hard work is the baseline, not the goal.

But that was just the start. Once Carter got PITCH down on paper, he was inspired.

Next came the Three Ws. This one was about self-competition versus external comparisons, another lesson he took from the mound into business school. In a draft blog post he shared with me titled, "Your Biggest Competition is You," Carter outlined a structured approach to continuous improvement. He encouraged his audience to ask themselves three, time-based questions:

W: What did I do better today than yesterday?
W: What's one thing I can improve this week?
W: What weakness can I turn into a strength this month?

As Carter continued developing content for his blog and LinkedIn posts, additional frameworks emerged. One of my favorites was his *Stop Overthinking, Start Executing* concept that came from observing both teammates and classmates suffer from analysis paralysis. "Ever watched a three- or four-year-old swing a baseball bat?" Carter wrote in one draft post. "It can be surprisingly smooth, natural, and efficient. They don't overanalyze their mechanics, they just see the ball and swing."

I had noticed this same phenomenon from my own son's baseball journey. Sometimes, it seemed like the more he was coached, the more he began to overthink what he was doing. But as Carter emphasized in his posts, preparation should build *confidence*, not create paralysis. I found these posts striking (no pun intended). Whether in sports, academics, or in business, our approach to preparation often *saps* us of our confidence.

Carter was determined to change that. His Three Cs applied the hard-won lessons from the pitching mound to the world of business pitching and interviewing, two areas that he noticed people often overcomplicated. The Three Cs stand for:

C: Confidence. When you're on the pitching mound or ready to give a business pitch, you're in performance mode. There's no time for doubt before you throw. You have to rely on the effort that led you to the moment. Confident pitches lead to strikeouts. Think of a business pitch as a performance, too. A confident delivery leads to a dominant performance, and ultimately, a win.

C: Clarity. On the pitching mound, there's no time for confusion, new ideas, or extra analysis. Only clarity. Sticking to the point leads to strikeouts. In a business pitch, clarity leads to action and results. Cut the extra slides and data and give your audience only what they need.

C: Connection. Focus on who you're there for. There wouldn't be baseball if there weren't fans. Whether you flash a smile, tip your hat to the crowd, or sign a ball for a young fan, focus on building connection. It's hard to overthink a pitch internally when you're focused on connecting with and pleasing your audience externally. The same is true for a business pitch. Focus on providing the connection your audience needs rather than staying stuck inside your head.

The more he focused on these powerful—and valuable—frameworks, the more Carter gained clarity about his purpose. "I want people to read my blog when I launch it," he told me. "I definitely want people to learn from it." He emphasized that he didn't want his blog to be just for recruiters or résumé-building, he wanted it to be for the next athlete figuring things out in higher education and in life. "I wish I'd had someone a couple steps ahead of me sharing what the transition was like," he said. "That's what I want to be for others."

This perspective has made service-first personal branding much easier for him to embrace. "I've thought about coaching, so it does appeal to me. It feels a lot more natural than self-promotion." In fact, Carter is so invested in this work that he even reached out to classmates (ideal customers) for feedback on his posts and frameworks. "I wanted to make sure what I was saying actually helped people. The conversations that came out of those posts made me realize I was onto something."

As of this writing, Carter is working on creating a website to house his ideas. He's not sure whether he wants to go into professional baseball, law, or business, "but the parallels in my brand stay the same regardless. I can't wait to share as I go."

I love Carter's story for many reasons, but I'd like to highlight a special aspect for you to think about. When he first walked into my class, Carter wondered if he was experienced enough to start a service-first personal brand because he hadn't had a full-time job yet. Even so, when we started talking about the things he *did* know, his brand quickly emerged. If you're wondering whether you have enough experience, knowledge, and wisdom to build a service-first personal brand, I hope Carter's story inspires you to find the same motivation.

More than that, I hope that you borrow one of Carter's keys to success: the power of frameworks. Frameworks add order to the thoughts and ideas that support your expertise. They are building blocks and instructions for your audience to apply, try, and succeed with your value. And while we often don't think of them in our day-to-day lives, frameworks are all around us. Just look at these familiar examples:

> *Stop, drop, and roll.*
> *See it, say it, remember it.*
> *Red means stop, yellow means caution, green means go.*

Sound familiar? All these frameworks make intuitive sense to us, but that's only because we understand their context. Red, green, and yellow, for example, had nothing to do with driving until stoplights became our framework for controlling traffic.

Frameworks are effective because: (1) They take a big idea and make it easy to understand, and (2) They make you look smart. How? By showing your audience that you've done the work and organized the chaos into actionable items that show the transformation they want to achieve. That's the value of frameworks that leads to visibility, and why frameworks are so essential to a service-first personal brand. In this chapter, you'll learn the ABCs of framework creation so you can lead your audience with authority.

> **Wait, What?**
>
> Frameworks aren't just for the internet, they work in meetings, interviews, and conversations. When you package your insights clearly and connect them to a human moment, you gain visibility for the value that you've taken the time to package.

Frameworks Boost Your Credibility and Make People Notice You

You're smart. If you want to look smart, start using frameworks. One of the fastest ways to gain trust and understanding, and to signal authority, is to put your ideas into clear structures with clear steps and a helpful acronym, as Carter did. Frameworks make abstract thinking feel real, they give your audience an easier way to remember information, and they boost credibility by elevating you from communicator to *teacher*.

Through frameworks, you show your audience a new way to think. And when your audience starts benefitting from your frameworks and repeating them to others? That's when you know it's working, and that's when you gain visibility.

According to the Elaboration Likelihood Model of Persuasion, people process messages in two ways: consciously and deeply (the central route) or subconsciously and quickly, based on surface cues (the peripheral route).[1]

A well-designed framework taps into both. It appeals to the analytical brain by offering substance and logic, but it also quickly signals authority, like, "Hey, I've thought this through." Even if a reader doesn't fully absorb every word, the structure itself communicates that you know what you're talking about.

Recent empirical work on persuasion knowledge adds another important dimension to the value of frameworks in the age of the internet and information skepticism. According to research, when communicators package insights into purposeful frameworks, audiences are less likely to feel manipulated and more likely to trust and apply what they learn.[2] So, not only do frameworks deliver a powerful punch when it comes to packaging, but they are also a key tool for trust building.

Finally, as I mentioned in Chapter 4, we don't stop our scroll for information we've heard before. Frameworks bring your counterintuitive, novel, or different viewpoints to the surface in a way that's easy for your ideal customer notice to understand.

Yes, frameworks make you look smart, but more importantly, they show your audience that you've done the work and organized the chaos into actionable items that show the transformation they want to achieve. And I'll shout it from the rooftops one more time: that's the value of frameworks that naturally leads to visibility.

The ABCs of Framework Creation

Every framework you create should include the following three elements, which I call "The ABCs of Framework Creation." Cheesy, I know. But it's also memorable, because it's. . . another framework! Let's break it down.

A Is for "Actionable"

Frameworks should be *actionable*. In Carter's Three Ws, he provides his readers with an actionable to-do that promises to yield quick results. The first W can be achieved in a day, the next in a week. Whenever you can create a way for your ideal customer to try something quickly and succeed, you create a trust-building opportunity. After all, when someone gives you advice and it helps you succeed, don't you immediately feel connected to them, appreciative of their value, and trust what they have to say next?

B Is for "Backup"

Your frameworks should also provide *backup* in the form of evidence or experience. Some of you will be teaching your audience concepts and practices based mainly on experience, like Kevin from Chapter 3, Eddie from Chapter 6, or Carter in this chapter. Some of you will also bring in more evidence and combine it with experience like Lisa from Chapter 2, Jennifer from Chapter 4, or Desiree from Chapter 5. Whether it's experience with or without the support of evidence, be sure to weave in that backup when you share your frameworks.

When Carter introduced his PITCH framework, his headline was, "How preparing for a seventy-four-strikeout season also prepared me for business school." It's hard to imagine a player achieving seventy-four strikeouts in a college-length season without years of experience under his belt. Make sure you back your frameworks with experience, evidence, or both, either in the headline text, lead-in text, or framework text itself.

C Is for "Core Concept"

Frameworks should revolve around a *core concept*. In Carter's Three Cs framework, he focused on one core concept: the tendency to overthink the business pitch. He also added a surprising approach by comparing the business pitch to the pitching mound in the explanation of each step.

Failing to adhere to one core concept is the most common area I see frameworks fall apart, because we are all tempted to try to teach too much at once. If your framework ever goes beyond five steps, reflect on what you're teaching. Chances are, you have more than one core concept.

In fact, even if you have a successful acronym, as Carter did with PITCH, you still might be able to break it down further. When Carter said he might turn his PITCH framework into a series of mini frameworks, I agreed. PITCH *is* valuable, but it also has several core concepts within it.

Remember, your knowledge is your most valuable asset. Give your audience just enough of it in each thing you teach so that they trust you enough to come back for more. Don't give away too much information, or they will know everything they need to know and won't need to come back to learn from you again.

> **Remember Your TRUTH**
>
> In Chapter 4, I described my TRUTH framework to help you define your entire brand, but the first three steps of it, TRU, are also helpful for developing mini topics within your brand:
>
> **T:** The trope your audience believes
> **R:** Your recognition of the real problem
> **U:** Your understanding of a better approach
>
> Remember, we only stop our scrolls for *new* information. Within your better approach lies the surprise, counterintuitiveness, or novel approach inherent in your knowledge. Carter's Three Cs are effective because they are counterintuitive to how we *think* we should do business: hefty analysis, long slide decks, and internal reflection. Instead, Carter suggests that the *opposite* will lead to true success: confidence in what you already know, concise points, and external reflection.
>
> If you find that your frameworks sound ordinary or like what everyone else in your industry or brand space says, remember the first three steps of the TRUTH framework, and you'll be sure to develop core concepts for your frameworks that are novel, counterintuitive, surprising, and ultimately, scroll stopping.

Finding Your Acronym

Once you have your ABCs, it's time to have a little fun. To find a structure for your frameworks, I recommend either using a representative word/acronym or alliteration (finding words for each part of your framework that all start with the same letter).

To find an acronym, write down as many words as you can think of that relate to your brand. For Carter, "pitch" was a perfect word to use, for obvious reasons. Other words like *team*, *lead*, *run*, or *home* could also work for his future frameworks. Feel free to use your AI tool of choice to brainstorm your list. Simply paste the steps that you are teaching in the prompt window and then ask it to generate ten one-word acronyms that could represent those steps in a framework.

After you have a list of appropriate-length words, start seeing which ones work with the steps in your framework. In my ABCs framework, I changed "evidence and experience" to "**b**ackup" to make it work with the "ABC" acronym. I could have also said "**b**ase it in experience, evidence, or both" but I thought that was too much of a mouthful. Again, AI tools can help you come up with alternatives if you're having trouble finding a word to match an acronym.

If you're using alliteration to name your framework, that's a little easier than finding a representative word. For this, let the strongest word in your framework guide you, and then use AI tools to come up with the other words. Carter's began with "confidence" for his *Three Cs*, because no other word sounded right as a replacement. He then changed "get to the point" to "clarity" and "focus on the external" to "connection" to make the rest work. He did this by asking ChatGPT what "C" words represented each of those two phrases.

Of course, there are other approaches to determining your acronym as well, like how Carter used three *what* questions for his Three Ws and how I used ABCs and AEIOUs for two of the frameworks that appear in this book. Those are not exactly representative words, but they *are* effective mnemonic devices. Again, have fun with this part, and don't be surprised if a word search leads you to clarify your core concepts even more. Carter, for example, told me he liked his Three Cs much more after he was forced to think of his phrases as key words. "It really became precise," he said.

From Framework to First Thought Leadership Post

Do you feel like a thought leader yet? I find that most clients and students start to feel a transformation right around the time that they start to develop their first framework. Believe it or not, once you have a framework, you're halfway done with your first thought leadership blog post. Now, you just need to add a story-based lead-in.

In the AEIOUs of service-first personal branding that I introduced in Chapter 5, recall that "I" stands for *involvement* in the experience of your ideal customers, and involvement creates empathy. If you've experienced something or observed it repeatedly, you can better imagine how someone else feels in a similar situation.

One recent study of the online space found that audiences are more likely to engage with and follow people when they perceive empathy and relatability in their content. Lead into your frameworks with storytelling that shows emotional insight and personal involvement, and your ideal customers are more likely to pay attention and connect.[3]

As a lead-in to his Three Ws framework, Carter wrote about an experience he had in Little League and then used that as a segue. Here's how a draft of that thought leadership piece looked:

> I remember when I stopped competing with others and started competing with myself. I was actually in Little League and made it my everyday practice goal to get better than a teammate. It almost ruined baseball for me because I would always be sad when he did better than me.
>
> One day, my coach told me that if I wanted to get happy, to focus on the things I (and only I) did better at each practice. By the end of the season, I was in love with baseball again. Today I realize that I was experiencing the power of intrinsic motivation. I've learned that my real competition isn't the other pitcher on the mound or the person with a better résumé, it's the version of myself from last week, last month, last year.
>
> Here are my Three Ws so you can find joy in your own improvement:
>
> **W:** What did I do better today than yesterday?
> **W:** What's one thing I can improve this week?
> **W:** What weakness can I turn into a strength this month?
>
> What's one way you push yourself to be better than you were yesterday? Drop your thoughts below!
> #PersonalGrowth #SelfImprovement #CompeteWithYourself #MindsetMatters #ContinuousImprovement

Carter's lead-in, combined with his framework for this thought leadership, covers my ABCs perfectly. He provides actionable steps in his three questions, which are based on his own experience playing baseball (that we know is extensive because he references his involvement all the way back to Little League), and he sticks to one core concept: self-competition. This post would stop my scroll on LinkedIn, Instagram, or your platform of choice. His advice is a bit counterintuitive (many of us assume we'll get better, not worse, by competing with others) and valuable, and that combined with his relatability make him visible.

In Chapter 10, we will go into further depth about how to create story-based lead-ins. But for now, go back to the overlap in your P/P Venn diagram from Chapter 2. Is there a story behind something you identified in that overlap that you can relate to the framework you're teaching? If not, how else might you be able to connect with your audience through a lead-in caption?

Personal stories and empathy are powerful, but if you ever want to vary your lead-ins, consider asking your audience a general question that they can relate to. You might recall that Carter used this alternative approach when he led into his Three Cs framework about overthinking by asking, "Ever watched a three- or four-year-old swing a baseball bat?" Then, he followed the question up with, "It can be surprisingly smooth, natural, and efficient. They don't overanalyze their mechanics, they just see the ball and swing."

This can be a great way to practice lead-ins in a less vulnerable way than telling your own stories. It can also be a good way to vary your content and involve your audience. Just be sure not to overuse this method in lieu of personal stories, because your own stories will always forge a deeper connection.

> **It's Your Turn**
>
> Now it's your turn to create your first thought leadership post. Start by creating a framework rooted in my ABCs to show your value. Then write a lead-in to add to the ABCs, create relatability by showing involvement, and ultimately amplify your visibility. Set a goal to post a thought leadership post once a week on LinkedIn for now, and in the next two chapters, I will give you strategies to expand on this.

Frameworks Go Beyond the Scroll

Tracy Fauver, a former client who you will get to know better in Chapter 11, is a social worker who has spent the last two decades of her career leading human services organizations. Tracy has worked with many at-risk populations who are often judged unfairly. She believes that the key to a more compassionate society, and the first step to helping others who are struggling, is recognizing shared experience from trauma. She explains this with her CARE framework:

> **C: Confront the impact.** Everyone has trauma that's affected them in some way. Acknowledge how it's affected you emotionally, mentally, physically, or spiritually.
>
> **A: Acknowledge shared struggles.** When you meet someone new, acknowledge their struggles and trauma rather than their flaws.
>
> **R: Reflect with compassion.** This is where empathy begins. What can you understand about someone, instead of judging them?
>
> **E: Extend empathy to others.** Turn your insight into action. Support, listen, show up. Don't just feel empathy, practice it.

Tracy takes this framework, rooted in her vast experience working with diverse populations, to every meeting, interview, public hearing, and experience. She's become known for her compassionate approach to managing organizations and diverse populations. It's gotten her professional opportunities, speaking engagements, and even helped her to form consortia on trauma-informed management. Her ability to communicate key steps to solving social problems in a digestible framework is central to her success.

Frameworks go beyond the scroll. They are powerful tools that you can use virtually anywhere to solidify your service-first personal brand and expertise. Memorize some of your key frameworks and use them at networking events, in interviews, workshops, meetings, speeches, and the like. Become valuable and visible everywhere.

Frameworks and Your First Thought Leadership Piece, at a Glance

Main Idea
This chapter shows how organizing your knowledge into frameworks can boost credibility, signal authority, and serve as a launchpad for your first thought leadership piece.

Key Takeaways
Frameworks shape your value. They make your ideas easier to understand, remember, and relate to, especially when paired with a story lead-in. This value and relatability naturally lead to visibility.

The ABCs of framework creation (action, backup, and core concept) ensure your audience can apply, trust, remember, and share what you teach.

Next Steps
Use the ABCs to build your first framework. Then lead into it with a personal story. This is the foundation of your first thought leadership post. Make it a goal to post one on LinkedIn each week.

How Long Does This Take?
It takes about two hours to create your first thought leadership piece.
    Framework creation: one hour
    Story lead-in: thirty minutes
    Final post draft: thirty minutes
    And there you have it: value *and* visibility

PART III
INFORM Your Audience with Impactful Content

9

Your Simplified Digital Funnel

> What if I could formalize this and build an entire personal brand based on coaching other first-gens about things like well-being, authenticity, financial literacy, and career building?
>
> —Marisol Ibarra

"The first time I posted about being the only English speaker in my household, people said, 'Thank you for saying this.' That's when I knew I had to keep going."

Marisol Ibarra didn't plan to start a podcast. It was the spring of 2020, and like many young professionals, she was stuck at home wondering what the pandemic meant for her future. "I felt like I was going to stay stagnant," she says. "I was a few years into my career, and all of a sudden, everything paused."

Marisol knew she needed to turn the pause into meaning, both for herself and others. She was a legislative staffer at the California State Capitol and had all the trappings of success. But much like Eddie from Chapter 6, she was a first-generation Mexican American and often felt lonely. On top of that, she was a woman trying to forge a corporate career. "I could really feel the double dose of adversity and isolation," Marisol says.

This longing led her to go on a journey of discovery. She journaled, sought out mentorship, and eventually hired a Latina coach. "She told me, 'You have a story to tell. You've got to start showing up. You're a talker, start a podcast,'" Marisol says.

Marisol found the idea nerve-wracking, but it stuck with her. "It took me seven months to hit record," Marisol says. "I kept thinking, 'Why would anyone want to hear my story?'" An inner voice told her that Latina women were supposed to blend in and be subservient. But with encouragement, she reframed. "My coach said, 'Try it like a science project. Test the hypothesis. If it doesn't work, that's data too.'"

"It was the push I needed," Marisol says. "Viewing it as an experiment took some pressure off." Marisol launched *Here Comes the Sun*, a podcast for and about first-generation professionals, especially women, navigating life between cultures, careers, and expectations. She invited guests to talk about imposter syndrome, caregiving, burnout, financial literacy, and cultural pride. "I wanted to create a space where we could share what it means to succeed while still carrying the emotional load of being the first," she says. "I wanted people to know they aren't alone if they are the only Latina in a boardroom, supporting their multigenerational families, or trying to show up authentically yet blended between cultures."

Each time Marisol posted a new episode, she would extend her podcast's reach. "I would post the podcast on several platforms, including Apple and Spotify, and then I would also post it on my social media platforms, like LinkedIn and Instagram. I would also email it to my subscribers."

As she kept going, the feedback rolled in. "The experiment seemed to be working," she says. "I would get DMs, like the one about being the only English speaker growing up in a family, and I knew I was breaking down barriers of isolation, fear, and impostor syndrome that we carry but don't talk about."

The more Marisol helped break down these barriers for others, the more she was doing so for herself. "I've always been the bridge in my family," she says. "I translate documents, book flights, explain retirement accounts to my parents in Spanish. The next day, I show up to work boldly and make my voice heard at the State Capitol. It's beautiful, but it's also exhausting and lonely. Now others with that burden were being seen and heard, and frankly, so was I."

As Marisol's podcast gained momentum, her vision expanded. She began to ask, "What if I could formalize this and build an entire personal brand based on coaching other first-gens about things like well-being, authenticity, financial literacy, and career building?"

To grow into that vision, she knew she had to show more dimensions of herself. In addition to promoting her podcast, she began posting snapshots of daily life from the halls of the California State Capitol to illustrate her love of fashion and culture. She rebranded from *Here Comes the Sun* to *Moments of Marisol*. "I wanted a name that gave me permission to evolve. Something that didn't box me in."

The new direction resonated. Direct messages (DM)s kept coming. One said, "Hey, I saw your reel, can we get coffee?" Another said, "I didn't know I could talk about work like this." Each one affirmed her path.

"People were benefitting," Marisol says. "If they wanted coffee, or if I was teaching them something they didn't realize, then I was already coaching them."

Marisol was thrilled with the response and the community she had grown, but virality or follower counts never mattered to her. "You don't have to have a huge following to have a personal brand. You can start with who you are, right now," she says. "My purpose is to help first-generation professionals, especially women, find their way. That's the mission I show up with each day, and then I combine that with intentionality to naturally build my subscription list."

This intention can be seen across Marisol's platforms. For example, when she wrote blog posts for the UC Davis Graduate School of Management, she made sure they linked back to her content. "Each time I used my reach to build my list, growth happened," she said.

Her central hub, for now, is Instagram. But her goal is to expand to channels she more directly controls (see Chapter 7). "I'm working on completing my website to formalize everything," she says. Marisol has also begun testing webinars for first-generation professionals, and she's also exploring future digital products, like a course or coaching program.

She's even considering a brick-and-mortar space someday, which would be part gathering spot, part coaching studio, part community showcase. "And maybe a fridge in the back for aguas frescas," she laughed, referencing her side business selling Mexican drinks at pop-ups. "It's literally just water," she says. "But it brings people joy, and it tells a story."

When I asked her what the ultimate goal for her brand is, she didn't hesitate to offer a service-first response. "I want first-generation Latinas, and anyone struggling with their identity, to know that we don't have to be lonely or wait to be chosen," she said. "We can build what we wish existed." I couldn't help but smile. She deserves every subscriber on her list.

And so do you.

Up until this point in the book, you've been in planning mode for your brand. In Part I (Chapters 1–5), you created your brand vision. In Part II (Chapters 6–8), you packaged it. Here in this chapter, and throughout Part III (Chapters 9–11), we're going to go from building to sharing, shifting our focus to the external so we can begin connecting as a brand with our audience.

As you move through the following lessons, remember: This doesn't have to be hard or overly complex. I've built a career on streamlining and simplifying the marketing process because, at its core, simplicity leads to consistency, and that is the key to success for your service-first personal brand.

> **Wait, What?**
> Instead of playing "online marketing darts" and facing burnout, anchor your thought leadership around one message and funnel it across the channels that matter. This keeps your messaging clear, your output sustainable, and your audience growing.

Simplicity Is the Secret to Success

Most people play "online marketing darts" to try to build their service-first personal brands. They post high volumes of content, often on several platforms, and with no purpose, just because they think they need to be everywhere and everything all at once on social media to be successful. This usually leads people to burn out and quit because such an effort is time-consuming and doesn't lead to results.

Instead of going down that unfocused path, build a simple funnel based on what I call "cornerstone content." Just in case you're not up on your marketing jargon, a sales or marketing funnel is a coordinated content and communication system designed to move your audience toward a specific action (e.g., buying a product, signing up for a course or membership, or even just subscribing to your newsletter). Cornerstone content serves as the foundation for that funnel by building a broad ecosystem of related materials each week. You will reuse this content strategically and often, both to keep your service-first personal branding workload small and to engage your audience better. (Yes, despite what you may have heard, *reusing content helps you engage your audience better*.)

Industry data show that when brands deliver a consistent message across platforms, even in varied formats, they see significantly higher returns in brand recall, trust, engagement, and revenue. They also experience substantial revenue lifts, often over 20 percent, because unified messaging strengthens recognition and reinforces the same story wherever customers encounter the brand.[1] Another industry-backed report emphasized that consistency in voice and presence helps brands stay top of mind and builds audience trust, especially when supported by regular, engaging posts.[2]

In short, consistency and redundancy help your audience recognize your value sooner, and that's not a bad place to be when we are deluged with the equivalent of 100,500 words a day. If you take a quick scan of Marisol's Instagram content, for example, you see the same themes and terms, like achieving financial literacy and finding belonging, come up in almost every piece of her cornerstone content.

While the funnel strategy that I am going to explain may seem simple, please keep in mind the science I shared above. The simplicity is *exactly* why it works. I've personally used it for two decades, with great results for brands of all sizes.

Your Cornerstone Content Funnel Map

Your cornerstone content will be the backbone of your service-first personal brand's funnel, and you've already learned how to create it. It's the thought leadership piece I taught you how to write in Chapter 8. Each week, one of those pieces will be your cornerstone content. (Note: If a weekly thought leadership piece feels too ambitious at first, set a once- or twice-a-month goal and work up to weekly.)

In general, there are three obvious formats for your cornerstone content:

- Written (like you learned in the last chapter)
- Video
- Audio podcast

You can choose any of these formats, based on your comfort level. Marisol is a self-described talker, so she chose a podcast format because she was comfortable with the technology. You might feel more comfortable starting with written posts or videos. Whatever initial format you choose, you can use a tool I call a "VABlog" (video and blog) to bring all the formats together and cover all parts of your funnel. In the VABlog approach, videos can be adapted to text, text can be adapted to audio podcasts, audio podcasts can be adapted to video, and so on. You're saying the same thing regardless of format, but this way, you're reaching your audience via their preferred method of consumption.

Once you've produced your cornerstone content, you will then share it via your website, social media, email, and text message each week (see Figure 9.1). This multiplies your reach, reduces burnout, and improves discoverability. Let's examine each component, step by step.

Step 1: Your Website

Your weekly website VABlog serves as a digital home base where all roads lead. It also helps you get more visibility to your website. According to HubSpot's large-scale annual marketing report, website/blog content remains among the highest return on investment (ROI) channels for modern marketers, driven in part by increased organic traffic and deeper audience engagement.[3]

Search engines find you, in part, through the keywords you use. More words added to a website each week mean a higher probability of being found. The more search engines come to rely on AI, the more this continues to be true. AI-generated summaries of search queries contribute to what is known as a "zero-click" ecosystem, in which many users find the answer to their question directly through these summaries. So in addition

CORNERSTONE CONTENT FUNNEL MAP

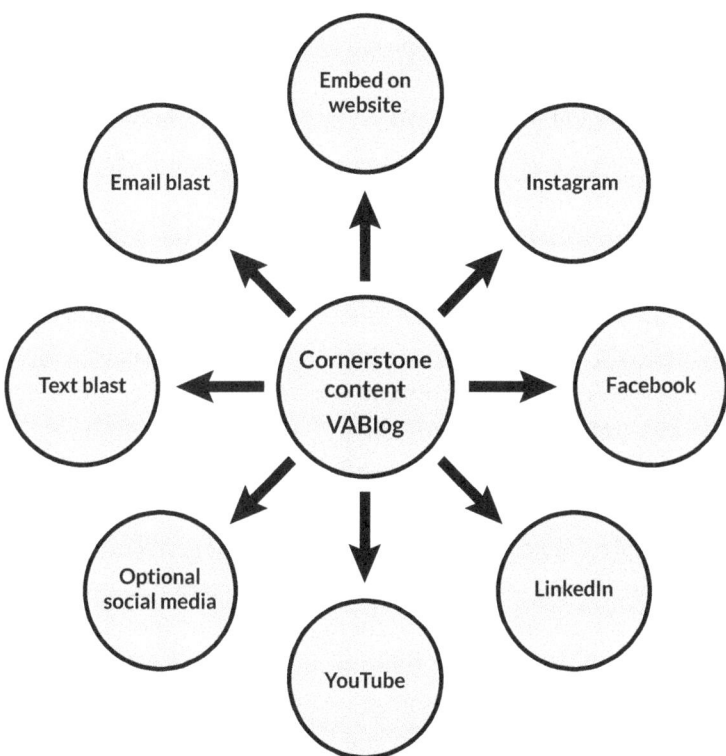

Figure 9.1 The Cornerstone Content Funnel Map helps you visualize where and how you are sharing your weekly cornerstone content.

to striving to be the first website listed, you should also strive to be listed in the search snippet.

One way to ensure that your website gets featured is to integrate "well-structured, novel information and frameworks" in your content. The large language models (LLMs) that AI tools use to find answers to queries rely not only on keywords, but also on information that connects concepts and answers key questions and prompts.[4] Packaging your cornerstone content with frameworks naturally provides the connection that

LLMs look for. That way, your content doesn't get aggregated into the same bucket as all the other content that says similar things. It will go into a bucket of its own, producing its own snippet that defies general categorizations and demands to be featured.[5]

So, where do you come up with all these frameworks? I suggest starting with the TRUTH framework (Chapter 4) to create your brand's unique point of view (POV) and then supporting that POV by following the framework strategies outlined in Chapter 8.

To brainstorm further ideas, ask AI to assist you. For example, Marisol might ask, "What are key questions first-generation Latinas ask about financial independence?" She can then form frameworks based on that information. Just like interviewing "ideal customers" (Chapter 3), AI can give you powerful insights into your customers' curiosities, queries, and keywords. We tend to jump straight to prompting and finding answers with AI, but if you remember to *question the question*, you'll be rewarded with insight.

For example, Marisol could ask, "What do first generation Latinas ask you about the most?" Or, "What do first generation Latinas say they struggle with the most?" After all, there are humans (potential audience members) behind each of the billions of queries and prompts that AI receives daily, and with them comes a treasure trove of information about how those humans think, feel, struggle, and act that you may have overlooked. But you have to remember to ask.

Once you have a framework or two in place, it's time to start creating your weekly VABlog pieces and posting them to your website. For this step, all you have to do is embed text of your first thought leadership post. There are two ways to approach this: video/audio-first, or text-first.

If your initial piece of cornerstone content is a podcast or a video, turn it into a piece of written content with just a few simple software tricks. First, create an audio transcript. (There are many software solutions that create transcripts, and some video and audio recording tools have transcript production options built in. Rev.com is a favorite of mine.) Then, run the transcript through an AI tool like ChatGPT and tell it to summarize each section with time stamps. To get the best prompting results, name each part of the framework you taught in your video or podcast so that the AI tool you choose to use can go look for, summarize, and stamp those specific cut points. Then, above the written text you just created, embed the video or podcast.

If your initial piece of cornerstone content is a written post, create a video lead-in (preferred) or use a photo to accompany the text. I'll cover the how-tos of both of these techniques in Chapter 11.

Step 2: YouTube

If you create a video blog, video lead-in, or video podcast, host it on YouTube. YouTube plays an important behind-the-scenes role in your funnel success. Since YouTube is owned by Google, having a presence there also gives your content a search engine optimization (SEO) lift, albeit passively. Industry research commonly notes that brands with embedded YouTube videos on their sites rank higher in search results and receive longer average page visits.[6,7]

Marisol has experienced this boost firsthand. "The episodes of my podcast on YouTube show up on the first page of Google every time I search my brand or my name," she says. Those are encouraging results, even if Marisol isn't trying to be a YouTube star. Many of her videos are simply the audio of her podcast branded with her logo as the visual, and that's fine. The goal is visibility for her value, and the passive SEO benefits of YouTube contribute to that. This is why the VABlog is so powerful. If you use video and written content on each blog post, you cover all aspects of the SEO equation.

If you're not ready for videos yet, remember: This system still works with photos. Don't let a lack of videos get in the way of progress.

Step 3: Baseline Social Media

If your website (see Chapter 7) is your brand's online home base, then social media is its discovery engine. In addition to sharing audio/video content to YouTube, I recommend sharing your weekly cornerstone content on LinkedIn, Instagram, and Facebook, which are still the best platforms for promoting brand discovery, are simple to use, and reach the widest audience. Here's why.

LinkedIn is the most trusted social platform, according to *Business Insider*'s Digital Trust Report.[8] It favors long-form content, professional insights, and personal storytelling, which is perfect for the particular style of thought leadership content I have taught you how to produce. Post your cornerstone content there each week. Marisol also uses LinkedIn to highlight events and guest blogs, like the ones she did at her business school.

Instagram users want to discover things. It's especially valuable for lifestyle, wellness, and career-related brands, and it remains the top platform for discovery, with 61 percent of social users turning to it to find their next purchase.[9] Marisol uses Instagram as a primary driver of her brand by recycling her weekly content into smaller snippets (which we'll take a deeper look at how to do next chapter). Simply post your cornerstone content as-is in the caption of a post each week, and if you created a video lead-in, post that as the visual. Share your reel (video) or post to Instagram stories for additional reach.

Sharing to Facebook from Instagram is easy, and despite shifting trends, Facebook remains a strong discovery and traffic tool, accounting for over 60 percent of all social media referral traffic and offering unmatched reach, especially among Gen X and Boomers.[10] It can generate a nice visibility boost with no additional effort. The catch is that you need to make sure your Instagram and Facebook profiles are either both set to personal pages or both set to business pages to enable auto posting from Instagram to Facebook. I recommend professional profiles because you get better analytics, which can help you make more informed decisions on what types of cornerstone content to produce next (as I will discuss in Chapter 10).

Remember, social media is your discovery tool, so make sure to use it with purpose.[11] Instead of playing "online marketing darts," use all your weekly cornerstone content posts to drive opt-ins to your email and/or text lists. Simply say something like, "Would you like these insights delivered to your email inbox (or phone) each week?" Then identify where your opt-in link is (comments, bio, etc.). Marisol is in the midst of launching her website, so she uses her Instagram bio as a powerful opt-in tool and constantly gives soft reminders as she puts out new episodes and reminds people, "Don't forget to subscribe to the link in my bio." Putting subscription and opt-in opportunities in your social bios is another great way to make sure your ideal customers have as many opt-in opportunities as possible.

One word of caution: As mentioned in the beginning of the chapter, social media has increasingly become a "zero-click" ecosystem just like website search results, thanks to the continuous supply of reels and the scrollability of feeds.[12] In such an ecosystem, visitors are trained and incentivized to keep scrolling, rather than click away to other sites. Knowing this, your job is to think of ways to get potential audience members to opt in without asking them to leave the platform when they see your opt-in invitation. This is what Marisol does by sending people to her bio. On my social pages and posts, I tell people to "screenshot this link" and ask them to come back to it when they are ready. That way, they don't have to click away from their current scroll, and it's the first thing in their camera roll when they open it next.

You might be nervous about posting the same information to so many different places, and you may even feel the urge to curate the formatting, filters, and captions for each platform. Resist the urge. Keep your approach simple and sustainable, so you don't burn out. If someone notices you're posting the same cornerstone content across platforms, thank them for noticing. It's hard to get an audience member to pay that much attention. Congratulations!

Before we move on, if you're reading this book ten years after it was published, social media may have vastly changed. If so, ask yourself this question: "Which platforms or places promote brand discovery, are simplest to use, and cover the widest audience or audience most important to me?" These are the places you should be posting your cornerstone content to each week to get discovered.

Step 4: Optional Social Media

As of this writing, channels like TikTok, Pinterest, Threads, or X (formerly Twitter) are optional. Consistency is more important than coverage, and you already have a lot of crossover coverage to these platforms by being on the platforms I recommended. If you already use them, add them to your list of places to post your weekly cornerstone content. If not, wait until you've created a sustainable system with the platforms I highlighted earlier, and then layer these other platforms in as you have time. Again, cross post with as much recycled content as you can. The consistency will reward you with both saved time and increased discoverability from your unified messaging we discussed earlier in this chapter.

Step 5: Email and Text

As you learned in Chapter 7, your owned audience is your most engaged audience. They are the ones who have taken the extra step to opt in and hear more from you. Email your thought leadership piece to them weekly. This nurtures and deepens the relationship you've already built. I recommend starting with the story lead-in in the body of the email, followed by a brief framework summary (first sentence of each step), and a call to action (CTA) like "Read the full post on my blog." This structure boosts engagement and click-through rates to your website (which in turn boosts its SEO).

Texting is also powerful. It currently comes with a 98% open rate.[13] A simple message like, "Check your email for my latest post: [Title]" keeps you top of mind. Remember: Your email list and/or your text list are algorithm-proof and owned by you.

As You Choose Your Weekly Topics, Take a Global Look

Here are a few examples of Marisol's podcast topics, all centered around navigating life as a first-generation professional:

- The Many Hats We Wear: Navigating Multiple Identities in Today's World
- Get Clarity About Your Business as a First-Generation Owner
- HOPE's College Leadership Program for First-Generation Latina Leaders

Let's pause and notice something. While Marisol has dozens of post and podcast topics, it only takes looking over a few to understand what her brand has to offer, even if you'd never heard her story before. This is because she repeats her brand's value proposition over and over again in varied ways with every piece of cornerstone content she creates. If you find yourself going off-topic often in your cornerstone content, go back to your brand statement for weekly inspiration.

Carrie Prince Uses Her Email List to Pivot

In Chapter 7, I mentioned that as Carrie Prince built her brand and got more clarity on her goals, she transitioned from being a dating coach to a leadership coach. As you may remember, she highlights several similarities in dating and leadership, especially when it comes to interpersonal communication and teamwork. When Carrie started her pivot to become a leadership coach, she didn't announce it on social media first. She announced it to her email list. "I knew that these people were the strongest part of my audience who trusted me the most," she explained. "It seemed only right to tell them first, but it was also strategic."

Because Carrie had consistently built and nurtured her email list through the kind of funnel work outlined in this chapter, she already had hundreds of people on her list who knew, liked, and trusted her. Of those subscribers, Carrie knew many of her dating clients might be interested in pivoting to leadership coaching with her. For those that wouldn't, Carrie knew that many trusted her enough to refer her services to someone else who needed them, thus helping her to expand her audience and clientele.

"My initial leadership coaching clients came from the email list I built as a dating coach," she says. "And by telling them first, I had clients, case studies and social proof before I even made my leadership coaching business public, which made the transition much stronger."

Your owned audience (email and/or text list) is a powerful asset. It will stay with you however your brand grows and changes. As you work on building out your funnel, from your website to your social channels to email and text, make sure you focus on growing and nurturing it. As technology changes, move with it. In ten years, we may have AI assistants opting into lists for us, but the idea is the same. There is a person behind the email, phone number, or even bot, and when they opt in, you own that contact in your audience. That's a much better place to be in than relying on rented audiences from third-party platforms.

Last, give this process time to grow and mature. The cornerstone content–driven funnel works because it capitalizes on social media as a discovery tool. It builds your website's SEO and LLM visibility. It gives you the opportunity to own your own leads by driving subscriptions to email and text lists, your most valued leads. It repurposes information, which avoids burnout on your end and strengthens the impression on your ideal customers' end. In short, by anchoring everything to one weekly idea, you create content that is consistent, efficient, searchable, sharable, and sustainable.

Now it's your turn. Build your own funnel by following the same design illustrated in this chapter. Draw a circle in the middle for your cornerstone content and then map out the key areas of the online ecosystem that you will cover with email, social media, and the like. Add methodically as your brand grows.

> **Your Simplified Digital Funnel, at a Glance**
>
> *Main Idea*
> This chapter introduces a system for publishing thought leadership consistently without burnout. By repurposing one weekly cornerstone content piece across your website, email/text list, and social media, you create a strategic funnel that increases your brand's visibility and trust while reinforcing your core message.
>
> *Key Takeaways*
> - You don't need to be everywhere, just consistent in the places you commit to.
> - Reusing content reinforces your core message and ensures that people see your value even if they find you on different platforms.
> - Focus your funnel on owned platforms (website, email, and text) and let social media serve as a discovery engine.
>
> *Next Steps*
> Map out your funnel and consistently share your cornerstone content throughout it each week.
>
> *How Long Does This Take?*
> Map your funnel: thirty minutes
>   Weekly content creation and sharing: one to two hours
>   This one comes with a bonus: As you do it each week, you will get faster at it.

10

The Words That Power Your Funnel

Five casts, ten braces, and counting.

Ella is eleven now, and in the eight years since we found her early onset scoliosis, those casts and braces heroically guided her spine away from her heart and lungs. After the first couple of years, the casts had pulled her spine so straight that only a couple of hints of curvature remained. Those curves were under ten degrees, which meant she could move to bracing instead of casting. The braces would hold the correction in place, ensuring that unless something out of the ordinary happened, she'd live a normal life and never require a surgical correction.

We thought the bracing would be a welcome change. The brace came with an hour break a day, and the break would be increased over the years to night bracing only. That meant a little bit of swimming, real showers, and soft hugs on a *daily* basis, even at first. But I'll never forget the night that she completely broke down. She'd been wearing the brace for months, and I had just told her that her "brace break" time was up.

She looked at me with complete sadness in her eyes and asked, "Why did it have to be me?" My heart sank. I had no acceptable answer for her. I told her we all have something hard that we have to deal with. I cited my tendency to over worry and overthink things, the continuous positive airway pressure (CPAP) machine my husband, Jay, wears at night, and the speech issues that Jack had to overcome. She didn't care. "I would rather any of those, mom. Do you know how awful this feels?" I didn't. I could only imagine.

Her sadness turned to anger as I searched desperately for something better to say. I wanted to take it all away: the constant discomfort, the tightness; gosh it always seemed *so tight*, take-your-breath-away-tight, when I pulled the Velcro to the right place. I held her and cried with her. An hour passed, then a little more, and she abruptly stopped crying.

"Mom? If we order those princess hair tools right now, what day will they get here?" I was already clicking *buy now* when I told her it looked like we could get them tomorrow.

In the years since that night, Ella would complain, but she always seemed to accept what she had to do. In fact, she went on to be incredibly athletic and active, always naturally good at the sports she tried. Her resilience was amazing to watch. She came home proud one day and told me that someone at school was sad that day and found her to talk to because "everyone knows" that she knows how to help. Who knew a cast could also shape a soul with so much bravery, acceptance, kindness, and empathy?

When Ella turned ten, her doctor told us that her spinal curves had recovered sufficiently to try weaning off the brace entirely. She looked at me with questioning eyes. I couldn't believe it either. After the first night out of her brace, Ella said to me "It was like the bed was hugging me all night. Is that what beds feel like all the time?"

Can you believe how much she'd tolerated?

It turns out, we were right to be skeptical. After two months, her curves regressed enough to indicate that she needed night bracing again, this time until she was done growing. We both took the news stoically. It would be at least a few more years before she felt those bed hugs again. We were so disappointed.

I didn't realize how much I'd compartmentalized everything to cope with what Ella had to go through over the years until Ella ran up to Jay and me a year later. "Jack's really hurt," Ella said. The panicked look in her eyes had us up in a split second, running toward him. He was writhing in pain.

An emergency room visit confirmed he'd suffered a buckle break in his left arm, a common injury for an active eight-year-old boy. He would have a cast for six weeks and then he'd be all healed up in time for summer. I was nauseous and sweating as I heard the news, and my heart pounded as they applied the cast. Ella was reacting too.

"Mom, will he get really hot?"

"Mom, he's going to feel so sad when he can't swim."

"Mom, will he be able to sleep okay?"

Her eyes were glistening as she held tightly to his "good" hand. A common injury, a simple cast, a panicked reaction for both Ella and me. Meanwhile, Jack was strangely calm.

No wonder we were reacting to Jack's routine cast in the way we did. It represented so much more to us than what it was. It took soft hugs away *and* bed hugs away. But Jack wasn't having the same reaction. Once he was over the initial trauma, he was proud. He told his story of injury and bravery to anyone who would listen. Jay told him that when he was little, he'd always hoped for a broken bone so he could look as cool as Jack did with his cast, but he never got one.

Jack picked bright orange for his cast color, and his confidence brightened with it. Jack wasn't focused on the downsides of his cast. He was focused on feeling brave and tough instead, because his cast experience was completely different from Ella's.

His confidence stuck around. Here's a moment I posted about on LinkedIn[1]:

Saturday musings: What's your jumbotron moment?

> A few weeks ago, my son broke his arm. To soften the blow (retroactively, I suppose), we took him to a Giants game. Our seats were near the dugout, so we arrived early, hoping he might get an autograph or two.
>
> As my son and daughter stood by the net, waiting hopefully, their faces suddenly appeared on the jumbotron (see Figure 10.1).
>
> In that split second: My normally outgoing daughter crouched behind her brother in shock. Then she took a few deep breaths, stood back up, and waved proudly.
>
> My normally shy son stayed steady, smiling stoically until the camera panned away.

CONFIDENCE AT THE GIANTS GAME

Figure 10.1 Ella (left) and Jack (right) wave at the jumbotron in Oracle Park, April 2025.

They each had their own reaction to being visible, and both were brave in their own way. Undoubtedly, people in the crowd smiled and experienced some joy because of it. I know my husband and I did.

Here's the thing:

The internet is a jumbotron. Every time you post, you step onto that big screen. Whether you're sharing joy, insight, or a moment of perspective, you're giving someone else a reason to smile, learn, reflect, or act.

Yes, there will be moments you need to crouch and take a breath, or hold on tight to that stoic smile, but the important thing is to step in

> because no one can learn from, smile because of, reflect on, or act on your value if it's not visible to them.
>
> So—What's YOUR next jumbotron moment? Who will smile, learn, reflect, or act because of you? #personalbranding #contentmarketing.

I made that post because I thought it would inspire others who were feeling nervous to launch their brands. Whether they needed a little breath like Ella because their bravery came with a little more baggage, or whether their challenge was fresh, like Jack's, maybe this could help them hit *publish*.

I also shared my story because I was living it in real time, and I often feel compelled to share my experiences. Like me, you are also living the middle of *your* story right now, and you also relate to all kinds of people in the middle of theirs.

But just because we're living our stories doesn't mean we're good storytellers. Often, when we try to tell our stories, we start at the beginning. The most successful storytellers—on social media, in public speaking, and the like—start right in the middle. This forces them to lead with the incident or conflict that led to the next step. It also leaves people wanting to know more both about the outcome and how it all started. In this chapter, you're going to learn the formula for expert storytelling that will stop the scroll on your service-first personal brand.

Wait, What?

When content is built from your lived stories and experience that align with your audience's needs, it creates trust, boosts visibility, and moves people toward transformation. This is the foundation of a sustainable and service-first content funnel, and it's sure to stand out if you don't start at the beginning or end, but right in the middle.

Social Media Is the Story of Our Lives

When I opened this chapter with Ella's story, you may have realized that you'd been wondering about how everything turned out for her. You may have even paid a little more attention when I came back to it.

There's a reason for that: Stories are powerful. We physically react to them. When we hear them, we release oxytocin, known as the "love" hormone. It's what makes us feel warm and fuzzy when we get a hug from a loved one or hold a sweet, furry friend. It also creates increased attention and trust, which is great for brands. Even sad stories, according to the research, can boost oxytocin levels (in addition to some cortisol) because oxytocin is related to empathy.[2] When we feel empathetic, which often happens when we hear or read a story we can relate to, we are more likely to gain trust through that shared understanding.

Stories also help us remember things better: 22 times better, to be exact.[3] In a world of information overload, being memorable is important. To test the power of stories, think back to Chapter 1. It's likely been a while since you read it, but you probably recall bits and pieces of what I told you about Ella's initial diagnosis and how it shaped me, maybe even more than you remember some of the other information I've shared in the pages since then. Maybe you even went back to Chapter 1 after you read the rest of the story in this chapter to refresh yourself.

Stories connect the dots. In Chapter 8, when Carter shared his story lead-in about some of his frustrating experiences in Little League and how those experiences connected to business, we were better able to understand, relate to, and remember his subsequent framework. Humans naturally think in the form of stories because that's how we experience the world.[4] By packaging your knowledge to fit the way people naturally think, you're better understood and able to help more people.

Social media is ideally suited for storytelling. In fact, I'd go so far as to say that social media *is* one big story. The biggest mistake people make on social media is forgetting that. Social media is just an extension of how we experience in-person life. That's why the most interesting people let you in to little snippets of their lives. That's why companies tell stories about their founders and customers. You can do this for your brand, too, and people will subconsciously come back for more.

To do this, let's start by creating a bank of long-form content. Then I'll help you take bits and pieces from that to build your short-form social media content and captions.

Your Long-Form Content Trifecta

When you're first starting out with your service-first personal brand, I recommend three pieces of long-form content: your "involvement story," your first piece of cornerstone content, and a BIO. You'll be surprised at how often you refer back to these to create short-form content.

How to Write the Involvement Story

In Chapter 8, we briefly touched on the story lead-in as a component of your cornerstone content. Your involvement story can be about yourself, someone you've helped, or even something you've closely observed. Whatever the subject, the story should highlight a common struggle your audience can connect with, so that you benefit from the "I" (involvement) in the AEIOUs of service-first personal branding, and the subsequent perceived empathy that comes with it.

My story about The Hug is a good example of an involvement story because many professionals can likely relate to a time where a hard-to-overcome moment of personal struggle caused them to reevaluate a professional or personal path.

Most involvement stories are ineffective and forgettable because they start at the beginning and skip the incident or setback. In doing so, they look like this:

Starting point → Action → Transformation

That's a logical, linear progression, but it's not compelling. Stories that connect with people and create empathy look like this:

Starting point → Incident → Action → Setback → Resolution → Transformation

Here's how my involvement story looks both ways:
Scenario 1:
Starting point. Ella has early onset scoliosis and I am contemplative. →
Action. Ella puts on casts and braces, and I fix my business. →
Transformation. Ella is cured, and I get the business I want.

Scenario 2:
Starting point. Ella has early onset scoliosis, and I am contemplative. →
Incident. I hug her for the last time before her first cast. →
Action. Ella puts on casts and braces, and I fix my business. →
Setback. Ella's brace doesn't totally work; Jack breaks his arm. →
Resolution. We learn lessons about confidence and bravery that are related to things I teach my students and clients. →
Transformation. Resiliency for ourselves and others.

Scenario 2 is clearly a lot more relatable because the incident and setbacks create empathy. My audience can relate to my struggles, even if they haven't experienced the same thing. But remember, we live most of our lives in the middle of stories, either responding to incidents with actions or trying to overcome setbacks to get a resolution. Your stories are more relatable when you highlight those moments and start in the middle as well. In Chapter 1, I started with The Hug (incident). In this chapter, I started with a setback when I explained that Ella's brace wasn't exactly the moment of freedom we thought it would be.

To cue yourself to start in the middle with either the incident or setback, one of my favorite prompts is, "I remember," because it forces you to home in on a specific moment—like hugging Ella for the last time before her first cast was applied, or Jack breaking his arm—and then work backward to the starting point and forward to the transformation.

Now, it's your turn to write your involvement story. Here's how:

1. Write "I remember" at the top of a blank page.
2. Then jot either of these down:
   (a) Incident → Starting Point → Action → Resolution → Transformation
   (b) Setback → Starting Point → Action → Resolution → Transformation
3. Start freewriting. Don't worry about errors, grammar, or getting it perfect. Just write.

One of the biggest mistakes people make is editing as they go. When you backspace or rewrite mid-sentence, you switch from the creative side of your brain to the technical side. Don't do it. Let the thoughts flow.

When you're done, review the organization first. Did you follow the story arc, or did you drift? Once the structure feels right, then you can polish it by either editing by hand or by running it through an AI tool. If you choose the latter, ask it to preserve your voice and wording but to help with clarity, grammar, and punctuation. The result should be a strong involvement story to pull from in your content.

Marisol Ibarra, who I introduced in Chapter 9, found this exercise especially powerful. "I started my story by saying, 'I remember when my teacher realized I was the only English speaker in my family,'" she says. "So many setbacks of being a first-generation Mexican American just flowed out. I had so many moments of escalation, setback, and resolution that helped me transform into a guide for others going through the same struggles."

You might recall that Jennifer Anderson from Chapter 4 remembered when she was staring out her kitchen window, sure other parents were also struggling with feeding their children. Dr. Lisa Hornick from Chapter 2 remembered when she looked up at the stage of an optometry conference and wondered if she could be up there as well.

I hope you enjoy writing your first involvement story. Just remember: You don't have to stop at just one. Write several of them as you get inspired. You'll need them as you build your brand for years to come.

How to Write Your First Piece of Cornerstone Content

Your first piece of cornerstone content is the same as the first thought leadership post I walked you through in Chapter 8. It includes a framework with a story lead-in, and your story lead-in comes directly from one of your involvement stories. Each week, you're going to need to create story lead-ins, so I've included a list of 52 prompts in the back of this book to get you started. Similar to the "I remember" exercise, these prompts drop you directly into pivotal moments, escalations, and setbacks to powerfully introduce your weekly cornerstone content.

The key to getting your cornerstone content to work is the segue. In the post about the Giants jumbotron I shared earlier, I segued by asking my readers about their own "jumbotron moment" and then pivoted into talking about how they might react to the opportunity to build a brand online. Some examples of segues are:

- Asking a related question. ("What's your jumbotron moment?")
- _____ is so closely related to _____.
- _____ reminds me of the moment when _____.

After the segue, simply drop in your framework.

How to Write Your BIO

You need a biography for your website, your social media platforms, and for public appearances and speaking engagements. Traditionally, biographies are boring because they are full of facts and figures with no stories to remember them by. But I'm talking about creating something more powerful: a BIO that delivers a more interesting impact with a descriptive phrase-based lead-in, a story, and the facts.

Here's how to write your BIO:

1. **Brainstorm.** Describe yourself in three words or short phrases. AI tools are your friends here. Remember when I taught you how to name your brand in Chapter 6? Use a similar process. Generate twenty or more options for these words and phrases about yourself so you can objectively choose without emotion.
2. **Inform.** List the main facts and accomplishments that you want people to know about you.
3. **Organize.** Write a story about yourself, followed by a fact-based paragraph.

I recommend writing in the first person rather than the third person for a more personal approach. Alternatively, you can write the story lead-in in the first person, followed with the fact-based information in the third person. Here's an example that follows the latter format from Jennifer Anderson (Chapter 4).[5]

I'm a mom, wife, registered dietitian, and the founder of Kids Eat in Color.

When I was a new mom, I learned that feeding kids is tricky. My first child started to fall off the growth chart as a little guy, and I realized how much effort can go into feeding a child. I took my angst and specialized in feeding children and picky eating. After months of research, I formulated an approach. I started making small, evidence-based tweaks at mealtimes hoping to end the food struggles and reduce our stress—and it worked!

Since then, I've been sharing my knowledge with other parents and built Kids Eat in Color and our team of experts to be the resource I wished I had when searching for ways to feed my kids. I'm professional and also a real-life parent, and I make sure that all our guides, courses and tools bring practical strategies to families.

So whether you are a parent feeling stressed about mealtime, defeated by extreme picky eating, or just need some help with meal ideas, the team and I are here for *you*.

Here at Kids Eat in Color, we know that small changes and a little color make big differences in children's health.

Jennifer Anderson is a registered dietitian and has a masters of science in public health from Johns Hopkins School of Public Health. In 2019, she founded Kids Eat in Color, an authoritative resource that helps families feed their children from their first bite of solid food through picky eating and elementary-aged nutrition needs. Prior to starting Kids Eat in Color she coordinated youth nutrition programs at a food bank, performed research in inner-city food deserts, and consulted for the USDA national office SNAP-Ed program. Her academic background is in public health nutrition, cultural anthropology, and economics.

The handy thing about this format is that you can snip and use the fact-based paragraph for more formal situations like speaking engagements and panels. You can also snip and use the beginning of it for short-form, three-phrase bios on social media platforms like LinkedIn and Instagram.

From Long Form to Short Form

The funnel I introduced in the last chapter includes one piece of long-form thought leadership content (your cornerstone content) each week (or at a slower starting interval, with the intent to work up to each week).

It's a fantastic place to start, but there are simple ways to repurpose your content further to increase your chances of being discovered on social media. A batching calendar will help you achieve this (see Figure 10.2).

Your Batching Calendar

A smart content strategy starts with batching, not just for efficiency, but for consistency and sustainability. Batching means writing a bunch of pieces of cornerstone content all at once. I encourage you to batch and plan twelve

---

BATCHING CALENDAR

WEEKLY THEME:				
		DAILY POSTS		
1	2	3	4	5

Figure 10.2 This is a batching calendar template for one week of content scheduling. Create twelve weeks of content at a time to maintain consistency and sustainability.

weeks of content at a time. This will help you avoid giving away too much information in a single piece of cornerstone content. Remember in Chapter 8 when I told you that if your framework goes beyond five steps, consider splitting it into two? Planning in advance allows you to zoom out and make sure you're saying as little as possible each week. Remember, you are going to be branding yourself for a long time. No need to explain it all away in the first post.

Next, repurpose pieces of your cornerstone content by breaking it down into mini-topics. Think back to Carter's Three Ws framework from Chapter 8:

- What did I do better today than yesterday?
- What's one thing I can improve this week?
- What weakness can I turn into a strength this month?

The three questions with a story lead-in are his cornerstone content. But then on each subsequent day, he can make shorter posts by reintroducing the framework and asking one question at a time. For example, he could say, "Yesterday I posted my Three Ws. What will you do better today than yesterday?"

As you break down your frameworks into daily reminders, depending on framework length, you'll realize that you have between four and six posts per week (cornerstone content, plus a three-to-five-step framework broken down over subsequent days). This is a powerful way to create your content because research shows that educational posts outperform purely entertainment-based posts.[6] You might even remember in Chapter 4 that when Jennifer Anderson focused on educational posts, her brand started to grow the most.

To fill out the rest of the days you aren't posting educational content, consider a few other types of posts.

Personal Posts

In this type of post, simply share a snippet of your story, or of the story of someone you've helped, without necessarily teaching anything. (But remember: Start in the middle, at a setback or action.) Whenever I make authentic posts about my kids or hobbies, I gain reach and engagement. Not only does this give my audience something varied to consume that's relatable and story based, but algorithms prioritize authentic and relatable sharing, even on business pages.[7] Personal posts that show vulnerability also tend to gain reach, even on LinkedIn.[8] After all, vulnerability inherently signals to your audience that you trust them, and that trust deepens their connection to your brand.[9]

Engaging Posts

Ask your audience a question related to your brand. In addition to generating engagement, this often leads to new content ideas. There's also a scroll-stopping benefit to asking questions. Research shows that headlines phrased as questions tend to drive significantly higher click-throughs than declarative ones. In one field experiment, question-style headlines, especially ones that reference the user (for example, "Are you making this common mistake?") increased readership by over 100 percent compared with statement-style headlines.[10] Questions also create agency among your readers, which means they perceive autonomy over their own opinions and actions.[11] For example, would you be more contemplative if Nike asked you why you do it, versus simply telling you to "Just do it"? When you tell your readers what to do, they might do it. When they answer a question and decide for themselves that they want to do something, they do it at a much higher rate.

Behind-the-Scenes Posts

Give your audience a peek into your world: your workspace, your process, your family, or your team. These posts humanize your brand and make your expertise more relatable. People also watch behind-the-scenes content longer than other forms of content.[12]

Combination Posts

Combining post types is often a winning scenario. In the LinkedIn post I shared at the beginning of the chapter, I combined a behind-the-scenes look at my family with an engaging question: "What's your jumbotron moment?"

Fun or Pop Culture

You've likely seen posts share something trending, funny, or culturally relevant. Many people think that being trendy is the key to virality, but it's not. Invoking emotion *is*, however, which you are doing every week with story-based lead-ins to your cornerstone content.[13] Topical posts can suck away a lot of time without a lot of reward. Use them sparingly; ideally, no more than once a month.

Some More Posting Tips

Here are some ideas that will ensure that you maximize the effectiveness of your posts.

Don't Forget the Opt-Ins

While content is fun to think about, remember: The goal of this funnel is to drive people to your website and ask them to opt in to your email and text lists. I recommend that you give reminders in at least half of your posts, especially your cornerstone content. Remember, social media has increasingly become a zero-click ecosystem, so try different approaches to this. For instance, as I recommended in Chapter 9, you could put opt-in links in social media bios or tell your audience to screenshot your content with a link that they can return to and then opt in later. That way they don't have to interrupt their scroll, but your brand will be top of mind the next time they open their camera roll.

Headlines, Subject Lines, and the First Sentence of Each Post

Headlines are the most critical element of content. They account for 62 percent of engagement gains, with optimized headlines driving a 78 percent increase in traffic and 71 percent longer attention spans.[14] In other words, you need to get the headlines right.

AI tools have made it much easier to create headlines or suggest alternatives. Each time you write cornerstone content, a short-form post, or an email or text, ask an AI tool to brainstorm twenty headlines for you. As with naming your brand or framework, this takes the emotion out of it and usually generates options you would never have thought of.

Be Inquisitive with AI

AI is evolving rapidly, but you can use timeless strategies to make sure that no matter how it changes, your content still stands out.

First, be warned: AI waters down content. Research from my colleague Beth A. Bechky and her coauthor Gerald F. Davis showed that, "while generative AI improves efficiency and the average quality of a creative product, it also tends to reduce the advantages of expertise and induce a homogenization of what is creatively produced as outputs."[15]

To avoid the risk of homogenization, that is, of having content as vanilla as everyone else, draft first, even if you're using voice-to-text. Talk to AI like it's a research associate. If you're trying to form a thought leadership piece, take it through the TRUTH framework, step by step. The more steps you take in your prompting, the more original your output gets. Be sure also to tell it your purpose when you prompt it (you want opt-ins and traffic to your website and owned lists, for example). Describe your ideal customer and your brand voice. Train it with writing you've done in the past.

When in doubt, as I mentioned in Chapter 9, *question the question*. Ask an AI tool questions about what your ideal customers wonder about most and incorporate themes and keywords from its answers into your content.

Observe Others

Find people whose brands are either competitive or complementary to yours. Follow them and keep a spreadsheet of the posts you like. Use those posts as inspiration for your own with an added twist. In entrepreneurship, the discovery rarely goes to the first person to try, but rather to the last person who perfects it.

Your competitors are an asset. Learn from them, use them for inspiration, and don't be shy to interact with them. You may even find yourself collaborating on a panel together someday.

It's Your Turn

Make your batching calendar. Start by defining your weekly cornerstone content. Then divide that into mini daily topics. Fill in the empty days with personal, engaging, or behind-the-scenes posts. When possible, combine styles. Use the trendy stuff sparingly. Whatever you do, remember your purpose. Half the time, use techniques to gain opt-ins to your owned online space. That's why you're doing all this work in the first place!

A parting word to the wise: If you fall off pace or lose momentum, pick right back up when you can. Consistency is key, and so is finding it again when you get off track. Think of falling off your funnel schedule like eating a big dinner full of junk food. It's easier to overcome when you get right back on track as soon as possible rather than giving up and eating junk food for weeks.

The Words That Power Your Funnel, at a Glance

Main Idea
This chapter shows how long-form content forms the foundation of your brand, and how short-form snippets, stories, and posts extend your reach across platforms. Through storytelling and a structured content system, you create connection, visibility, and impact.

Key Takeaways
- Your long-form content trifecta consists of your involvement stories, cornerstone content, and BIO all of which can be repurposed into short-form content.
- The story arc (starting point, incident, action, setback, resolution, transformation) helps build empathy and trust by highlighting relatable struggles, especially when you start right in the middle.
- Snippets from longer content increase social media engagement and can be batched using a weekly-to-daily system.
- A variety of post types, including personal, engaging, and behind-the-scenes posts, enhance relatability, increase reach, and serve your funnel goals.
- Headlines are critical: They drive up to 78 percent more traffic and improve attention spans by 71 percent.
- AI can enhance content strategy when used intentionally, after your original ideas are drafted.

(continued)

(*continued*)

Next Step

Map your batching calendar. Start with weekly cornerstone content and divide it into daily snippets. Fill empty days with personal, engaging, and behind-the-scenes posts. Use AI to brainstorm and optimize your headlines and content, and always lead with your voice and purpose.

How Long Does It Take?

Cornerstone content: two hours/week

   Snippets and other posts: 1–1.5 hours/week

   Batching calendar creation: one hour/month

   Recommendation: Batch 12 weeks of content at a time for consistency, efficiency, and ease.

   And as with the steps I discussed at the end of Chapter 9, the bonus of consistency here is that the more often you do this, the less time it will take you.

11 The FaceTime Effect

> I was so nervous to make videos at first, and I'll always say you made me do it. Don't tell anyone that I kind of enjoy it now.
> —Tracy Fauver

"It's not that hard to hold up this cup of water right now," Tracy Fauver explains in a video, arm straight out in front of her, holding a small glass of water in a paper cup. "But I would probably get impatient if I had to hold it up for a full 10 minutes. Can you imagine if I had to hold it up for several hours? My arm would definitely start to shake, my elbow might bend, water might spill. I might give up."

You might remember Tracy from Chapter 8. A social worker, Tracy has worked with diverse populations, from children in foster care to individuals experiencing homelessness. Uniting her work is the belief that we too often treat symptoms, rather than the root cause, when people fall into addiction or other social disparities. "Rather than just treat symptoms of the problems," Tracy says, "addressing the underlying trauma and its outcomes with compassion instead of judgement is the first step to finding solutions to provide social safety nets that truly work." This belief lies at the heart of her CARE framework (**c**onfront the impact; **a**cknowledge shared struggles;

reflect with compassion; extend empathy to others). She's fascinating to listen to.

With a focus on childhood trauma and its long-lasting effects, Tracy educates others on the topic of stress as it relates to the widely cited adverse childhood experience (ACE) study.[1] In the video I quote from at the beginning of this chapter, she compares "green-light stress" to the nervousness she felt making the video or to taking a math test as a child. It's brief, mild, and often positive. In other words, a little nervousness before a test can actually help you succeed. Yellow-light stress, she continues, could stem from something like the death of a loved one. It's more serious but can be buffered by strong relationships. "A grandparent might pass away when a child is young," Tracy says, "but that child can overcome the stress if she is well supported by parents." Red-light stress, Tracy reveals, is something entirely different. It's prolonged and intense, and those experiencing it often don't have supportive relationships to buffer it. Tracy explains that it's, "like if your mom worked the night shift and you never knew if your dad was coming home drunk and angry or sober and happy as you faced him alone. Imagine always living in that kind of fear as a child. Imagine always holding this paper cup of water," she says to the camera.

ACEs are tricky. Unmitigated red-light stress, and even unmitigated yellow-light stress, can lead to physical and mental health problems later in life. Tracy continues, "We now have scientific evidence that a completely healthy 40-year-old can have an unexpected heart attack or stroke and trace it back to chronic red-light stress, especially when it occurs in childhood."

Tracy made this video when she was the executive director for Yolo County Court Appointed Special Advocates (CASA) in California. She was both fundraising for and recruiting advocates who form voluntary, one-on-one relationships with children in foster care so that they can help advocate for them in court and in life. "Wouldn't it be a gift if you could be the buffer for a child who has undoubtedly experienced red-light stress?" she asks, as she puts the water down and sighs a breath of relief, symbolizing the difference a volunteer could make for a child. It was a simple but moving video, and it got results.

After her tenure at Yolo County CASA, Tracy went on to work as the executive director of Davis Community Meals and Housing, an organization serving people who are either in danger of or experiencing homelessness. In another video, she again explains the effects of trauma on that population. "The stories are incredible," Tracy says as she sits in the backyard of a transitional housing shelter run by her organization. "Everyone has their own idea about what causes adults to be hungry or lose their homes. But if you have a compassionate conversation with anyone in these situations, you can pinpoint the [childhood] trauma." She then provides powerful examples and introduces the "We're all in it together campaign," for compassion and understanding. "Explore the stories on our website and social media," she tells her viewers, and "find common ground." It's no surprise that people did, and still do.

Every organization Tracy works for, and most importantly the people those organizations serve, seem to grow and thrive in her presence. Tracy would tell you that the way she inspires people can be replicated. She'll also humbly tell you that she simply, "points the camera at herself and tells stories with a lesson."

I beg to differ. I think she has a bit of magic, but I've had the pleasure of seeing that magic evolve over the years. She was always good, but now she's effortless because she knows how to connect with her audience on camera by sincerely sharing her novel points of view. "I was so nervous to make videos at first, and I'll always say you made me do it," she jokes as she remembers how uncomfortable she was at first. She continues, "Don't tell anyone that I kind of enjoy it now."

It's always struck me that what makes most people nervous about videos—looking sincerely at the camera and speaking candidly, risking an imperfect appearance and even a blooper—is exactly what your audience wants. It's the same with photos (bring on the face-forward candid shots). Even if we try not to be, we're always more self-conscious and self-critical about ourselves than our audience will be. In fact, the things we criticize about ourselves the most are often the things that endear us to others.

This chapter is a signed permission slip to you to stand in front of the camera and be authentic. Those videos and images, bolstered by a bit of strategy behind them, are the authentic connection you need for your brand to matter deeply to your audience.

> **Wait, What?**
> People trust people, not robots or perfection. Your imperfect presence on video or in a photo tells your audience that you're real, relatable, and ready to help. That's the foundation of a service-first personal brand.

Mistakes Make People Watch

In Chapter 9, I told you that I would explain how to make a video lead-in, which is a video summary of a written blog entry intended to draw more attention across social media channels and improve search engine optimization (SEO) on your website. Even if most people understand the value of a lead-in, many get anxious at the thought of making videos for their brands. Again: Relaxing and accepting imperfections, mistakes, and bloopers is the secret to success here. Flawed videos convert better.

I'll say it again. Flawed. Videos. Convert. Better.

I've always known this intuitively, but now we have scientific proof. A 2023 study comparing Instagram video content found that user-generated videos featuring casual language, unscripted moments, and visible flaws were significantly more effective at fostering purchase intent than brand-produced videos, even when both had similar complexity.[2] Another 2025 study of social media influencers found that when creators proactively pin their bloopers ("flop videos"), it significantly increases viewers' purchase intent by boosting perceived authenticity.[3]

In other words, user-generated, imperfect face-to-camera videos consistently outperform polished, professional ones because they feel more authentic and trustworthy to viewers. Think of it this way: Have you ever been nervous to talk to someone, and then a little relieved when they revealed a human flaw like saying "um" a lot? We relate to imperfection because we're all imperfect. It's called the pratfall effect.[4] And in the age of AI, I expect viewers will demand even *more* authenticity, not less.

Face-to-camera videos also capture attention and build trust. A recent study shows that when a speaker faces the camera, it increases viewer attention by over 40 percent.[5] Additional research shows that direct eye contact (which face-to-camera videos mimic) and a conversational tone also increase attention.[6] For these reasons, I will focus on teaching you how to create natural, conversational, and inevitably imperfect face-to-camera video snippets to introduce your weekly cornerstone content.

To Create Your Video, Think SPLIT

Five key elements to creating a high-converting, authentic video are summed up as SPLIT: **s**cript; **p**lacement; **l**ighting; **i**ntonation; and **t**ripod. Let's explore each, one-by-one.

Script

One thing that makes Tracy's videos so effective is that they sound unscripted, but they didn't start that way. Tracy rehearsed a lot, but here's the key: She never used a script; she used bullet points. "If I memorized a script word for word, I sounded programmed," she said. And she's not alone. Memorization kills authenticity, but preparation earns it. To sound authentic while telling the story you intend to tell, do exactly what Tracy did. Start by listing bullet points that prompt your story. Resist the temptation to make the bullet points too detailed. Think of them as memory triggers, not memorized language. Here's what Tracy's bullet points looked like for her ACEs video:

- Introduce the evidence-backed ACEs study.
- Green-light stress, childhood math test.
- Yellow-light stress, death of grandparent, good relationships buffer it.
- Red-light stress. Alcoholic father. Home alone.
- Long-lasting effects of ACEs.
- Mitigating effects of relationships connect to why Yolo County CASA needs money and volunteers.

If you reread Tracy's story from the beginning of this chapter with these bullet points in mind, you can see how they serve as triggers for her main points. Once you have your bullet points, read them out loud to yourself without trying to memorize them. Then, read them twenty more times. The trick is, don't do this twenty times in a row. Space it out instead. When people read or hear something repeatedly, such as lyrics, catchy phrases, or lines in a song, their memory is strengthened naturally through spaced, incidental exposure, building deeper, more accessible memories over time. Forcibly trying to memorize via mechanical repetition, on the other hand, often creates only a shallow memory that fades quickly.[7] If you've ever wondered why song lyrics that you hear often but not intentionally are so easily stuck in your head, while you can't seem to remember a code you just received no matter how many times you repeat it to yourself, you've experienced the difference.

To achieve this type of sticky memory with your bullet points, carry them with you or put them on a counter you pass often. I tell my students to tally each time they pass by and reread the bullet points to be sure to get to at least twenty. That way, when you make your video, your words will come out as naturally as a song in the shower, rather than like a memorized code.

Another part of your script is the opening sentence. Because this statement is make-or-break in terms of grabbing your audience's attention, I do recommend memorizing that one part word-for-word. Tracy's first sentence was, "It's not that hard to hold up this cup of water right now, but I would probably get impatient if I had to hold it up for a full ten minutes." She wrote that out word-for-word above her bullet points to memorize it and make sure it came out flawlessly. Once you get the first sentence out, there might be an um here or a stutter there, but you should absolutely keep going. Remember, we like that authenticity. If you lack a confident start, though, it's hard to continue.

Placement

Your face-to-camera video can be jarring if it's framed improperly. Try your best not to cut off the top of your head or leave too much space on top. As a guideline, follow the "rule of thirds," a common photography and videography practice that divides the frame into nine equal parts using equally spaced horizontal and vertical lines. Use this grid concept to place key visual elements along the intersections of these lines to create balance and visual appeal. You can even install a three-by-three grid with the camera settings in your phone to help you with placement each time you take a video.

TRACY FAUVER FACE-TO-CAMERA

Figure 11.1 Tracy Fauver speaks face-to-camera in a video for Davis Community Meals and Housing. Using a grid as a guide for the "rule of threes" creates a professional appeal for the video. (Obtained with permission.)

Here's how to apply the rule of thirds to your on-screen image. If you're sitting at a desk or standing at a counter, your face should take up the top third of the video frame, and your torso should take up the bottom two thirds (see Figure 11.1). If you're taking a close-up of your face, it should take up the top two-thirds of the video frame, and your neck and the top of your shoulders should take up the bottom third. Be sure that your face is centered.

Lighting

You will get the best results when your video is "front lit." This means you'll want to face a light source. If you're inside, facing a bright window on a sunny day might be enough. On darker days or in the evenings, you'll want to face a light source. There are a variety of lights on the market for taking selfie videos. For simple, face-to-camera videos like the ones I am describing, I recommend purchasing a ring-shaped light that distributes light evenly by encircling the camera lens. Ring lights are also easy to set up and are designed for close proximity, which means they are good for small spaces like desktops or offices.

A note of caution: Being front-lit shouldn't mean you have to squint. If you find that you're squinting (this happens when we are told to "face the sun" for better lighting) or if you realize that you are too harshly lit, move fifteen to thirty degrees to one side. A small rotation like this ensures you won't get shadows on your face. Please do a couple-second practice video to work this out. The last thing you want to do is to have a great take of a video, only to realize that viewers can't see half of your face. And remember, your body moves and so can your light. If you have a good background, and you are using a light but see a shadow, move the light, not your body. Of course, if you're squinting in the direct sun but have a good background, you have no choice but to move your body a bit.

Finally, clean your phone lens. You're going to be taking selfie, face-to-camera style videos, which means you're going to be using the camera on your phone. That lens smashes against the oils of the side of your ear and face when you use the phone to talk in the normal orientation. Wipe it off before you take a video so it's not blurry. Even the slightest smudge can make light refract in weird ways.

Intonation

Think about the last time you yelled at someone. Was your voice higher or lower pitched? When we speak at a louder volume, our voice automatically gets a higher pitched tone to it. It also becomes less varied, and humans don't like listening to fast, monotone voices. Instead, we like listening to lower pitched voices, which naturally happen when we speak at normal volumes in a varied, conversational tone.[8] The biggest mistakes people make on video are speaking too loudly or too quickly, or both. Being aware of this is the first step to avoiding it.

Avoiding background noise is also important, both to keep your voice at a natural volume (we naturally speak louder to stand out from noise) and for your video quality. Beware of airplanes, leaf blowers, lawn mowers, cars, construction, and other sources of ambient noise. If possible, consider purchasing a non-amplifying lapel microphone.

Tripod

Buy a tripod for your face-to-camera videos. It provides steady footage, giving you less to worry about (it's almost impossible, not to mention distracting, to hold your phone still). I recommend getting both a desktop tripod and a floor tripod so that you have a variety of setup options.

That said, don't let the absence of a tripod stop you from starting. You can absolutely prop your phone up using books, boxes, or any sturdy surface that brings the camera to eye level. Use a mug or small object behind your phone to keep it from slipping and place it on a windowsill or bookshelf for natural lighting. The key is to make sure your phone is steady and your face is well lit. If you absolutely need to hold your phone, rest your elbow on a table or desktop so that it's as steady as possible.

Additional Video Tips

Here are some other tips that will help your videos look great.

Start Strong

After you start your video, smile and count to five. This gives you the opportunity to cut the first few seconds of your video and appear smiling and ready at the start. Your phone comes with simple built-in editing tools to do this. Simply click Edit, use the scissor mode to make a cut right before the point where you want the video playback to start, then delete the portion of the video prior to the cut.

Consider purchasing a remote video starter. You can search for "phone camera remote," "selfie remote," or "Bluetooth remote shutter" to find one. Check your tripod first, though. Some include remotes when you buy them.

Finally, take your hands out of your pockets and let gesturing happen naturally. Remember, we don't want robot videos, we want authentically human ones. If you are having trouble knowing what to do with your hands at the start of the video, clasp them at your waist first, and then release them when you start the video. You'll likely naturally raise them in a gesture when you release them, making the beginning of your video look natural and lively.

Practice Until You're Sick of Yourself

To get comfortable on camera quickly, practice until you're sick of yourself. The best way to do this is to look in the mirror for five minutes straight and practice your opening line and bullet points. Be sure to time a full five minutes. That doesn't seem long, but it will feel long when you do it, and it will likely make you eager to get on camera and just get the video done.

Add Subtitles

Most social media platforms have the option to auto-generate captions. Please enable this, as most videos are watched on silent, at least at the start. Software like Rev.com or Adobe Premiere can also embed the captions ahead of time if you want more sophisticated editing or translation capabilities.

Never Delete

Instead of deleting takes you don't like, mark the ones you do like as favorites. We learn more from our mistakes than our successes. Just like athletes trying to improve their plays, you can rewatch your bloopers and learn how to improve next time. You might even decide you want to post a blooper for an engagement boost.

Cut and Correct

As you use the cut tool to adjust the beginning of your video, you might get good enough at video editing to salvage a video that has a few mistakes but is otherwise good. Enable this kind of edit by leaving giant pauses after mistakes. For example, if you completely fumble or forget a phrase, pause and count to ten in your head, then restart the phrase and continue. That will give you plenty of room to make a cut later and delete the flawed portion (and you can easily find the flawed portion because the sound bar will be flat for ten seconds). Then just bring the part of your video that's after the cut to meet the part of the video before the cut, and it will flow seamlessly together.

Have Fun

Above all, have fun with your videos. Remember how Tracy said she even started enjoying hers? I have no doubt that you will, too. Experiment with editing and various setups. Have your kids or pets join you for behind-the-scenes looks. And eventually, hit Post. Done is better than perfect.

Kevin Leung Skipped the Viral Videos and Played the Long Game

When Kevin Leung (from Chapter 3) first started building his social media presence on his Instagram account, he tried complex camera setups and mimicking viral trends, and he struggled. The traditional influencers he was gaining inspiration from, "wake up every morning. . . they brush their teeth in the same spot. . . it's very consistent. And it's also rhythmic. The sound edit is good. The sound bites are good. The video quality is good. That's what I aspired to be," Kevin says.

And then he realized, after his first two videos, that he physically couldn't do what these other influencers do. Not only was it a lot of work, but he was wasting what people had always told him was his best attribute: his personality. That's when he decided to be front-facing and treat his videos like a FaceTime call. This face-to-camera approach built his presence consistently over time. "You might not go viral because you posted a trend, but you can count on consistent growth," Kevin says.

Kevin also knew that there was value in varying his content every once in a while. "Video is obviously the most preferred type of content, but when I varied my content with still photos and carousels, I always saw a boost." And there's evidence to prove Kevin's theory. LinkedIn, for example, has outright stated that its algorithm doesn't prefer a particular format and encourages users to incorporate variety.[9] Instagram users also find engagement boosts in variation of creative formats, especially when carousel posts combine videos and photos.[10]

Make a SPLASH with Photos

To create a great photo, focus on SPLASH. Six key components to engaging photos are **s**egmentation; **p**oints of interest; **l**eft to right; **a**void chaos; **s**pace; and **h**orizontal and vertical formats.

Segmentation

The rule of threes for video also applies to photos. It's hard to find a photo in Kevin's Instagram feed where he isn't using the rule. Figure 11.2 shows one of my favorite examples of the horizon in the top third and him in the bottom two-thirds. I also like how he puts himself in the right third vertically. It creates great lines and harmony in the photo. When Kevin takes a standing photo, he always has his head in the top third and his body in the bottom two-thirds.

Points of Interest and Angles

Photos can help you set the mood and tone of a post. Figure 11.3 shows Kevin looking out into the wilderness. You can practically feel him taking it all in, and his caption is about appreciating nature. To get perspectives like this in your own photos, take pictures that show your viewer where you want to take them. For example, you could take a picture from the bottom of a hill to show the journey ahead, or from the threshold of a bridge.

Left to Right

We tend to visually scan images in the same direction we read. In cultures where text is read left to right (like most of North America, South America, and Europe), studies show that people often prefer photographs and objects that flow from left to right and whose main subject faces toward the right side of the frame. That means you can often make your images feel more natural and compelling by creating them so the viewer's eye enters on the left and travels toward your most important element on the right.[11,12] (In multiple countries in the Middle East as well as some in Central and South Asia, this reverses from right to left.) Notice how Kevin puts himself to the right in Figures 11.2 and 11.3 so that he is the focal point. In Kevin's official *Survivor* cast photo, he is also off to the right.

KEVIN LEUNG EXPERTLY USES RULE-OF-THIRDS

Figure 11.2 Kevin Leung frames this photo using the "rule of thirds" by putting the horizon in the top third and himself in the bottom-right two-thirds. (Obtained with permission.)

Avoid Chaos

Studies show that we gaze longer at symmetrical, simple images than asymmetrical, chaotic scenes.[13] Pursue these types of aesthetics. When in doubt, just as with video, a face-to-camera photo is always your best bet. You'll get the same bonus trust because your gaze at the lens simulates eye contact with your viewer. So much of Kevin's Instagram feed is an invitation in which he posts simple face-to-camera pictures and videos, making eye contact with us, inviting us to trust him and relate to him.

KEVIN LEUNG USES ANGLES AND POINTS OF INTEREST

Figure 11.3 Kevin Leung takes the viewer along with him in this photo, as he uses angles and points of interest to show the depth of the wilderness. (Obtained with permission.)

Space

Consider leaving white space like a blank wall for text or a logo, especially for branded content. Graphic design software tools like Canva are great for embedding this kind of information into photos. And when you take this type of photo, you should ideally look or point in the direction of the information you're trying to highlight, as Kevin did in the example below, pointing to the Barry's logo (see Figure 11.4).

Horizontal and Vertical

Take time to orient your phone both horizontally and vertically whenever you take a picture. Not only is it handy to have photos in both formats for social media, but in branding we have a rule: Crop, don't zoom. Sometimes a photo in horizontal format taken from a distance crops better to vertical format when you want to get closer on the subject, and vice

KEVIN LEUNG USES SPACE TO HIGHLIGHT A FOCAL POINT

Figure 11.4 Kevin Leung highlights the Barry's logo by leaving space for it at the top of the photo. You can do this by taking a photo against a blank wall and inserting a logo or words as well. (Obtained with permission.)

versa. The greater the variety of photos you take in original form, the more freedom you have for editing.

An Extra Tip: Make Uniform Backgrounds

If you have a text-only post for a platform like LinkedIn, consider bump-out text with a branded background. Use the same font as your logo and a branded background color. Tools like Canva work well for this. Tracy does this often to announce new posted stories for her "We're in it Together" campaign (see Figure 11.5).

All these tips help you to achieve one key thing: authenticity, which leads to relatability. Remember, we like real content and face-to-face human connection.

TRACY FAUVER USES A STOCK PHOTO WITH BUMP OUT TEXT

Figure 11.5 Tracy Fauver uses a stock photo of broken handcuffs to illustrate Rosa's story and add attention to a text-only LinkedIn post. (Obtained with permission.)

Give It a Try

Follow SPLIT to create your first story lead-in video. For in-between posts and to vary the algorithm, create photo-based posts with SPLASH. For text-only posts, create a JPEG with a branded bump-out quote.

The FaceTime Effect, at a Glance

Main Idea
This chapter explores why authentic face-to-camera videos and well-composed photos are the most powerful tools in your service-first personal branding tool kit.

Key Takeaways
- Flawed, unscripted videos outperform polished ones because they feel real.
- The pratfall effect, eye contact, and authenticity all contribute to stronger engagement and trust.
- Use the SPLIT method (**s**cript, **p**lacement, **l**ighting, **i**ntonation, **t**ripod) to confidently record story-driven, face-to-camera videos.
- Use the SPLASH method (**s**egmentation, **p**oints of interest, **l**eft to right, **a**void chaos, **s**pace, **h**orizontal/vertical) to create scroll-stopping photos.
- Your story and your face are enough. Done is better than perfect. Imperfect content builds perfect connection.

Next Steps
Use the SPLIT method to film your first story-based lead-in to a cornerstone content video. Then create one or two supporting photo- or text-based posts using SPLASH. Aim for consistency, not polish.

(continued)

(*continued*)

How Long Does This Take?

Video bullet point prep: thirty minutes

    Mirror practice: five minutes

    Filming and editing your first video: one hour

    Photo post and caption: forty-five minutes

    Recommendation: Batch one video and three supporting posts in a single 2.5-hour content block. Rewatch and reuse your own "blooper" footage to keep learning and improving.

    You'll be amazed at how quickly you feel more confident in front of the camera.

PART IV
CULTIVATE a Presence That Grows and Scales with You

12

Should I Charge for This?

> I've had something like twenty million impressions on Reddit. So, I knew the content was liked. The question was: Would people pay for this?
>
> —Taylor Stanton

"There's so much more beauty out there, and not everyone is able to get there [to see it]," Taylor Stanton says. "That was one of the driving forces for me, opening up and democratizing the backcountry."

The desire to make wild spaces feel more accessible and revered sits at the heart of Taylor Stanton's service-first personal brand. *Beyond Yosemite Valley*, his independently published wilderness photography book, isn't just a visual showcase. It's an invitation to see America's most iconic landscapes in a new way. "Yosemite is not Disneyland for the outdoors. I want to reframe that. These are public lands, yes, but they're also sacred lands. And they should be treated with reverence, not like an amusement park."

Taylor's dream has always been to combine his passion for national parks and photography with his background in marketing. After nearly fifteen years in the field, he realized that while he had helped shape countless campaigns and brand stories for others, he hadn't taken the time to build something of his own. "A lot of people in my space get comfortable marketing other people's products," he muses. "And they wake up one day and realize they've made a salary, but they haven't developed their own brand. They've just worked."

At first, Taylor thought that personal branding was a form of sales. But he quickly realized that it was really about "believing in yourself and your brand enough to take risks. To put yourself out there into the market of public opinion. Because if you don't do it, no one else will."

I reminded him that done is better than perfect. "I hadn't heard that before, but it got me thinking in a new way about the MVP [minimum viable product] approach [that startups use]," Taylor says, "I'm a marketing and communications person. I'm used to ghostwriting quotes for billion-dollar CEOs. You don't get it right on the first, second, or third try. It goes through multiple rounds of revision. That made me a perfectionist. If you keep thinking like that on your own, though, nothing's going to get done. I had to stop worrying about every little detail. The moment you start putting yourself out there, even imperfectly, is the moment people can start paying attention."

So, he got to work. He blocked off time, stopped overthinking, and produced the book he'd been thinking about for years. He drew on a decade's worth of wilderness photography, much of which had already gone viral on Reddit and Facebook. "I've had something like twenty million impressions on Reddit," he says. "So, I knew the content was liked. The question was: Would people pay for this?"

The answer came quickly. *Beyond Yosemite Valley* quadrupled his investment within the first forty-eight hours. "It was intensely and pleasantly surprising how quickly I sold a thousand copies, and then more and more," he says. "I've made it profitable on just organic content marketing. I haven't paid for ads. And part of the reason it's taken off is because I've been building relationships in the [US] national park community, especially with park rangers. They've been promoting it in their own networks."

The success of the book came with an unexpected career opportunity. "The same year I published the book, I got a job working with the largest congressionally chartered foundation supporting public lands."

Despite this, Taylor is quick to point out that the book isn't just about his own success, but rather, it's about serving a broader purpose. "There are two big problems I'm trying to address," he says. "First, equitable access. Not everyone can get out there. I'm a somewhat fit person, and even for me, some of these places are hard to reach. I wanted to create something that enabled people to see what they might not be able to see themselves."

The second goal is a mindset shift. "National parks aren't just bucket list items," he says. "It's not about going just to say that you've been there. It's about having a personal experience with the wilderness. I'm trying to take people there with the book."

And Taylor doesn't plan to stop with Yosemite. He plans to turn the book into a full series. "The next one will be *Beyond Arches*, and then *Beyond Canyonlands*. I've already done the analysis, and this content doesn't exist right now, at least not in a way that focuses on the lesser-known places with strong visuals and narratives."

Looking ahead, Taylor hopes a *Beyond* series will be more than a creative side project. He sees a lot of possibilities. "I wish I'd started developing this kind of a personal brand sooner," he says, "where you become known for the things you teach and share instead of dancing in front of a live feed." Taylor hopes that his brand helps him continue to combine his skills to serve what he cares about most. "Someday, I'd love to be the CMO of a wilderness association. Something focused on recreation and public land access. That's always been the dream: to use my marketing background in service of the places I care about most."

But for now, he's proving what's possible when a personal brand isn't just about self-promotion or sales, but about serving and sharing a deeper vision. "No one's going to push you to do it," he says. "You have to push yourself. And if you keep waiting for the perfect time, it'll never happen. Sometimes you just need to suck it up, block off the time, and get it done. The rewards are on the other side of that discomfort, for you and the people you serve."

There may come a time during your service-first personal branding journey where, as Taylor did, you ask yourself, "Would people pay for this?" By the time you ask that question, you're already overlooking the answers you already have. Taylor just wishes he had started earlier. "Sometimes I wonder where I'd be if I did this when I first had the images ten years ago."

The concept of a minimum viable product, or MVP, that Taylor referred to in his story was made famous by Eric Ries in his book, *The Lean Startup*. As Ries explains, the MVP is the smallest version of an idea that allows you to gather *validated learning* with minimal effort and risk.

Taylor did exactly that, but he did it long before *Beyond Yosemite Valley* became a book. He *really* did it when he first began sharing his message and visuals on Reddit and Facebook, earning millions of impressions between the two platforms. In lean startup terms, that's not just tinkering; it's validation. People (more than twenty million of them) were not only paying attention, but they were engaging. And as Ries argues, it's actual customer behavior, not compliments, that tell you if your idea has potential.[1]

That's the beauty of a service-first personal brand built around expertise instead of aesthetics. Because traditional influencers have a broad and undifferentiated audience, they must grow a huge audience first, often by exploiting ephemeral trends, before they can monetize through brand sponsorships. When you build a service-first personal brand around a specific, framework-supported TRUTH, you validate potential MVPs every time you share a piece of cornerstone content. Taylor had his validation when his images and narratives went viral ten years before he actually monetized his product with the book. The book looked deeper, which further contributed to his success.

> **Wait, What?**
>
> Not everyone who builds a service-first personal brand will choose to monetize, but if you do, it's one of the best positions to be in. You already have real data and validation from your audience showing what they value most. Take it slowly, start with a minimum viable product, and validate, validate, validate. The good news? You don't need a massive audience to succeed, just a dedicated one.

Determining What People Would Pay For: The Engagement Ratio

Let's take a moment to compare two hypothetical people on Instagram. Mary is an aspiring world traveler. She talks about the places she wants to see someday; she muses about saving money for travel; and she even posts pictures of outfits she'd wear on a plane flight. . . someday. Jane, by contrast, also likes travel, but she often posts pictures from the places she's been and insights from what she's learned from her travels.

If I were the marketing director for a luggage company, I might assume that both Mary and Jane are good bets for my audience. But in reality, Jane has a much higher chance of following through and making a purchase decision than Mary because she's already behaving in a way that indicates she needs luggage. *Interest*, like Mary's, is an *indication*. Despite her strong interest, she may never actually travel someday and need luggage. *Behavior*, like Jane's, is *validation*. She needs luggage because she is *already* traveling. Be sure to make the distinction between interest and behavior when you ask, "Would people pay for this?"

This is exactly what Taylor did as he looked deeper into those twenty million impressions of his content. "I loved the impressions I was getting," Taylor says, "But when I compared impressions to engagement, I was fascinated by which photos led in terms of engagement."

Premium accounts on LinkedIn or business accounts on other social platforms include dashboards that display performance metrics for your accounts and individual posts. The data on these dashboards tell you both how many people were shown your post (impressions) and how many people commented on or liked your posts. The latter actions are indications of engagement, and those are behavior metrics.

To figure out which pieces of cornerstone content are driving the most engagement (behavior), go to the "posts" section of the respective dashboards of your social media platforms. First, make sure dashboards are set to twenty-eight days or longer, so you'll have a long enough time window to see patterns develop beyond the typical seven-day default. The posts will be sorted in order of impressions (high to low), but that only tells half the story. Consider engagement metrics like comments, shares, reposts, or likes, as well. Some platforms will even give you a summary "engagement" metric and allow you to sort your posts from high to low engagement. If there's no engagement metric, make your own by combining the counts on comments, shares, reposts, and likes. Then divide that by impressions. Take note of the posts with the highest ratios of engagement to impressions. They represent your best work. As Taylor realized, "The posts with the most impressions didn't always lead to the most engaging conversations and vice versa. I paid attention to that when I chose images for my book, and it worked."

Engagement ratios are important because they correct for outside components that might make a post visible, but not necessarily valuable. My cute labradoodle always gets more impressions than an educational post, for example. And while this visibility is important to your brand building because it invites more people to see your value, it's not an effective way to validate ideas for monetization (or every brand would be about puppies). Look for the concepts that your ideal customers are telling you hold the most value, because that's what they will ultimately pay for.

> **Remember All Those Interviews You Conducted?**
>
> In Chapter 2, I encouraged you to interview people you trust to ask them what stands out about you so that you could discover whether their answers align with your intended brand direction. In Chapter 3, I suggested interviewing your ideal customers to better understand what drives them. Some of those conversations may have hinted that people would actually pay for your knowledge, services, or products. Pay close attention to those sentiments. They are additional layers of validation that complement your social media analytics. While data can reveal insightful patterns and trends, it doesn't always tell the whole story.
>
> Look for consistent patterns, both in what people say to you directly and what you observe online. This will strengthen your confidence in what you're building. It's also a great way to validate your ideas when you have a small social media following. As Taylor said, "Early validation didn't just come from social media. It came from people who looked at my photos before I even posted them and told me I had a different point of view that I needed to show people."

Monetize Incrementally

I don't love the word *monetize*. It sounds technical, even transactional. In practice, though, monetizing your service-first personal brand is often just the next step in a natural progression. Taylor, for example, shared photos and stories that resonated with his audience. When the feedback kept coming, he turned those same photos and that same momentum into a self-published book. You might be sharing frameworks that help people overcome shyness, like Kevin, or that treat the underlying cause versus the symptoms of dry eye disease, like Lisa. You might even be sharing cooking techniques, like Eddie. Whatever topic you decide to share about, if people are engaging with that content in the form of comments, resharing, and reaching out, you're collecting valuable validation.

The simple next step in the progression could be turning one of those frameworks into something more in-depth or experiential, such as a live workshop, for example. You don't need anything fancy: Zoom or a quiet conference room will do. Your first attempts at monetization might not match your final product, but they are valuable tests. You'll earn some money, yes, but more importantly, you'll gather feedback. That feedback becomes data you can use to refine the next iteration. Over time, your products or services might evolve into an e-book, a coaching program, a membership, or even a full-fledged academy or nonfiction book.

Formats for Packaging Your Product

Once you start thinking incrementally, you'll realize there's no one right format for turning your value into a product. Some of my clients and students have launched workshops. Others have sold art prints, clothing, digital workbooks, courses, recipes, or consulting services. The format should fit both your content and your capacity.

Remember, if you're testing something beyond your cornerstone content, like a product or design, you don't have to wait until it's fully built. You can post a t-shirt mockup before printing inventory, or share a sample page of your recipe guide before formatting the whole thing. What matters is deducing how people respond, not just in impressions, likes, or views alone, but in the engagement ratios they create and the in-person feedback you get as well.

Finally, be sure to compile the feedback from online comments, direct messages, emails, texts, and your personal interviews. You might look back and realize that you have some testimonials to share from those interactions, or that the feedback suggested a powerful next step, kind of like how one of my students suggested I teach a class on personal branding. As I'll share in a short story at the end of this chapter, there's even at least one brand that literally got its start because people repeatedly commented online and in-person, "You should sell this!"

Your Monetization Checklist

Here's a checklist of items that you should make sure you've explored before you start charging people for your work.

Incorporation

If you're exchanging intellectual property, services, or physical products for money, even just a few sales, you're running a business, and it's important to make it official. That usually means registering your business with the appropriate city, state, and federal entities.

Requirements vary depending on where you live, so take time to research what's needed in your location. You may need to register in more than one place, and you'll need to decide on a business structure, like a sole proprietorship, LLC, or S corp, depending on your goals, liability concerns, and tax preferences. Local chambers of commerce, small business lawyers, or accountants can point you in the right direction or help you make the best choice for your situation.

Legal Protection

When you begin turning your ideas into paid products like live workshops, it's natural to worry about others copying your ideas. Fortunately, at least in the United States, the mere act of creating and sharing your original work online already gives you some automatic protection. Under US copyright law, your content is protected the moment it's "fixed in a tangible medium," which includes blog posts, PDFs, videos, and even social media posts or captions. If you've posted it with your name on it, you've created a digital trail of authorship.[2]

That said, if you're developing products or services core to your business, like a course title, tagline, or signature framework that you plan to build around, you may want to formalize legal protections. Registering a copyright or trademark gives you added legal power to prevent or block competition. A copyright protects the expression of your ideas (like written text or video content). A trademark protects brand identifiers like names, phrases, or logos used in commerce.

You don't need to trademark everything before launching. In fact, you may not need to at all. Remember, owning your work starts by showing up confidently and consistently under your own name or brand. Putting your ideas out there helps establish your reputation, and in many cases, your originality becomes your best protection. Just remember to check and make sure that your name isn't already in use by someone else. As I mentioned in Chapter 6, Trademarkia is a good tool for this.

Sales Tax Requirements

If you're selling physical products, or certain digital goods and services, you may be required to collect sales tax from your customers.[3] Sales tax laws vary by state and sometimes even by city. Some states tax digital downloads or online courses, while others don't. You may even owe sales tax in states where you don't live if you earn more than a certain threshold.[4] Many e-commerce platforms like Shopify or Etsy will help calculate and collect sales tax for you, but you're still responsible for making sure it's collected correctly, and for filing the returns and paying the tax. To be safe, get a lawyer's or an accountant's opinion.

Get Your Software in Order

When you're just starting to monetize your ideas, it's tempting to patch things together with free tools or DMs, and for a while, you probably can. But the sooner you set up streamlined, professional systems, the easier it becomes to scale, stay compliant, and earn your audience's trust.

- If you're selling digital products (like templates, guides, or workshops), platforms like Teachable or Thinkific can help you deliver content securely, manage payments, and even build simple landing pages.
- For physical products, tools like Shopify and Etsy, or WordPress plugins like WooCommerce make it easy to build a store and track inventory.

- If you're invoicing for services like coaching, make sure you have proper accounting software like QuickBooks or Wave.

Finally, make sure your email and text opt-in systems are working. As I discussed in Chapter 9, a key part of your funnel is your owned leads. Landing page optimization software like Leadpages, ClickFunnels, or Unbounce can increase lead acquisition by 30 percent or more.[5,6] Be sure to use the A/B testing features to get the most out of these platforms.

Validation Generally Comes in Small Batches

Armaan Bhattal (Chapter 2) is on a mission to revitalize Sikh culture so that traditions and values don't fade away. "With each generation, we're losing more and more," Armaan says. "If we don't do our part now, it's going to keep getting lost. And what we lose isn't just language or tradition. We lose a way of serving the world. *Seva*, or service, is a huge part of who we are. We feed hundreds of thousands of people for free at our festivals. We fight injustice. We uplift others. If we lose Sikh culture, we lose those values, too." While Armaan's brand is an arbiter of cultural awareness now, it didn't start that way.

Armaan's brand actually started as a concept for clothing. Unlike Taylor, who saw early signals of traction through millions of impressions, Armaan Bhattal validated his brand to a much smaller audience of just a few hundred Instagram followers and a circle of supportive friends. Those friends had seen Armaan's paintings and apparel designs, most of which he kept private at first. "Designing was sacred to me," he says. "It was my escape." But their repeated encouragement gave him the push he needed. "They would say things like, 'you *have* to sell these.'"

Finally, Armaan came around. "If I was going to share the most personal thing I had," he says, "I was going to do it right." He designed his own website, filmed a launch video, and took the stage at a Sikh dance competition in downtown Los Angeles, where he introduced his designs to a live audience.

From there, Armaan began selling his art and apparel designs at Sikh festivals across California. His tables at these events weren't just merchandise booths, they were gathering places. "People who had bought something last year would come back looking for me," he says. "They brought their kids, their cousins. They saw it as more than a t-shirt. It really meant something to them."

It meant more to Armaan, too. He had lived through discrimination, been physically attacked for wearing a turban, and worked in communities across the United States where people had never met a Sikh person. "I was the only one who looked like me," he says. "That meant I had to represent my culture with even more care." Those experiences shaped his desire to use storytelling as a form of cultural preservation and education, in addition to selling his merchandise. He added QR codes and opt-ins to his booth displays, collecting emails and phone numbers to "ultimately connect people to the deeper message" behind his work.

His mission became to uplift the Sikh community while educating others. "It's about helping people feel seen," he says, "and showing young Sikhs that they don't have to hide who they are." In a way, Armaan reverse-engineered his service-first personal brand by monetizing first and then working backward to develop his TRUTH framework and educational components. That's common with service-first personal brand journeys. Often, they launch seemingly out of order, or by accident. The important thing is to seize the momentum and continue to gain visibility to share your value.

As I mentioned in Chapter 5, Corporate brands spend millions of dollars trying to engineer the kind of authenticity that both Armaan Bhattal and Taylor Stanton created with their personal TRUTHs. They invent mascots like the Geico Gecko or the Energizer Bunny to humanize themselves, or they hire spokespeople to inject purpose into their messaging. But service-first personal brands already have that built in. In that way, it's the most natural brand you can build.

Now it's your turn to validate your monetization potential. What's one incremental creation that you can develop so that you can start earning money from the brand value you've already built and validated? Keep notes as you go, and don't forget the monetization checklist.

Should I Charge for This? At a Glance

Main Idea

This chapter shows that monetizing your service-first personal brand isn't about chasing trends, representing other brands for money, or "selling out." It's about noticing what people already find valuable in your work through interviews, in-person encouragement, or social media engagement, and taking a small next step to package that value into something people can pay for.

Key Takeaways
- Monetization can be incremental. A workshop using your frameworks or a live presentation can be a low-risk starting point.
- Feedback from both ideal customer interviews and online analytics can help you identify which products or ideas are worth testing.
- Your original content is protected by copyright the moment you share it with indications of your ownership, but you may still need to consider incorporation, taxes, and trademarking as you go.
- Selling platforms and tools can help deliver your product.
- While corporate brands spend money trying to create purpose through mascots or campaigns, service-first personal brands already have it built in.

Next Steps

Choose one framework, product idea, or story that people have already responded to, either online or in person. Brainstorm a simple way to offer it as a paid experience or resource. Could it be a sixty-minute workshop over Zoom? A table at your next community event? A for-sale PDF?

How Long Does This Take?
First, spend fifteen minutes identifying a framework, story, or piece of content that's already gotten a strong response (use the engagement ratio as a best practice for validation).

Next, spend thirty minutes brainstorming one or two simple ways to turn it into a paid experience (e.g., workshop, PDF, live session).

Set aside one or two hours to create a basic version (slides, outline, or draft content), and then another thirty minutes to share it with a few trusted people or post online to test for interest.

13 | Surprising and Uncommon Marketing Strategies

> None of that would've happened if I hadn't been consistent in my personal values and carried them over to my company's values.
> —Ryan Wilson

When Ryan Wilson first heard about personal branding, he didn't buy in. "I didn't like doing it. I really didn't," he says. "I thought, why am I even posting this online? I don't want to talk about myself." He'd spent ten years in the US Army, earned degrees in finance and computer science, and was on track for a solid corporate career. In his mind, his work should speak for itself. Pursuing visibility felt unnecessary, maybe even a little silly, but he reluctantly did it as part of an assignment in my class. "You made me do it, so I did," he says, "And it felt as uncomfortable as I thought it would." But then he did it again, and it got easier.

He talked about things that were important to him, like transitioning from the military and seeking an internship in finance, but being a veteran was what really drove his posts. "It's something I'm really passionate about," he explained. Ryan had always tried to make a difference for people both in the Army and as a veteran. When he was in the ranks, he advocated for women's rights and equality. As a veteran, he advocated for other veterans in general. "Believe it or not, there are still a lot of holes still in the ecosystem," he says. His network thought so, too, and started paying attention. "Whenever I made posts about being a veteran and ideas for helping other veterans, people shared, commented, and messaged me."

Ryan did more than just talk about helping veterans. He implemented his ideas. During his MBA program, he launched the first Veterans MBA Association at UC Davis. The group became a hub for networking, mentorship, and career support. It also became a mirror. As Ryan reflected on his experiences, he realized just how many leadership stories he'd never told. "I always thought that was just my job," he says. "But when you list it all out, when you actually put it on paper, it's like reading the story of who you've become. Veterans don't always realize that." He went on to tell me that veterans have undoubtedly led dozens of decisions by the time they leave the military and combat, decisions that could be a matter of life and death. "When you don't have another comparison, you don't realize the magnitude of it."

Ryan always had a secret dream of starting a business with his brother, a gifted mechanic and, in Ryan's words, "a technical genius." But he also thought he should work in finance to give stability to his young family. When he got a finance internship at Intel, he thought he'd "made it," but the dream of starting a commercial fleet services business in his hometown with his brother kept tugging at him. As his internship came to an end, his brother reminded him again about their shared dream. "I knew I needed to take the risk with him," Ryan said, "or I would always wonder."

He and his brother got to work. Ryan used his business and marketing skills to build the business, and his brother started working on the fleets of trucks. Their approach was rare and refreshing. "Companies sign a 'partnership agreement' with us when they sign on. We take a preventative approach. A broken-down truck shouldn't drive our business. It should be the other way around. If we do enough preventative maintenance, there should be no breakdowns in the first place."

He elaborated further. "Our values come from the military. Our operations are precise and proactive, our shop is clean, our communication is clear, our turnaround time is fast." Even the color scheme, navy and white, was intentional. "Those are the old and new colors of the infantry," he says. "Everything we do ties back to our identity. Military values. Military precision. Mechanical excellence. Local impact."

Starting with one truck bay, the business quickly scaled to a 30,000-square-foot facility with eleven employees, but Ryan never abandoned his mission to help veterans. He spoke at veterans' associations, sponsored veterans' events through his business, and stayed active on veterans' issues. "That part of my brand never wavered," Ryan says, "and never will." And while this commitment was never part of his plan, it also created opportunity.

One day, an executive was scrolling LinkedIn when he saw one of Ryan's posts about fleet readiness. He read more. He noticed Ryan's support for veterans and his unique approach, and he reached out. That single post led to a multi-location expansion opportunity with one of the biggest names in the fleet services business.

"None of that would've happened if I hadn't been consistent in my personal values and carried them over to my company's values," Ryan said. "We wouldn't be looking at expansion this fast. We wouldn't be less than a year in business and already fielding calls most companies wait years for."

WilsonTech Fleet Services is now a certified Disabled Veteran Business Enterprise (DVBE), and Ryan actively partners with other veteran organizations for hiring. "Being a veteran isn't just a label," he says. "It's how I think, how I lead, how I live. I think people trust us because they can feel who we are."

Ryan's long-term vision is to scale WilsonTech across the entire I-80 corridor from San Francisco to Reno, and eventually up and down I-5. "I want a company that never fades," he says. "One that supports my kids, my grandkids, and helps a lot of people in the process."

Before I ended our interview, Ryan said something that made me chuckle, "Thanks again for that super uncomfortable assignment."

This book is built around a redefined, service-first approach to personal branding, and with that comes a rethinking of how we show up in the public eye. Traditional marketing relies on paid exposure like ads and sponsorships. Traditional public relations rely on earned exposure like media coverage, interviews, and headlines. But both of those channels are now noisier and more hype-driven than ever.

The average person sees between 4,000 and 10,000 ads each day. Even if we consciously register just 2 percent of them, that still means we actively notice 80–200 ads daily.[1,2] News organizations publish hundreds of headlines per day, amplified across websites, apps, and social platforms.

Having a marketing and public relations plan will help your brand grow faster, whether or not you've monetized your brand. But given how crowded the online space and our human brains already are with ads and headlines, it's a smart tactic to layer other, less-cluttered paths to visibility in the mix, especially for new or young service-first personal brands.

> **Wait, What?**
>
> In a digital world flooded with ads and headlines, it's easy to assume that visibility comes from shouting louder or paying more. But for service-first personal brands, there's a better path: *Service-first visibility* that comes from expanding reach through action, value, and community.

Service-First Visibility

Service-first visibility is a powerful alternative to conventional public relations and marketing. Your service-first personal brand is already built on helping and teaching others, so service-first visibility takes this a natural step forward. Service-first visibility can take the form of cause marketing, like partnering with a nonprofit organization, aligning your service-first personal brand with a mission that matters, creating a cause that supports your service-first personal brand, or making a donation to or sponsoring an organization that aligns with your values. This way, instead of fighting to get featured in someone else's story or to be seen on someone else's newsfeed, you'll naturally show up there because you helped in places that reflect your values and make an impact.

Service-first visibility like this often leads to earned media, word-of-mouth referrals, and organic digital recognition. Brand expert David Aaker has long championed the idea of brand purpose, arguing that companies that align with authentic causes build stronger emotional bonds and longer-lasting trust.[3,4] Cause-based partnerships also create what Aaker calls a "credibility rub." The trust and goodwill earned by a respected cause transfers, in part, to your brand.

However, this only works when the partnership is genuine. Performative support or opportunistic branding is easy to see through. This is why Ryan's work with veterans helped him launch and grow WilsonTech. Not only did it align with Ryan and his brother's company values, but it also helped get them in front of new audiences, both online and in person. While Ryan was helping at veterans' events, those audiences were sharing stories about his support and the support of his business on their social channels.

Ryan has built a business around this sort of service-first visibility, but you can do this work even if you haven't monetized your brand. Dr. Lisa Hornick, who we met in Chapter 2, has volunteered at health clinics to screen for vision problems. Carter Delaney, who we discussed in Chapter 8, could volunteer at a local Little League organization.

These and countless other examples show how seeking service-first visibility is a natural way to multiply your audience and start a powerful ripple effect. In the following sections, we'll look at a few of the most common starting points as you pursue new opportunities.

Local Speaking Opportunities

In-person appearances are one of the fastest ways to build buzz around your service-first personal brand. Even better, the practice is time-tested, evergreen, and becoming increasingly valuable in the digital age. The more remote our world becomes, the more we crave seeing and speaking with each other.[5]

In fact, people don't just seek connection, they seek action. When given the opportunity, people don't just listen, they share and act. A single talk can lead to Instagram posts, LinkedIn mentions, additional speaking invitations, or new leads, just don't forget to ask for them. Connect the dots with opt-in links or QR codes on postcards, slides, or table stands to leave with your audience.

Skeptical? Research shows that making the online-offline connection is a smart marketing move. According to McKinsey, branded, in-person events like workshops and pop-ups create trust-filled, immersive moments that fuel digital engagement and even sales.[6] In fact, 75 percent of content marketers say live events are their most effective strategy.[7] For Ryan, a Reno airshow honoring veterans became one of his biggest opportunities. "It was strategic because it was in a city that we wanted to expand to, and it was mission oriented. I received a lot of leads at my booth and in the informational chats I gave."

If your brand is new or has a smaller following, local speaking opportunities can be an especially effective move to boost visibility. Start with a local service club or chamber of commerce, most of which are constantly looking for speakers. Other great opportunities include alumni events, local festivals, and industry panels.

As for what to say? You've already worked that part out. Just tell your TRUTH! Your TRUTH-based, service-first frameworks are portable, pre-tested online, and built to teach, inspire, or spark action. Just make sure to record your talk so you can reuse snippets of the content later for social posts, your website, and applications for bigger speaking opportunities in the future.

Local Media Links

Media links build authority because they act as third-party endorsements or signals that a trusted source relies on your expertise. This aligns directly with Robert Cialdini's principle of authority, which states that people are more likely to trust and follow recommendations from credible, recognized experts or institutions.[8] You've experienced the power of this type of authority if you've seen media links on a website and found yourself trusting the brand more.

In addition to authority and trust, media links are great for website search engine optimization (SEO). Google's own SEO Starter Guide confirms that links from other reputable sites help search engines assess a website's credibility and relevance. In fact, high-quality links remain one of the most important ranking factors in search algorithms. And the benefits don't stop there. Large language models (LLMs) like ChatGPT or Google's Gemini will find, trust, and cite your content, especially if it's presented in a novel framework (looking at you, Chapter 8). Because LLMs are trained on data scraped from high-ranking, authoritative sources, links from reputable media outlets improve your search visibility and topical authority, making your site more likely to be included in training data or cited in real-time tools. In essence, a media mention becomes a signal of credibility not only to humans, but to algorithms.[9]

If your brand is just starting out, it will be a long shot to get cited in a publication like *Forbes*, the *New York Times*, or the *Associated Press*, but starting local and working your way up is an effective tool. Local broadcast and print outlets are often on daily or weekly deadlines and need to fill their broadcasts or publications with interesting content. If you notice that a journalist is reporting on something similar to your brand, send them a story idea. Cause-based stories are especially helpful in this regard. In fact, Ryan was featured on several local radio stations for his involvement in the veterans' airshow he sponsored and earned leads from those radio interviews.

Once you have a media link, use it. Share it on your website and feature snippets of the sound, video, or pull-out quotes of the article on social media, too. Be sure to send it to your email and text lists as well. Next time, pitch to a bigger, more well-known media outlet, and incrementally climb from there. Pretty soon, you could get featured in once out-of-reach publications.

Source of Sources

I met Peter Shankman over twenty years ago at a Press Club event, back when digital PR was still in its infancy. Even then, Peter had a clear vision: Make it easier for journalists to find credible sources and for everyday experts to get media exposure. He brought that idea to life with Help a Reporter Out (HARO), a platform that revolutionized media outreach and was eventually acquired by the PR giant Cision. Now he's doing it again with a more accessible and streamlined tool: Source of Sources.

Unlike traditional PR platforms, Source of Sources flips the script. Instead of experts pitching journalists, journalists post what they're looking for, and then you get emailed the full list of inquiries twice a day. If something fits your expertise, you simply respond. Ryan, for example, might respond to an inquiry about how AI will impact the trucking industry. Once you've signed up at the Source of Sources homepage, you'll get high-quality media requests from journalists who are already on deadline and actively seeking voices like yours. It's visibility without the chase, and a direct way to grow your service-first personal brand.

To sign up, go to sourceofsources.com, enter your name and email, and start receiving high-quality media requests from journalists who are already on deadline and actively seeking voices like yours.

Guest Blogging and Podcasting

Guest blogging and podcasting are time-tested tactics that can be very effective when done locally and incrementally, similarly to media links. Look for people in the same stage as your brand with dozens, hundreds, or a few thousand followers, and seek opportunities there. Chances are they're like you: Creating a blog to gain visibility before having a huge following or monetization.

Another great strategy is to pitch complementary brands. For example, Ryan Wilson might benefit from writing a blog post for a tire company about how to service your fleet's brakes to make your tires last longer. That tire company might in turn write a post for Ryan's blog about which tires hold up best in inclement weather. In this way, both you and the brand you're partnering with get cross-promotion.

When you contact brands to write guest blogs or appear on podcasts, point out the cross-promotion effects. Be sure to show them your past work (any of your cornerstone content will do) and share your email and/or text message list size in addition to your follower counts. Don't hesitate to share your ripple effect with them. For an example about how to quantify that effect, see Dr. Lisa Hornick's story in Chapter 2.

Making the Pitch

You've already written half your pitch: It's your story-based BIO and fact-based paragraph. To complete the pitch email/DM, start your message with a paragraph about what you intend to cover and why you think the person you're writing to would benefit from cross-promotion with your brand. This should give you a great start with minimal effort.

The Nano-Influencer Network

A nano-influencer is anyone with fewer than ten thousand followers. While that may sound small in the world of viral content, nano-influencers often have a much greater impact per follower than larger accounts. Why? Because smaller audiences mean greater intimacy. They've likely met or personally interacted with many of the people who follow them, which creates higher trust and engagement.

That intimacy fuels social proof. When someone sees a trusted peer or someone just a few degrees removed endorsing a product, idea, or mission, the influence is stronger than a generic ad or celebrity post. Studies show that consumers perceive recommendations from nano-influencers as more authentic and reliable than traditional ads or celebrity endorsements.[10] I'd much rather people post to a couple hundred people who trust them than to hundreds or thousands who followed on a whim. Try cross-posting with influencers who complement your brand, and remember, you're an influencer too. If you have even a few followers, you have influence, so be sure to reciprocate.

A New Approach to Advertising

Digital ads on platforms like Meta can accelerate audience growth, especially when grounded in human psychology. Instead of jumping straight to the call to action, begin with a low-friction content ad, like a brief informational video or educational post where you introduce yourself and deliver something valuable, *without* asking for an opt-in. Video-view campaigns tend to cost less per engagement than click-based ads, and they allow your audience to self-select into your funnel. Next, retarget anyone who watched at least ten to fifteen seconds of that content. These "warm leads" have shown genuine interest, making them far more receptive to opting in on the next ad. Because they're already familiar with you, your cost per acquisition (CPA) with this layered ad strategy is dramatically lower than targeting cold audiences with an opt-in ask directly the first time.[11]

This approach also mirrors how trust naturally forms: through repeated exposure and providing value before any ask (this is the same way you are building your brand organically). By leading with teaching, you replicate real-world rapport online and the actions that helped you grow without ads in the first place. Layered retargeting campaigns consistently achieve click-through rates nearly ten times higher than cold-audience campaigns, with better conversion rates, as well.[12]

In short, even though this method uses multiple ad steps, the tighter targeting of warm leads reduces your overall ad spend and builds a more engaged, responsive list. Ironically, most marketers still spend the majority of their ad budgets targeting cold audiences. Since you are your own marketer, using a warm-lead funnel strategy gives you a distinct advantage in both cost and conversion.[13]

Maikhou Thao Is Using Service-First Visibility to Empower Hmong Women

Maikhou Thao didn't set out to be a disruptor, but it's the role she's most proud to own.

As a first-generation Hmong American, Maikhou grew up navigating the tension between honoring her heritage and questioning the gender norms within it. She remembers vividly the moment that crystalized her purpose: her father's funeral in 2017. "I felt completely silenced," she says. "The men made all the decisions. The women, including me, were expected to just listen and follow." That moment sparked a deep conviction: Hmong women deserve to lead, not just hide behind the scenes.

Today, through her role as Director of Movement Building Initiatives at Everyday Impact Consulting in Sacramento, Maikhou partners with nonprofits working across sectors like health equity, education, and environmental justice. Her work is already shaping leadership pipelines within these organizations, helping them recognize and invest in the leadership potential of women from marginalized communities.

Maikou has plans to take the service-first visibility she's built through these nonprofit partnerships and activities even further. Her TRUTH really stood out to me. It's a culturally responsive leadership model designed to support Hmong and AAPI women as they step into leadership roles. "We're not asking people to abandon their culture," she says. "We're asking them to expand it, to recognize that cultural pride and progress can coexist. Before this, the widely accepted belief was that it had to be one or the other."

In fact, her long-term goal is to launch her own organization dedicated to cultivating a new generation of Hmong women leaders. "I want to build a space I didn't have growing up," she says. "A space where women are encouraged to lead, be vocal, and challenge traditions that no longer serve us."

She envisions hundreds of Hmong and AAPI women stepping into leadership across sectors including education, tech, healthcare, and nonprofits, without feeling like they must choose between their cultural identity and their personal ambition. "We need to normalize seeing Hmong women in boardrooms, on panels, in decision-making spaces," she says.

Maikhou's impact is already felt. Her classmates, colleagues, and even older siblings describe her as a leader they look up to. One former roommate, now a social worker, credits Maikhou's mentorship and recommendation with helping her get into graduate school.

"My vision is to build a generation that doesn't have to unlearn what I did," Maikhou said. "I want women to show up as themselves: loud, proud, rooted in tradition, but not confined by it."

I hope Maikou's example shows you that you don't have to wait until you have a full-fledged service-first personal brand or business to form partnerships and spread your message. When Maikhou launches her brand and website officially, these experiences will be a catalyst to form her base and grow, whenever she takes that next step. If you're not ready to launch your entire brand yet, you can use this approach as well.

Surprising and Uncommon Marketing Approaches

Main Idea

This chapter reframes traditional marketing by showing how visibility can grow more naturally through community engagement, cross-promotion, and a revised approach to common practices.

Key Takeaways

- You don't have to rely on ads or headlines to be seen. Layer in less competitive visibility strategies like nonprofit partnerships, local events, and peer collaboration.

(continued)

(*continued*)

- Service-first visibility builds trust faster. Ryan Wilson's veterans-focused approach helped his brand gain traction with both clients and the media.
- In-person opportunities like speaking events and local press often lead to digital mentions, social shares, and credibility boosts.
- Tools like Source of Sources (a new version of HARO) help service-first personal brands get PR coverage without pitching cold.
- Guest blogging, podcasting, and cross-posting with other nano-influencers can drive visibility without requiring a huge following.
- Ads can still work, but warm-lead funnels using educational content first tend to convert better and cost less than targeting cold audiences.

Next Steps

Choose one visibility strategy that feels achievable right now: a non-profit partnership, a local event, a podcast outreach, or even a guest blog. Write a pitch using your story-based BIO and your TRUTH-based message. Bonus: Register for Source of Sources and keep an eye out for media requests that align with your expertise.

How Long Does This Take?

As you consider how you'll create your own service-first visibility, here are some time estimates:

- Pitching a podcast, blog, or local event: one hour
- Attending or speaking at a live event: two to four hours
- Drafting a guest blog or article: two hours
- Setting up Source of Sources: ten minutes

I recommend choosing one "earned visibility" action to complete this week, whether it's local or digital, and treat it like part of your brand building, not an afterthought.

14

Your Working Brand Plan

> I always thought branding was about standing out and I've never been someone who seeks that. It didn't dawn on me that standing out through service is both brand-building and proof of concept at the same time.
>
> —Shannon McPartland

"A perfect scenario would be that we have no unidentified bodies," Shannon McPartland says. "That my tissue storage room did not have jawbones of people who we're still wondering who they are."

I first introduced Shannon, a senior coroner technician, in Chapter 4. For more than two decades, she's worked in the aftermath of tragedy, helping families find closure after unimaginable loss. While she's witnessed the fallout of fires, overdoses, homicides, and disappearances, her future mission is as much about the living as it is the dead. "I want to give families closure and healing. I want every lost body to be sent home," she says.

Shannon's interest in forensic science began early. As an undergraduate at UC Davis, she pursued internships that would look good on her med school applications, an experience that reconnected her with an early passion. "I have always been interested in forensic science," she says. "Ever since

I was a young kid, I watched shows on Court TV and was fascinated by solving crimes through science." That curiosity led her to the Sacramento County Coroner's Office, where an internship turned into a career-defining calling.

Among the many cases she's worked on, one early case remains etched in her memory: a woman murdered in Oakland whose body had been buried in Natomas (a community within Sacramento). "We got a whole bunch of bags of dirt and were going through all the dirt looking for the bones," Shannon says. "It was amazing to be able to put her all back together. We found everything except for a kneecap, I think. Because of our work, they arrested the suspect, he was convicted, and the family got closure. I knew I'd found my career."

Not every case gets that kind of attention, though, and that's the problem Shannon wants to fix. As she brainstormed about her service-first personal brand, she realized that it's the cases that aren't associated with crimes that need the most help. Unlike the high-profile criminal investigations, which she calls the "*Dateline* cases," unidentified cases that involve everyday deaths are underfunded and often overlooked by professionals in the field. "Being a coroner is a hard job," Shannon says. "The emotional rush of solving a cold case or an active crime case is undeniable. But the fulfillment of reuniting families is unmatched."

As I mentioned in Chapter 4, this passion stemmed in part from Shannon's work on a 2018 wildfire in California. "Out of the eighteen sets of remains we worked on, we were able to bring seventeen families the closure they needed. When I reflected on that, I imagined how it would feel if I were missing someone from such an unexpected event. I would desperately want closure. I know this is not the type of closure people were hoping for, but it's better than the torture of wondering."

As Shannon formed her service-first personal brand plan, she thought about the need for a platform to raise awareness about the overlooked and underfunded everyday deaths. "I've done the same job for over twenty years, and I never really thought about starting anything on my own, but something shifted." After decades of service in a field that rarely gets public recognition, Shannon began to envision how her experience could serve a broader purpose. What if she could bring dignity to the thousands of unidentified individuals stored in coroners' offices around the country? "I would love to be able to start a brand that could help get these people identified," she says. "I just know this matters."

At first, she thought about her brand from the perspective of the families of lost loved ones, but then she pivoted. "I remember starting off with the idea to raise awareness to families, but it wasn't making sense," she recalls.

Then she thought of it from other coroners' point of view, and it became clearer. "I thought I would talk about the fulfillment of solving the unidentified everyday cases and shine the light on the bodies waiting to be returned home as a call to action to my industry . . . to get every piece of human remains off the shelves, crime or not," Shannon says. The idea sounded promising, but she still didn't feel like that alone would solve the whole problem.

As Shannon thought more about her long-term plan, she realized her brand needed to go deeper. She remembered a conversation she once had with another coroner who was passionate about identification work. "I wish someone would start a nonprofit," the colleague had said. And now Shannon understood why. "If I could both raise awareness and fund the everyday deaths that aren't currently prioritized, that fills a big gap," she says.

And if she can also figure out a way to identify remains not associated with crimes for less than $10,000 per case, "That would be the trifecta: to raise awareness, fund the gap, and figure out a way to keep the costs down when crimes aren't involved," she says. "It seems like we could streamline costs in the everyday cases."

To give a haunting example of why she's so passionate about this work, Shannon says, "We received a young man who died of an overdose. We had fingerprints, we had photos, we had all of his clothing, and nothing came back. His fingerprints didn't come back to anybody. But someone is missing him. How do we create a better system for those kinds of cases?"

This story fuels Shannon's core belief, "Every case is a cold case to somebody." She emphasizes, "Whether it's the justice system or just a family out there missing their loved one, it matters."

Shannon imagines a nonprofit that could support identification work by funding genetic testing, training staff, and raising awareness. "Awareness would come before the money," she says. "Most people don't know. They think about homicides. They don't think about people who have just. . .disappeared."

When Shannon launches her brand, she will define success by the reunifications her work helps achieve. "Each reunification will mean that we've achieved our three goals. We will have created awareness, raised the funds, and made the costs attainable enough," she says. "And I can guarantee that even though we weren't able to bring them back their loved one alive, the family will still be really grateful that we were able to tell them what happened. Closure matters so much."

You might recall from Chapter 4 that Shannon initially wasn't even sure she wanted a personal brand, but she changed her mind entirely when she realized that it wasn't the personal brand she didn't want, it was the hype she thought she had to engage in to grow it. "I always thought branding was about standing out and I've never been someone who seeks that. It didn't dawn on me that standing out through service is both brand-building and proof of concept at the same time."

If you've gotten this far in the book, you've already taken many steps to create a powerful, service-first personal brand. But sometimes it's the very last step, the working brand plan, that gives your brand concept final polish. Shannon, for example, first thought about targeting families of lost loved ones to gain awareness. Then she pivoted to others in her industry, like coroners and medical examiners, as a target audience. It wasn't until she zoomed out and thought about her long-term plan, though, that clarity came, and she realized that she wanted to have a way to fund her ideas as well. "I will raise awareness among coroners and medical examiners as I build my brand," she says, "but I will also foreshadow the future. I will talk about a future nonprofit, cost streamlining, and all the things we can do to actually make sure that all the jawbones go home."

When Shannon thought about the long-term and worked backward, everything made sense. There's massive value in zooming out and making a working brand plan. It's a simple, five-step slide deck that serves as your brand's blueprint for future success, and you can create it all through reverse engineering.

> **Wait, What?**
>
> A service-first personal brand without a plan is like a business without a strategy. "Reverse branding" gives you space to experiment, build trust, and validate your ideas. Meanwhile, planning with the long-term in mind helps you identify audience segments, content strategies, and future funding models, before you even need them.

Your Five-Slide Brand Plan

Service-first personal brands can evolve in two ways. You might be like Shannon and have plans to eventually become a consultant or business owner. Or you might want your service-first personal brand to help you move through your career by opening doors and boosting credibility.

Regardless, having a plan is important for determining both how your content will evolve and how you will measure your results. Brand plans run the gamut from simple to complex, but one thing most have in common is that the plans change as they grow. A simple five-slide brand plan is just enough to help you set your goals and vision. It doesn't take very much time to create and is easy to update as inevitable changes happen with growth.

Here's the overview:

- **Slide 1: Identity.** Include your name, logo, brand statement, and TRUTH answers.
- **Slide 2: Goal.** Define your five-year, one-year, one-month, and current actions. Update regularly.
- **Slide 3: Website map** (pull from Chapter 7).
- **Slide 4: First piece of cornerstone content** (pull from Chapter 8).
- **Slide 5: Funnel map** (pull from Chapter 9).

Notice anything? That's right: You've already done all this work. Now, all you have to do is put it all together into a short slide deck.

Slide 1: The Basics

Slide 1 will represent the basics of your service-first personal brand (see Figure 14.1). Divide it into quadrants:

- Upper left, brand name and URL.
- Upper right, logo.
- Lower left, brand statement.
- Lower right, your answers to the TRUTH framework in Chapter 4.

This slide will ultimately keep your brand on track.

BRAND PLAN TEMPLATE, SLIDE 1

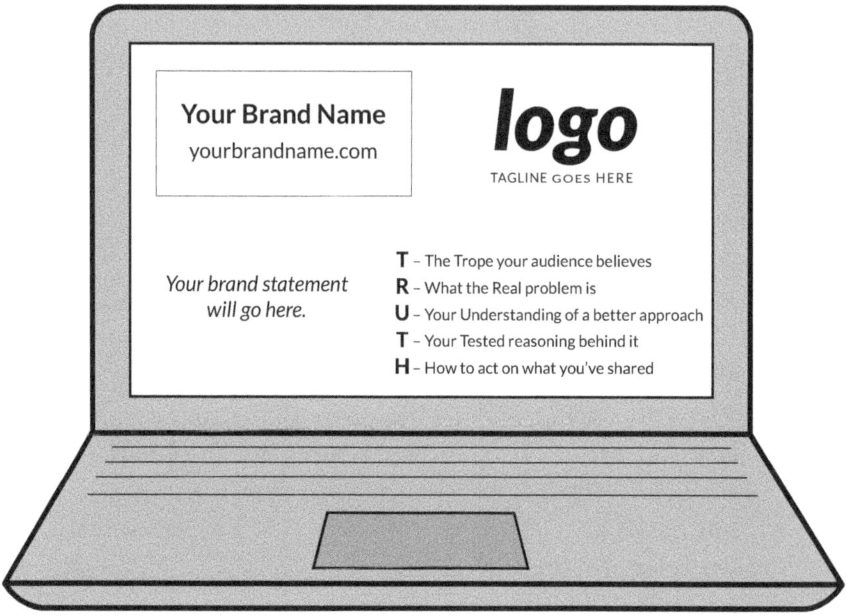

Figure 14.1 Use the first slide to describe your basic brand structure.

Shannon refers back to her brand statement often as she plans launch content. "I have it memorized," she says, "Through enhanced monetary resources, cost streamlining, and awareness, I empower coroners, medical examiners, and people who support the cause to return every body home."

Her TRUTH also helps keep her on track.

- **T (common trope):** Cold cases are the important ones.
- **R (real problem):** Dozens of everyday cases are going unidentified in coroners' offices.
- **U (understanding):** Every case is a cold case to someone, but we need more money and will to solve them.
- **T (tested reasoning and evidence):** Purpose and closure felt by both coroners and family members.
- **H (how to act):** Donate to the cause or join the cause.

"The bottom of the first slide is my motivation," Shannon says. "It keeps me goal-directed, and it powerfully and simply reminds me of my 'why.'"

Slide 2: Goals

The second slide should also be divided into quadrants (see Figure 14.2):

- Upper-left: five-year goals
- Upper right: one-year goals
- Lower left: one-month goals
- Lower right: what you're consistently doing right now

The bottom of this slide will be updated often. The top will be the anchor, guiding your short-term actions with your long-term goals.

Figure 14.2 Use the second slide of your brand plan to describe your brand goals.

In Shannon's case, her plans are as follows:

- **Five years:** Launch a nonprofit to bring all remains home. Establish myself as a trusted voice in body identification and funding for it.
- **One year:** Publish at least forty regular thought leadership posts on LinkedIn to grow credibility, test audience resonance, and help my industry understand the need for identifying the everyday cases.
- **One month:** Purchase URL, launch a website, complete twelve-week content calendar.
- **Today:** Begin drafting my first piece of cornerstone content.

When you make your goal slide, start with your five-year plan and work backward. Ask yourself: What do I need to do in a year, a month, and today to make this happen? To stay active working on your goals, change the bottom of slide 2 daily, and update it monthly when applicable.

Optional Slides

After you create your first two slides, pull in the rest of your brand plan. If you've followed the advice in the previous chapters, you already have it:

- In Chapter 7, you created a website map. That should be slide 3.
- In Chapter 8, you created your first piece of cornerstone content. That should be slide 4.
- In Chapter 9 you created a funnel map. That should be slide 5.

Together, these slides create a clear implementation plan.

Next, validate your five-slide brand plan with the ideal customers you interviewed in Chapter 3. What do they think? When Shannon did that, one of them told her, "I like how this also shows decision-makers the importance of funding decisions." Shannon took that information and immediately added county supervisors to her list of industry professionals, joining coroners and medical examiners. "If increased awareness leads to more legislative decisions to provide funding for all the remains and not just the cold case remains," she says, "that is a huge win for their families. I'll keep that audience in mind as I create content."

The Power of Reverse Branding

Shannon's story follows a path that yours might, too. She plans to lead with her service-first personal brand before launching her nonprofit. "The whole funnel you taught, that will build a coalition for starting my nonprofit. It will also help me find other resources like vendors for genetic identification," she says. "I never saw a business or a nonprofit as an extension of a personal brand, but now it seems like a natural progression."

She's right. This reversal has multiple benefits:

- It gives her time to find the right audience.
- It helps her test concepts without pressure to monetize right away.
- It allows her to refine her positioning through the analytics she collects.

By the time she's ready to scale, Shannon won't just have a business idea; she'll have a loyal audience, tested content, and clarity about what works. Her brand provides both proof of concept and a pipeline.

Set Benchmarks with Service

Perhaps Shannon's most important insight came at the very end of the process, when she talked about her excitement over identifying the first body through her nonprofit. "That will be the ultimate proof of concept, but then there's math to do," she says. "If we identify five bodies a month in the first year and get the costs down to $8,000 per body, we know that we need around half a million dollars a year to do this."

But Shannon acknowledges that her results only begin there. "Another result that's harder to measure, but that I hope to achieve just through my cornerstone content and thought leadership pieces, is that a coroner might find a reason to take an everyday case off the shelf. They might use my frameworks to advocate for why they need to do it. Maybe that will happen again and again."

Five-Year Plans Uncover Holes

If this book has helped you realize that you've already been building a service-first personal brand without knowing it, then you have something in common with Christine Nguyen. Her service-first personal brand, Pink Grubz, began as a creative outlet during her MBA program and blossomed into a community-minded food and lifestyle platform. A full-time project manager at Comcast by day, Christine uses her nights and weekends to spotlight small businesses and cultural experiences, particularly those rooted in her Asian American heritage. Her thoughtful, visually appealing, and family-friendly content serves as a digital scrapbook of where she's been and who she's supported. Whether it's restaurants, city events, or niche experiences like cake-building nights or mulberry-picking, Christine brings warmth and visibility to local gems that might otherwise be overlooked.

In fact, the heart of her brand is generosity, and she was passionate about supporting struggling restaurants during the pandemic. But as her brand, primarily established on Instagram and TikTok, grows, she wonders, "Is this still a hobby, or could it be something more?"

In other words, Christine finds herself right at the intersection of a passion project and a viable business. "I've started getting contracts and making some money for posting, but the long-term viability of this model makes me nervous, especially considering the uncertainty around TikTok's future." Christine has a point. Social media companies like TikTok often find themselves caught up in various cultural and political headwinds. If they aren't being required to divest from their founding company to continue operations in the United States (as TikTok was in the process of doing as I wrote this book), they may just be faddish and eventually fall out of style.

Knowing this, Christine made building infrastructure her next step, including a website, a logo, and a formal process for gathering leads. She's already experimenting with engagement strategies and cross-platform content and is exploring YouTube to diversify her income, as well. Finally, she's thinking about formalizing some sort of business-building consulting program "so that small, local brands can get help showcasing themselves through working with people like me."

Now, as Christine plans out her content, she's thinking about how to translate showcases into frameworks. "I am excited to diversify," she says. "I have several product ideas that are independent of social media. For example, a workbook on how to plan a trip around food discovery and off-the-beaten-path events could be a neat merchandise item to sell."

This idea only came to Christine when she thought about her five-year plan. "Thinking about the long-term is forcing me to think about the short-term," she commented.

You may not have a five-year plan mapped out yet like Christine. While it's common in business circles to create such a document, it's not essential to building your service-first personal brand. However, if you're pretty far down the service-first personal branding path, it never hurts to zoom out and make sure that the actions you're taking today are fulfilling the goals you have someday. Once Christine got aligned with her five-year plan, for example, she realized the importance of going back and designing a logo and creating a website, adding further dimensions to her brand.

> **Your Working Brand Plan, at a Glance**
>
> *Main Idea*
> This chapter explores how to turn your long-term vision into a strategic, visual brand plan that guides your actions today. A five-slide format outlines how brand clarity, goal setting, and reverse branding can generate traction, test ideas, and attract the right audience before monetization begins.
>
> *Key Takeaways*
> - Your brand plan should be simple: A five-slide system with your brand identity and goal timeline provides clarity and structure.
> - Reverse branding, which is building a service-first personal brand before launching a business, allows you to test ideas, gather feedback, and refine your message in public.
> - Your five-year vision often reveals strategic gaps (audiences, funding, and content strategy) that shape what actions you should take today.
>
> *(continued)*

(*continued*)

Next Steps

Create your own five-slide brand plan:

- Slide 1: Identity
- Slide 2: Goal
- Slide 3: Website map
- Slide 4: Cornerstone content
- Slide 5: Funnel map

Then validate your plan with ideal customers and use their feedback to refine your direction and positioning.

How Long Does This Take?

Time estimates per component of your working brand plan:

- Slide 1: thirty minutes
- Slide 2: thirty minutes
- Slides 3–5 (if done in earlier chapters): one hour
- Customer feedback: two to three hours

I recommend blocking out one full day to complete your slides, revisit your earlier brand work, and get validation from your target audience.

15

You'll Never Be Ready. Start Anyway

> My personal brand is this portable thing. Opportunities begin and end, but my brand is always with me, helping others and opening doors.
>
> —Leticia Garay

Leticia Garay lives with a condition called complex post-traumatic stress disorder, or C-PTSD. It's similar to post-traumatic stress disorder (PTSD), an anxiety condition triggered by a traumatic event in a single moment of time. But C-PTSD is different. It's an anxiety condition triggered by a series of traumatic events stretched over years.

I'll never forget meeting Leticia for the first time. She told me that one of the biggest reasons she was pursuing her graduate degree was to face her fears head-on after a nearly decade-long relationship left her feeling broken, unsure, and lost. Instead of keeping her struggles private, she said, she wanted to use them to raise awareness, "as vulnerable as that felt."

When she began her MBA, she also started an Instagram profile, @leticialivingincolor. It became a space where she could share her journey with C-PTSD and help others with the same condition or similar struggles feel less alone.

In class, she quickly realized that her profile could also be her service-first personal brand. "I knew that I was already talking about valuable things on my profile," she says, "but I couldn't be ignorant anymore. I knew I had to create a website, collect information about my audience, and get more structured about my content schedule."

Leticia told her TRUTH. And part of her truth had to do with defying the very definition of a diagnosis. She pointed out that even though people say they aren't defined by their mental health diagnosis, many immediately become fearful of what they can and can't do, and when they might break down next. Leticia challenged her audience to think differently; to see her, someone with C-PTSD, enrolled in a rigorous MBA program, showing up anyway.

She didn't just write about it. She modeled it.

In one blog post, she shared[1]:

> The thing is, I'm not crazy. And if you have a mental health diagnosis, you're not either. Stop gaslighting yourself (that's tough love, my love). Accept where you are, take the breath you've been holding (you didn't even know you were doing that, huh?), and give yourself grace. Now, you're ready to tackle not the world, not even the day, but just one step and one breath at a time. I am not C-PTSD. I just live through it. Sometimes it colors my personality, but it does not define me—it just changes the lens through which I see the world.

From there, Leticia made guides for others struggling with mental health issues. She started saying yes to speaking engagements. At one such engagement, she opened with: "I feel like an impostor being up here, and I am sharing this vulnerability because I know many of you share these feelings. But if you get any value out of what I say today, remember that you only heard it because I stopped gaslighting myself and came up here, despite my misgivings."

When Leticia started creating her service-first personal brand, she was working as a transfer student admissions officer at UC Davis while beginning her MBA there. As she wrote, she also achieved. She was given a prestigious leadership award from UC Davis and was ultimately selected as the class speaker at her graduation. Her topic? Vulnerability, taking chances, and resisting the urge to gaslight yourself.

As Leticia's brand grew, so did the ripple effects. "People would come up to me and thank me for sharing hard things. They would tell me they were suffering and finally made a breakthrough. Someone even said the words, 'Your writing saved me.'"

By the end of her MBA, Leticia came to another crossroads. She was burned out and decided to do another hard thing: quit the job she'd held for over a decade. During that time, she built her brand even more and was soon recruited to work in admissions for the MBA program she'd just completed. "It was a full-circle moment, and I was honored," she says.

As she shared with me later, Leticia attributes her success in pivoting careers to her work building a service-first personal brand. "My personal brand is this portable thing. Opportunities begin and end, but my brand is always with me, helping others and opening doors," she says. "It's a piece of security in a fast-paced world of constant change that can feel really insecure at times."

Her success didn't stop at landing a new job, either. Recently, she was invited to submit a proposal to speak at a university-wide conference about mental health and careers. "That's what I mean," she says. "There is so much impact to having a personal brand, both in your own growth and in other people's growth."

The Readiness Myth

Leticia's story proves it: Don't wait until you feel ready. Leticia sure didn't. She felt like an impostor, but she started anyway.

I wasn't ready when I set out to pivot my business from a time-for-money consultancy to a hybrid consultancy and professional training company. I started by setting up speaking opportunities, from national conferences to regional chambers of commerce to local Rotary clubs to online forums and more.

I'll never forget the first keynote speaking invitation I received, nearly a decade ago. This was a regional speaking opportunity in my own community. People who had been successfully in business for years were coming to learn from me. In a full-circle moment, I realized that one of my most influential mentors would even be there. Like Leticia, I, too, wondered if I really belonged there at all. In fact, the night before that speech, I was convinced I had a stomach bug as waves of nausea hit. At one point, I commented to my husband, "I can't believe how unlucky this is."

But I wasn't sick. I was terrified.

That keynote meant more than any professional endeavor or talk I'd given before. It wasn't just a speech—it was the launch of my new training programs. If it went well, doors would open. If it didn't, I'd stay stuck trading time for money only.

When I walked onstage the next morning, I still didn't feel ready. I cracked a bad joke, as I often do at the beginning of speeches and classes (it can only go up from there, right?) and loosened up.

Then I did what I teach every student and client to do: I told my TRUTH. I showed them why their marketing was too complicated, and I gave them tools to simplify it. I told them, "If this is the only time you ever see me in your life, I want you to walk away being able to do some of this."

I ended by asking everyone in the room to close their eyes and remember who they wanted to help when they went into their profession or created their business. I gave them permission to let that value be the crux of their visibility, rather than the mysterious pay-per-click, chatbot world that left them confused and tired.

"So can you do that instead?" I asked, "And trust that the value that you provide consistently will be the best and most fulfilling marketing program you've ever implemented?" I then gave them permission to open their eyes. I did too. . .but no one was sitting anymore. I was getting a standing ovation. My mentor bought trainings for his company. Dozens more lined up behind him.

That day taught me something I mentioned in Chapter 1 that I want to remind you to carry with you: It's not that you're an impostor or not ready, it's that you'll *never* feel ready to share something new. By definition, your ideas (which you worked hard on creating through your TRUTH) haven't been shared before. Of course it feels uncomfortable. Of course you doubt yourself. But that discomfort isn't a sign you're a fraud. It's a sign you're onto something worth sharing. Something for which there is no comparison or measuring stick yet, because your TRUTH is novel and valuable.

Leticia wasn't an impostor when she stood on stage and shared her TRUTH either. She was simply in uncharted territory. She was showing a new way to face C-PTSD. Rather than managing triggers, she encouraged others to invite them in and walk through them, one breath at a time.

Ordinary People, Extraordinary Impact

Every case study in this book has reinforced the same circumstance: ordinary people who didn't wait until they were "ready" to create extraordinary impact.

Take **Dr. Lisa Hornick.** At first, she worried that dry eye disease was too narrow, too unglamorous of a niche. Would anyone really care? She could have waited until she had more recognition, or a broader focus. Instead, she started sharing what she knew. Today, she's helped over seven million people live better lives and she's become the industry expert for the most complicated cases. Her brand began with what felt to her like "small" knowledge, but it became life-changing knowledge for others.

Or **Kevin Leung**, who set a goal to appear on *Survivor*. Kevin questioned whether he fit the mold. He didn't see people like himself reflected often in mainstream reality television. But the whole point was to break the mold, so he chose not to wait until he felt like he belonged, and went for it anyway. In doing so, he not only made his dream come true but also redefined representation for thousands of followers and millions of viewers. He proved that your brand can be as much about *who you are* as what you do.

Jennifer Anderson also began in what seemed like an unremarkable space: helping parents of picky eaters. She wasn't sure picky eating was a "big enough" topic to build a business around but made an Instagram profile to help some friends she knew must have also been struggling. She shared her TRUTH, that complexity wasn't always needed to "fix" picky eating, just an incremental approach with creative ideas. Today her content has reached millions of parents, she's expanded into other specialty areas, and families are finding joy at the dinner table again because Jennifer decided to begin.

For **Carrie Prince**, service-first personal branding began in the unexpected world of dating advice. She started by helping hundreds of clients navigate relationships and shared her insights on social media. Over time, she realized her frameworks for authentic communication weren't just about dating. They applied to leadership and professional growth, too. Carrie didn't wait until she had the perfect niche carved out. She started with what she knew, and her brand evolved. Now her work is transforming not just relationships, but boardrooms.

Marisol Ibarra didn't wait for a title or a corner office before she spoke. She shared her insights as a first-generation Latina balancing family obligations with professional ambition. She taught her audience about financial planning while supporting relatives, about showing up boldly in spaces where women like her were often underrepresented. At first, she doubted herself, but she kept going. Today, more than 40,000 people have learned from her content, and countless women have stepped more fully into leadership because she didn't wait to get her message out.

Tracy Fauver hated the idea of putting herself out there. But she had knowledge and approaches that could change lives, and she couldn't keep them inside. When she started showing up, everything changed. Her work has now helped hundreds of children in foster care find advocates, guided hundreds more experiencing homelessness toward housing and recovery, and created entire communities of allies. And she even began to *enjoy* video. Not because it felt completely comfortable and effortless, but because she saw the difference it made.

Taylor Stanton didn't think sharing his back-country images mattered. He was just one person with a camera, hiking through landscapes few others would ever see. At times, it felt self-indulgent to post his photos, but he shared anyway. Now, more than twenty million viewers have experienced those wild, inaccessible places through his lens. He turned private passion into a brand that expands people's imaginations and connections to the natural world.

And then there's **Christine Nguyen**, who could have stayed quiet when the pandemic threatened small businesses. Instead, she showcased them online, amplifying their voices and keeping doors open when they might otherwise have closed forever. Today, she continues to empower businesses with tools that will help them thrive for the long term. Her decision to start when it mattered most made all the difference.

None of those I've profiled were famous. None of them were "ready." Most of them also felt like impostors in uncharted territory. They were just like you and me. But they walked into the discomfort and started. And because they started, they changed lives, including their own.

Flip the Script on Your Limiting Beliefs

Still hesitating about starting your own service-first personal brand? Here is the truth behind common misconceptions.

Small Audiences Are Actually a Gift

Remember the 90–9–1 rule from Chapter 1? It states that on social media and online communities, 90 percent of people just watch. Nine percent engage occasionally. Only 1 percent post consistently.[2]

If you post once a week, you're already in the top 1 percent of visible contributors. And a small audience? That's your lab. You get to make mistakes in public with your closest people before thousands or millions of eyes are on you. How great is that?

You Have More Expertise Than You Think

In Chapters 4 and 5, I wrote that expertise is different from authority. Expertise isn't always about degrees and accolades, it's about *insight*. When Carter used baseball training as a metaphor for business school success, he redefined value. When Lisa Hornick challenged other optometrists and primary care doctors to stop using eye drops as a Band-Aid, she created a movement. When Leticia sought out triggers for her C-PTSD rather than avoiding them, she empowered others to follow along and join her. People stop scrolling when something sounds different.

What are your "Wait, what?" insights? Those are your expertise builders.

You're Already Online, but You're Not in Control

Still afraid to press *publish*? Consider this: You already have a digital footprint. People Google you. People search for you on social media. The question is: Do you want to control the story, or let others fill in the blanks?

People Will Say Mean Things. . . but That's a Good Sign

They will. Especially when your content starts gaining traction.

There is no single evidence-based strategy for how to respond. But here's what I know: Failing to prepare emotionally makes it harder. Instead, I suggest this:

- **Have a plan before it happens.** Will you respond or delete? If you respond, keep it to one comment and stop. And if you want to delete the comment, please do; despite arguments to the contrary, there's no evidence showing that's a bad strategy. So if it makes you feel better, just delete.
- **Decide what feedback gets your energy.** Constructive questions? Answer them. Cruel jabs? Delete.
- **Recognize that controversy creates traffic.** If people disagree, they comment. If they comment, algorithms prioritize the content. Conflict can fuel your visibility.
- **Use the growth as data.** If you're getting negative comments, that often means you're finally being seen. It's a milestone.
- **Add a simple boundary to your instructions to others.** Something like "Pause and reflect before you post" in your comments section can reduce toxicity, as found in a recent digital emotion regulation study.[3]

Most important: Don't let the fear of one person's comment keep you from helping a hundred others.

Keep Going Exactly When You Feel Like Giving Up

When you make your first few cornerstone content posts, you will undoubtedly feel a rush of excitement, amplified by any positive reactions to the post that comes with it. But there will inevitably be a time where things seem stagnant, or worse, a post doesn't get as much attention as your previous ones. This will make you tired, even panicked, and you'll likely want to give up. That initial success made you feel great, but now you're realizing you have a long way to go and you might not be as good as you thought at service-first personal branding. Welcome to the Dunning–Kruger effect (see Figure 15.1).

The Dunning–Kruger effect is a cognitive bias discovered by psychologists David Dunning and Justin Kruger, who found that people with low ability at a task often overestimate their competence.[4] In other words, the less you know, the more confident you feel. Therefore, as your knowledge grows (or as you do something longer), your confidence usually dips before it climbs again. That dip is where most people quit.

Now that you know this, the key is not to mistake awareness of what you don't know for failure. Feeling overwhelmed is not a sign to stop, it's actually a sign to keep going because it means that you're growing and gaining experience. And eventually, confidence will come with that, which will get you to the other side of the U-curve.

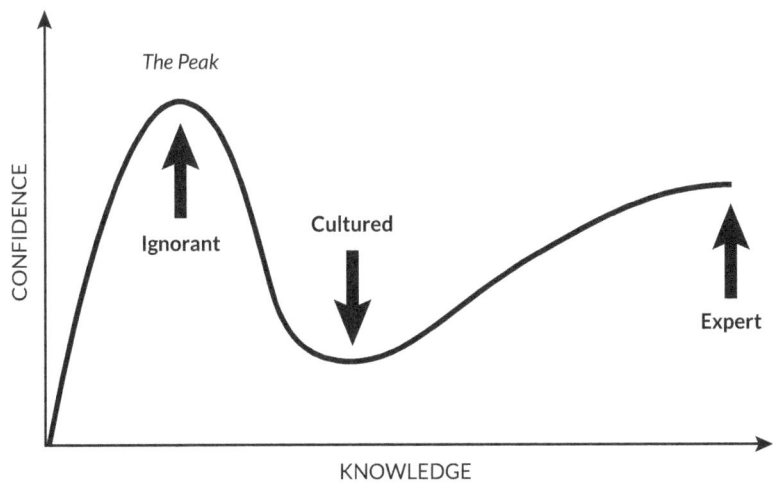

Figure 15.1 The Dunning–Kruger Effect illustrates that as you learn more, your initial confidence drops. With time, confidence increases as knowledge increases.

As you implement your service-first personal brand, it will be fun to brainstorm what that brand is and find your expertise. It will probably be fun to name your brand and make a logo, too. As you set up your website, make posts, set up list opt-ins, and all the rest of the detailed steps you need to follow, things will start to get complex. Please remember that when this happens, you are at the very bottom of the U-curve.

You are the only person who will get in the way of getting to the other side, so keep going.

Think Forward: The Future of Personal Branding

So where does all of this lead?

Life will change; that's the one guarantee we get. You'll change jobs. You might move across the country. Relationships may end. New ones may begin. Even your own ideas will shift with time. The ground beneath you will never stop moving. Rhythm and routine are fragile things in life.

But your service-first personal brand is different. Built on your TRUTH and your AEIOUs, it isn't fragile. It evolves with you. It doesn't evaporate when circumstances do. It's portable. It's yours. It's the thread you carry through transitions, setbacks, and reinventions.

Leticia proved this. Her brand carried her through burnout, through the leap of leaving a decade-long job, and into new opportunities she could not have predicted when she first started writing about C-PTSD. Each chapter of her life looked different, but her brand: her voice, her honesty, her TRUTH, endured.

This is bigger than personal shifts. The world itself is changing fast. Technology is rewriting the way we connect and share. AI now churns out words at lightning speed, compressing the internet into summaries of what most people already think. But here's the thing: Machines will generate content, while humans will still generate *trust*. Algorithms, especially those of large language models (LLMs), flatten the majority opinion into a blur. It's the novel, surprising, contrary ideas that break through, and that's where you come in. I want you to be the line worth highlighting, the perspective people stop to notice because it feels alive and new.

Life itself, not just the internet, is a series of questions in search of answers. Hungry? You ask where to eat. Confused at work? You search for insight. Facing a complex problem in your industry? You look for a new way forward. In every case, you gravitate toward those whose perspective you trust, and who can give you information you don't already know. In real life and on social media, your service-first personal brand tells your potential audience: *I am that person. I can help you find the answer.* On search engines and LLMs it tells them: "*Highlight this information.*"

That's why the future belongs to service-first personal brands. Not the loudest, trendiest, or most polished images, but the brands that are specific, sharp, helpful, and impactful.

As the future unfolds, reputation, not résumés, will be what opens the most doors. Already, employers search for information about you before they meet you. Already, collaborators and clients check your online presence before deciding whether to reach out. As AI continues to screen résumés and automate selection, your service-first personal brand will matter even more. It will be the pull marketing effect you create through it that bypasses the automation, or better yet, makes it unnecessary in the first place. People will think, "I know someone who would be great at this. Have you read his stuff?" Or, "I want to buy from her because she taught me how to use this." In short, you'll be recruited for the opportunity instead of having to fight for it. Christine Nguyen saw this firsthand when she began showcasing small restaurants online during the pandemic. Her reputation as someone who could elevate others preceded her, and she's sure it helped her get a corporate promotion.

Maybe when you opened this book, you doubted whether you had anything truly original to say. But look at what's happened. You've uncovered your TRUTH. You've clarified your AEIOUs. You've seen your own expertise emerge.

If a hundred people stood in a room, maybe ten of them would think they have something genuinely new to share off the bat. But my hope, and one of the reasons I wrote this book, is that following the simple guidance I've shared here would mean that every person in that group of one hundred would realize the uniqueness of their respective ideas.

For me, it all started with *The Hug*. That last moment, when Ella's heartbeat pressed against mine before it was enveloped in her first body cast and stolen from my reach. That was my turning point. Life was too short to wait until "someday."

And I hope you don't wait until someday, either. How could you feel more joy if you took a step toward pursuing your dreams now rather than later?

One more time for the people in the back: No one has ever been ready to share new things. The doubt you feel about sharing your novel information or point of view is proof you need to do it. You don't have to wait until you're ready because you never will be. None of us are.

Start today. Start with what you know. Start with who you are. Start with impact over image. That's your service-first personal brand: to make an impact for others, to show the world your value, and to unlock your authentic visibility.

> **Now It's Your Turn**
>
> If this book is the only time you ever interact with me in your life, my hope is that it will empower you to take at least some of what I've outlined with you to build your service-first personal brand. And if you'd like to keep learning more on your service-first personal branding journey, I'm here for you at vanessaerrecarte.com.

Appendix: Fifty-Two Power Prompts for Story Lead-Ins

Here are some prompts to inspire a year's worth of story lead-ins for your weekly cornerstone content, referenced in Chapter 10.

(1). I remember _____.
(2). I almost gave up when _____, but then I _____.
(3). I was never so scared as when _____, but I _____ anyway.
(4). I've never been happier than when _____.
(5). I am so proud of _____ because _____.
(6). I'll never forget when I made _____ mistake.
(7). My hero is _____ because _____.
(8). I love this _____ shortcut because it saves me time and sanity.
(9). The best advice I ever received was _____.
(10). When I can't sleep, it's usually because I'm thinking about _____.
(11). If I could pick anyone to meet, I'd choose _____.
(12). No one ever believes me when I tell them _____.
(13). To my younger self, I'd say _____.

(14). The biggest doubt I hear from _____ is _____.
(15). My most prized possession is _____ because _____.
(16). Don't tell _____, but I just _____.
(17). If I could talk to my _____-year-old self, I would say _____.
(18). _____ was my most memorable teacher because _____.
(19). I love _____ because _____.
(20). One piece of advice I didn't want to hear but needed was _____.
(21). My favorite season is _____ because _____.
(22). Right now, _____ is really bothering me because _____.
(23). I wish _____ were a word because I would use it all the time.
(24). When I really want to quit, I remind myself that _____.
(25). My day doesn't feel complete until I _____.
(26). One belief I've outgrown is _____.
(27). Whenever I eat _____, I'm reminded of _____.
(28). The scariest item on my bucket list is _____ because _____.
(29). _____ makes me feel vulnerable because _____.
(30). You'd never guess it by looking at me, but _____.
(31). _____ was a pivotal moment because I finally realized _____.
(32). My favorite ice cream flavor is _____—not for the taste, but because of the memory.
(33). Everyone believes _____ is true. But here's why I disagree.
(34). To me, happiness means _____.
(35). _____ was a life-changer for me.
(36). I used to think _____, but now I think _____.
(37). My happiest moment last week was _____.
(38). My most frustrating moment last week was _____.
(39). I feel most confident when I'm _____.
(40). I ate _____ for breakfast, and it reminded me of _____.
(41). My favorite kind of weather is _____ because _____.
(42). My favorite holiday is _____ because _____.
(43). _____ is something I'd really like to forget.
(44). I can't wait for _____ because _____.
(45). When it all comes down to it, I think _____ is really about _____.
(46). My favorite color is _____ because _____.

Appendix: Fifty-Two Power Prompts for Story Lead-Ins 229

(47). I just finished watching _____, and now I can't stop thinking about _____.
(48). The scariest goal I have right now is _____.
(49). My best friend understands that I _____.
(50). My favorite sport is _____ because _____.
(51). One thing I've never said out loud (until now) is _____.
(52). I never imagined I would _____, but here I am.

Notes

Chapter 1: Redefining Personal Branding

1. Todd Rose, "This One Research Study Will Change How You Think About Your Entire Life," interview by Mel Robbins, *The Mel Robbins Podcast,* 143 Studios, 29 September 2025, video, 1:27:57, https://www.melrobbins.com/episode/episode-329/.
2. Jakob Nielsen, "The 90–9–1 Rule for Participation Inequality in Social Media and Online Communities." Nielsen Norman Group, 8 October 2006, https://www.nngroup.com/articles/participation-inequality/
3. Roger E. Bohn and James E. Short, *How Much Information? 2009 Report on American Consumers* (University of California, San Diego, 2009), https://www.researchgate.net/publication/242562463_How_Much_Information_2009_Report_on_American_Consumers.

Chapter 2: Your Vision, Their Breakthrough

1. WellBiz Brands, "Drybar." *WellBiz Brands*. Accessed November 2025. https://www.wellbizbrands.com/our-brands/drybar/
2. Bloomberg News, "FIGS Shares Surge in Debut After $4.4 Billion IPO." *Bloomberg*, 27 May 2021.
3. Megan Thomas, "How Figs Founders Built a $4 Billion Business Modernizing Medical Scrubs." *CNBC Make It*, 1 June 2021.
4. Ayşegül Acar et al., "The Role of Brand Identity, Brand Lifestyle Congruence, and Brand Satisfaction on Repurchase Intention: A

Multi-Group Structural Equation Model." *Humanities and Social Sciences Communications* 11, no. 1 (2024): 1102. https://doi.org/10.1057/s41599-024-03618-w.
5. Sheryl Sandberg. *Lean In: Women, Work, and the Will to Lead*. (Alfred A. Knopf, 2013).
6. Jennifer L. Aaker, "Dimensions of Brand Personality." *Journal of Marketing Research* 34, no. 3 (1997): 347–356. https://doi.org/10.2307/3151897.

Chapter 3: Audience First, Always

1. Andrew Hargadon, *How Breakthroughs Happen: The Surprising Truth About How Companies Innovate*. (Harvard Business School Press, 2003).
2. Joni Salminen et al., "Use Cases for Design Personas: A Systematic Review and New Frontiers." *Proceedings of the 2022 CHI Conference on Human Factors in Computing Systems*. https://doi.org/10.1145/3491102.3517589.

Chapter 4: Tell the TRUTH to Stop Their Scroll

1. David Rock, *Your Brain at Work: Strategies for Overcoming Distraction, Regaining Focus, and Working Smarter All Day Long* (Harper Business, 2009).
2. Pablo Briñol, Michael J. McCaslin, and Richard E. Petty, "Self-Generated Persuasion: Effects of the Target and Direction of Arguments." *Journal of Personality and Social Psychology* 102, no. 5 (2012): 925–940. https://doi.org/10.1037/a0027231.
3. Robert B. Cialdini, *Influence: Science and Practice*. 5th ed. (Allyn & Bacon, 2009).
4. Source: Kids Eat in Color Instagram Post: https://www.instagram.com/p/DEVf897Bodp/. Used with permission.

Chapter 5: Add Relatability to the TRUTH

1. Jonah Berger, *Contagious: Why Things Catch On* (Simon & Schuster, 2013).
2. Valarie A. Zeithaml, "Consumer Perceptions of Price, Quality, and Value: A Means-End Model and Synthesis of Evidence." *Journal of Marketing* 52, no. 3 (July 1988): 2–22. https://doi.org/10.2307/1251446.

3. Robert B. Cialdini, *Influence: The Psychology of Persuasion*, rev. ed. (Harper Business, 2006), 143, 178.
4. Shailendra P. Jain and Steven S. Posavac, "Pre-Purchase Attribute Verifiability, Source Credibility, and Persuasion." *Journal of Consumer Psychology* 11, no. 3 (2001): 169–180. https://doi.org/10.2139/ssrn.256230
5. Brené Brown, "The Power of Vulnerability," transcript, Farnam Street. Accessed 2 July 2025. https://fs.blog/great-talks/power-vulnerability-brene-brown/
6. Jennifer Anderson, *Instagram*, 5 March 2025. https://www.instagram.com/reel/DHbIU3CAUgk/

Chapter 6: Name and Claim What You Stand For

1. Yanhui Zhao, Roger J. Calantone, and Clay M. Voorhees, "Identity Change vs. Strategy Change: The Effects of Rebranding Announcements on Stock Returns." *Journal of the Academy of Marketing Science* 46, no. 5 (2018): 795–812. https://doi.org/10.1007/s11747-018-0579-4
2. Yanhui Zhao, Roger. J. Calantone, and Clay Voorhees, "Identity Change or Business Model Change? The Effects of Rebranding Announcements on Stock Returns." *Journal of the Academy of Marketing Science* 46, no. 5 (2018): 795–814.
3. Saim Kashmiri and Vijay Mahajan, The Name's the Game: Does Marketing Impact the Value of Corporate Name Changes? *Journal of Business Research* 68, no. 2 (2015): 281–290. https://doi.org/10.1016/j.jbusres.2014.07.007
4. Véronique Pauwels-Delassus and Raluca Mogos Descotes, "Brand Name Change: Can Trust and Loyalty Be Transferred?" *Journal of Brand Management* 20, no. 8 (2013): 656–669. https://doi.org/10.30656/lontar.v10i2.4948.
5. Bylon Abeeku Bamfo, Courage Simon Kofi Dogbe, and Charles Osei-Wusu, "The Effects of Corporate Rebranding on Customer Satisfaction and Loyalty." *Cogent Business & Management* 5, no. 1 (2018): 1413970. https://doi.org/10.1080/23311975.2017.1413970.
6. Laurent Muzellec and Mary Lambkin, "Corporate Rebranding: Destroying, Transferring or Creating Brand Equity?" *European Journal of Marketing* 40, no. 7/8 (2006): 803–824.

7. Dig Insights, *"Apple's Logo: The Evolution of The Iconic Shape."* DigInsights.com. Accessed 29 December 2025. https://diginsights.com/resources/apple-logo-evolution/
8. Susan M. Fournier et al., "Naming the Brand," Harvard Business School Teaching Note 502-029 (Harvard Business School Publishing, 2002).
9. Felipe M. Affonso and Chris Janiszewski, "Marketing by Design: The Influence of Perceptual Structure on Brand Performance." *Journal of Marketing* 87, no. 5 (2023): 736–754. https://doi.org/10.1177/00222429221142281
10. Jonathan Luffarelli, Mudra Mukesh, and Ammara Mahmood, "The Influence of Logo Descriptiveness on Brand Equity (Let the Logo Do the Talking)." *Journal of Marketing Research* 56, no. 5 (2019): 862–878. https://doi.org/10.1177/0022243719845000
11. "Color Wheel – Color Theory and Calculator," Canva. Accessed 16 November 2025. https://www.canva.com/colors/color-wheel/
12. Straits Research, "The Key Role of Color in Branding and Marketing," 27 June 2024. https://straitsresearch.com/statistic/role-of-color-in-branding-and-marketing
13. Jill Morton, *A Guide to Color Symbolism* (Colorcom, Honolulu, 2010). (Based on the Global Color Survey and the website ColorMatters.com.)

Chapter 7: From Digital Renter to Digital Owner

1. Sheena S. Iyengar and Mark R. Lepper, "When Choice Is Demotivating: Can One Desire Too Much of a Good Thing?" *Journal of Personality and Social Psychology* 79, no. 6 (2000): 995–1006. https://doi.org/10.1037/0022-3514.79.6.995
2. Alexandre N. Tuch, et al., "The Role of Visual Complexity and Prototypicality Regarding First Impression of Websites." *International Journal of Human–Computer Studies* 70, no. 11 (2012): 794–811. https://doi.org/10.1016/j.ijhcs.2012.06.003
3. Barry Schwartz, *The Paradox of Choice: Why More Is Less,* revised edition, (Ecco, 2016).
4. Patrick Spenner and Karen Freeman, "To Keep Your Customers, Keep It Simple," *Harvard Business Review,* May 2012, 108–114. https://hbr.org/2012/05/to-keep-your-customers-keep-it-simple.

5. "Ultimate Email Marketing Benchmarks for 2022: By Industry and Day," Campaign Monitor. https://www.campaignmonitor.com/resources/guides/email-marketing-benchmarks/
6. "2022 Digital Trends Report," Hootsuite. https://www.hootsuite.com/resources/digital-trends
7. "Monetate Ecommerce Quarterly Benchmarks Q1 2022," Monetate, May 2002. https://monetate.com/resource/ecommerce-quarterly-benchmarks-q1-2022/
8. "20+ SMS Marketing Statistics (With Sources) to Know in 2025," Emarsys. https://emarsys.com/learn/blog/sms-marketing-statistics/
9. "43 SMS Marketing Statistics for 2025: Open Rates, CTRs & More," OptiMonk. https://www.optimonk.com/sms-marketing-statistics/
10. Nathan Ellering, "45+ texting and SMS marketing statistics to know in 2023," SimpleTexting (blog), 31 May 2023. https://simpletexting.com/blog/2023-texting-and-sms-marketing-statistics/.

Chapter 8: Frameworks and Your First Thought Leadership Piece

1. Richard E. Petty and John T. Cacioppo, "The Elaboration Likelihood Model of Persuasion." *Advances in Experimental Social Psychology*, 19 (1986): 123–205. https://doi.org/10.1016/S0065-2601(08)60214-2.
2. Rolf Reber, Norbert Schwarz, and Piotr Winkielman, "Processing Fluency and Aesthetic Pleasure: Is Beauty in the Perceiver's Processing Experience?" *Personality and Social Psychology Review* 8, no. 4 (2004): 364–382. https://doi.org/10.1207/s15327957pspr0804_3.
3. Agata Mirowska and Jbid Arsenyan, "Sweet Escape: The Role of Empathy in Social Media Engagement with Human versus Virtual Influencers." *International Journal of Human-Computer Studies* 174 (2023): 103008. https://doi.org/10.1016/j.ijhcs.2023.103008.

Chapter 9: Your Simplified Digital Funnel

1. Envive.ai, "40 Brand Voice Consistency Statistics in eCommerce in 2025." Accessed 17 November 2025. https://www.envive.ai/post/brand-voice-consistency-statistics-in-ecommerce.

2. Alicia Branham, "Mastering Social Media Marketing for Maximum Impact," *Supply House Times,* 11 July 2024. https://www.supplyht.com/articles/105963-mastering-social-media-marketing-for-maximum-impact.
3. HubSpot, Inc., *The 2025 State of Marketing Report.* Accessed 17 November 2025. https://www.hubspot.com/state-of-marketing.HubSpot
4. Alexandre Hoffmann, "Keyword Research for LLMs." *Passion Digital.* 28 March 2025. Accessed 17 November 2025. https://passion.digital/blog/keyword-research-for-llms/
5. Purpose Brand, "Super-Snippet SEO: Generative Engine Optimization for AI Overviews," *Purpose Brand Blog,* January 6, 2025. Accessed 14 July 2025. https://purposebrand.com/blog/super-snippet-seo-optimize-ai-overviews/.
6. SE Ranking. "How Videos Impact Your SEO Rankings." November 27, 2024. https://seranking.com/blog/videos-impact-seo-rankings/
7. Storykit. "Video for SEO: How Embedding Videos Boosts Your SEO Rankings." March 11, 2025. https://storykit.io/blog/video-for-seo
8. Business Insider Intelligence. "The Digital Trust Report 2023." *Business Insider,* 2023.
9. Jacqueline Zote, "26 Instagram Stats You Need to Know for 2025," Sprout blog, February 21, 2025. Accessed 14 July 2025. https://sproutsocial.com/insights/instagram-stats/.
10. Brent Barnhart, "26 Facebook Stats Marketers Should Know in 2025," Sprout blog, February 20, 2025. Accessed 14 July 2025. https://sproutsocial.com/insights/facebook-stats/.
11. Pamela Bump, "How (& Where) Consumers Discover Products on Social Media," HubSpot. Accessed 14 July 2025. https://blog.hubspot.com/marketing/social-media-product-research.
12. Cucu, Elena. "Zero Click Content for Social Media: Data & Insights." *Socialinsider Blog,* October 9, 2025. Accessed 17 November 2025. https://www.socialinsider.io/blog/zero-click-content.
13. Constant Contact. "SMS Marketing Statistics: The Numbers You Need to Know in 2024," updated 2024. https://www.constantcontact.com/blog/sms-marketing-statistics/.

Chapter 10: The Words That Power Your Funnel

1. Vanessa Errecarte, "Personalbranding #contentmarketing." *LinkedIn.* 23 May 2023. https://www.linkedin.com/posts/vanessa-errecarte_personalbranding-contentmarketing-activity-7326969277847080960-5Sj2
2. Paul J. Zak, "Why Inspired Stories Make Us React: The Neuroscience of Narrative." *Cerebrum* (February 2015). https://www.ncbi.nlm.nih.gov/pmc/articles/PMC4445577/.
3. Jennifer Aaker, *Harnessing the Power of Stories*, VMware Women's Leadership Innovation Lab. Accessed 14 July 2025. https://womensleadership.stanford.edu/node/796/harnessing-power-stories.
4. Raymond A. Mar, "Stories and the Promotion of Social Cognition." *Current Directions in Psychological Science* 27, no. 4 (2018): 257–262. https://doi.org/10.1177/0963721417749654
5. Jennifer Anderson, "Meet Jennifer." *Kids Eat in Color.* Accessed 17 November 2025. https://kidseatincolor.com/jennifer-founder-of-kids-eat-in-color/
6. Jamia Kenan, "Perfecting Your Edutainment Social Media Content Strategy." Sprout blog, 20 November 2024. https://sproutsocial.com/insights/edutainment-social-media/.
7. Natalie Slyman, "The Decline of Organic Reach: Are Social Media Ads the Only Way Forward?" Benchmark blog. Accessed 15 July 2025. https://www.benchmarkemail.com/blog/the-decline-of-organic-reach/.
8. Shani Orgad, "Posting Vulnerability on LinkedIn." *New Media & Society* 27, no. 8 (2024): 4822–4841. https://doi.org/10.1177/14614448241243094.
9. Brené Brown, *Daring Greatly: How the Courage to Be Vulnerable Transforms the Way We Live, Love, Parent, and Lead* (Avery Publishing Group, 2012).
10. Linda Lai and Audun Farbrot, "What Makes You Click? The Effect of Question Headlines on Readership in Computer-Mediated Communication." *Social Influence* 8, no. 4 (2013): 283–297. https://doi.org/10.1080/15534510.2013.847859
11. Jonah Berger, "Mastering the Art of Persuasion." *HBR IdeaCast,* episode 753, 11 August 2020, audio, 28 min., 04 seconds. https://hbr.org/

podcast/2020/08/mastering-the-art-of-persuasion. This episode features Wharton professor Jonah Berger's advice on using questions to foster autonomy and reduce reactance when persuading others.

12. Sagar Malviya, "Influencer Content Holds Attention Significantly Longer Than Traditional Branded Content: Kantar." *Economic Times*, 11 July 2025. https://economictimes.indiatimes.com/industry/media/entertainment/influencer-content-holds-attention-significantly-longer-than-traditional-branded-content-kantar/articleshow/122387073.cms.

13. Jonah Berger and Katherine L. Milkman, "What Makes Online Content Viral?" *Journal of Marketing Research* 49, no. 2 (2012): 192–205. https://doi.org/10.1509/jmr.10.0353.

14. Terri Walter, "From Clicks to Engagement: The Enhanced Art of Writing Headlines." Digital Content Next blog, 13 November 2017. https://digitalcontentnext.org/blog/2017/11/13/clicks-engagement-enhanced-art-writing-headlines/.

15. Beth A. Bechky and Gerald F. Davis, "Resisting the Algorithmic Management of Science: Craft and Community After Generative AI." *Administrative Science Quarterly* 70, no. 1 (2024): 1–22. https://doi.org/10.1177/00018392241304403.

Chapter 11: The FaceTime Effect

1. Vincent J. Felitti et al., "Relationship of Childhood Abuse and Household Dysfunction to Many of the Leading Causes of Death in Adults: The Adverse Childhood Experiences (ACE) Study." *American Journal of Preventive Medicine* 14, no. 4 (1998): 245–258. https://doi.org/10.1016/S0749-3797(98)00017-8

2. Khalil Israfilzade and Sakina Baghirova, "Comparing the Impact of Brand and User-Generated Video Content on Online Shoppers' Purchasing Intentions." *Management of Organizations: Systematic Research* 88, vol. 1: (2022) 69–84. https://doi.org/10.2478/mosr-2022-0013

3. Y. Jiang, et al., "Do 'Flops' Enhance Authenticity? The Impact of Influencers' Proactive Failure Disclosures on Purchase Intentions." *Behavioral Sciences* 15, no. 7 (2025): 971.

4. Elliot Aronson, Ben Willerman, and Joanne Floyd, "The Effect of a Pratfall on Increasing Personal Attractiveness." *Psychonomic Science* 4, no. 11 (1966): 227–228. https://doi.org/10.3758/BF03342263.
5. Kizilcec, René F., Kathryn Papadopoulos, and Lalida Sritanyaratana, "Showing Face in Video Instruction: Effects on Information Retention, Visual Attention, and Affect." In *Proceedings of the SIGCHI Conference on Human Factors in Computing Systems*, (2014): 2095–2102. https://doi.org/10.1145/2556288.2557207
6. Yi Huang and Siti Hajar Mohamad, "Examining the Impact of Parasocial Interaction and Social Presence on Impulsive Purchase in Live Streaming Commerce Context." *Frontiers in Communication* 10 (2025): 1554681. https://doi.org/10.3389/fcomm.2025.1554681.
7. Kang, Sean H. K. "Spaced Repetition Promotes Efficient and Effective Learning: Policy Implications for Instruction." *Policy Insights from the Behavioral and Brain Sciences* 3, no. 1 (2016): 12–19. https://doi.org/10.1177/2372732215624708
8. Jason Ingyu Choi and Eugene Agichtein, "Quantifying the Effects of Prosody Modulation on User Engagement and Satisfaction in Conversational Systems," *CHIIR '20: Proceedings of the 2020 Conference on Human Information Interaction and Retrieval* (ACM, 2020). https://arxiv.org/abs/2006.01916.
9. Andrew Hutchinson, "LinkedIn Has Outlined Its Recent Algorithm Updates, Which Focus on Broadening Content Formats," *Social Media Today*, June 26, 2019. Accessed July 2025. https://www.socialmediatoday.com/news/linkedin-has-outlined-its-recent-algorithm-updates-which-focus-on-broadeni/557609/.
10. Jenn Herman, "How to Improve Instagram Post Engagement: 4 Tips." *Social Media Examiner*, May 27, 2020. https://www.socialmediaexaminer.com/how-to-improve-instagram-post-engagement-4-tips/.
11. Chahboun, Sobh, Andrea Flumini, Carmen Pérez González, I. Chris McManus, and Julio Santiago. "Reading and Writing Direction Effects on the Aesthetic Appreciation of Photographs." *Laterality: Asymmetries of Body, Brain and Cognition* 22, no. 3 (2017): 313–339. https://doi.org/10.1080/1357650X.2016.1196214
12. Nittono, Hiroshi, Haruka Shibata, Keita Mizuhara, and Shiri Lieber-Milo. "Which Side Looks Better? Cultural Differences in Preference

for Left- or Right-Facing Objects." *Symmetry* 12, no. 10 (2020): 1658. https://doi.org/10.3390/sym12101658
13. Alexis D. J. Makin, et al. "Spontaneous Ocular Scanning of Visual Symmetry Is Similar During Classification and Evaluation Tasks." *i-Perception* 11, no. 5 (2020): 1–12. https://doi.org/10.1177/2041669520946356.

Chapter 12: Should I Charge for This?

1. Eric Ries, *The Lean Startup: How Today's Entrepreneurs Use Continuous Innovation to Create Radically Successful Businesses* (Crown Business, 2011).
2. Per the U.S. Copyright Office, copyright exists from the moment the work is "created and fixed in a tangible form." Accessed 22 July 2025. https://www.copyright.gov/help/faq/faq-general.html.
3. Gail Cole, "State-by-State Guide to the Taxability of Digital Products." Avalara Blog (North America), 1 August 2025. Accessed 18 November 2025. https://www.avalara.com/blog/en/north-america/2019/02/state-by-state-guide-to-digital-products-and-sales-tax.html.
4. South Dakota v. Wayfair, Inc. 585 U.S. ___ (2018). https://www.law.cornell.edu/supremecourt/text/17-494.
5. HubSpot, "16 Landing Page Statistics For Businesses." HubSpot Blog, November 24, 2023. Accessed 18 November 2025. https://blog.hubspot.com/marketing/landing-page-stats.
6. Marcin Hylewski, Artur Pluskota, and Błażej Abel, "The Effect of Landing Page Design and Structure on Conversion Rates." *Applied Marketing Analytics: The Peer-Reviewed Journal* 10, no. 4 (2025): 324–335. https://doi.org/10.69554/ANNV1551.

Chapter 13: Surprising and Uncommon Marketing Strategies

1. Ron Marshall, "How Many Ads Do You See in One Day?" Red Crow Marketing, 10 September 2015. https://www.redcrowmarketing.com/blog/many-ads-see-one-day/.
2. Albert Badalyan, "How Many Ads Do We See a Day—Top Trend & Statistics." Digital Silk, 30 June 2025. Accessed 24 July 2025. https://www.digitalsilk.com/digital-trends/how-many-ads-do-we-see-a-day/.

3. David Aaker, *Aaker on Branding: 20 Principles That Drive Success* (Morgan James Publishing, 2014).
4. David A. Aaker, *The Future of Purpose-Driven Branding: Signature Programs That Impact & Inspire Both Business and Society* (Morgan James Publishing, 2022).
5. Amy Novotney, "The Risks of Social Isolation." *Monitor on Psychology* 50, no. 5 (May 2019): 32–36. https://www.apa.org/monitor/2019/05/ce-corner-isolation.
6. McKinsey & Company, *Reimagining the Role of Physical Stores in an Omnichannel Distribution Network* (McKinsey & Company, July 2021).
7. S. B. Barnett and M. Cerf, "A Ticket for Your Thoughts: Method for Predicting Content Recall and Sales Using Neural Similarity of Moviegoers." *Journal of Consumer Research,* 44, vol 1 (2017): 160–181. https://psycnet.apa.org/record/2017-25852-009
8. Robert B. Cialdini, *Influence: The Psychology of Persuasion,* Rev. ed. (Harper Business, 2021).
9. Google Search Central, *Search Engine Optimization (SEO) Starter Guide* (Google, 2024). https://developers.google.com/search/docs/fundamentals/seo-starter-guide.
10. Marijke de Veirman, Veroline Cauberghe, and Liselot Hudders, "Marketing through Instagram Influencers: The Impact of Number of Followers and Product Divergence on Brand Attitude." *International Journal of Advertising* 36, no. 5 (2017): 798–828. https://www.tandfonline.com/doi/full/10.1080/02650487.2017.1348035
11. Manisha Saini, "50+ Retargeting Statistics Marketers Need to Know in 2025." Accessed July 2025, CropInk. Retargeting campaigns deliver a 50 % lower cost-per-acquisition than traditional ads and 10x higher CTR.
12. AdSpyder, "Don't Let Potential Customers Slip Away: Master Retargeting Ads." Accessed July 2025. https://adspyder.io/blog/dont-let-potential-customers-slip-away-master-retargeting-ads/. Retargeted visitors are 70 percent more likely to convert, CTR up to 400 percent higher.
13. Jon Loomer, "The 80–20 Rule: Facebook Ads, Remarketing, and Your Budget." *Jon Loomer Digital*, 1 June 2023. https://www.jonloomer.com/80-20-rule-facebook-ads-remarketing-and-your-budget/.

Chapter 15: You'll Never Be Ready. Start Anyway

1. Leticia V. Garay, "Complex Trauma (C-PTSD): The Gift That Keeps on Triggering." *Latina Living Blog*, 3 September 2025. https://leticialiving incolor.com/latinalivingblog/complex-trauma-c-ptsd-symptoms
2. Jakob Nielsen, "The 90–9–1 Rule for Participation Inequality in Social Media and Online Communities." Nielsen Norman Group, 8 October 2006. https://www.nngroup.com/articles/participation-inequality/
3. Akriti Verma, Shama Islam, Valeh Moghaddam, and Adnan Anwar, "Encouraging Emotion Regulation in Social Media Conversations Through Self-Reflection." *SSRN*, 13 March 2023. https://doi.org/10.2139/ssrn.4376558.
4. Justin Kruger and David Dunning, "Unskilled and Unaware of It: How Difficulties in Recognizing One's Own Incompetence Lead to Inflated Self-Assessments." *Journal of Personality and Social Psychology* 77, no. 6 (1999): 1121–1134. https://doi.org/10.1037/0022-3514.77.6.1121.

Acknowledgments

This book began as a belief that personal branding had been lost in a sea of self-promotion and vanity, and a conviction that we could make the world better by reframing it around service, impact, and genuine authenticity. It became a reality because of the support, insight, and shared belief of many remarkable people.

I am deeply grateful to Dean H. Rao Unnava, Associate Dean Joe Chen, and my colleagues at the UC Davis Graduate School of Management, who believed this idea was worthy of its own course. Their trust became the foundation on which *Valuable & Visible* was built. Thank you to Professor Andy Hargadon for giving me early insight into the trade nonfiction publishing process. To Amy Russell and Professors Mike Palazzolo and Ashwin Aravindakshan Nair, thank you for being a trio of texts, calls, coffees, or lunches away as I polled ideas and sought feedback.

A team of smart and dedicated people in the publishing industry helped me bring this book from concept to completion. My early framing for this book was strengthened considerably by Josh Bernoff, my developmental editor and thought partner. Josh helped me refine my concepts, clarify my voice, and navigate the publishing process. His wealth of knowledge, connections, and willingness to answer my "quick question" texts (many of which were not actually quick) made the process feel possible and success feel palpable.

I am also grateful to Jessica Guerrieri, a gifted fiction author and friend, whose candid advice and strategic encouragement helped me navigate the publishing landscape as a first-time author with both realism and heart.

This manuscript would not be what it is without Chas Hoppe, my developmental and line editor. His precision, insight, and steady encouragement added magical finishing touches that sharpened the message and strengthened the whole (and his sense of humor is truly awesome). And to Jessica Resnick, my copy editor, thank you for bringing a keen eye for detail that polished the manuscript to the point where I could finally stop having dreams about missing a typo.

Thank you to my team at Wiley: Shannon Vargo, Michelle Hacker, Jeanenne Ray, and Raven Buckler, who brought patience, professionalism, and genuine passion to this project. They treated this book with a level of care that helped it become its best.

My thanks also go to Sandra Smith, Emily Willette, and the team at Smith Publicity, who understood the heart of this book from our very first conversations and helped ensure it reached the readers it was meant for.

I feel incredibly fortunate for Heather Olah, my exceptional graphic designer and friend. She has an unmatched ability to turn complex ideas into clear, meaningful visuals, and to cheer me on while doing it. She also brought the cover of this book to life, never resting until we achieved the level of concept and refinement we desired.

To all of the incredible people whose case studies I featured in this book, thank you for trusting me with your stories, and for having the courage to put them out into the world. Lisa Hornick, DO, joined me for several idea sessions, offered thoughtful feedback, and poured over details with me as if the book were her own. Her insistence, along with Taylor Stanton, Tracy Fauver, Ryan Wilson, and Kevin Leung's that I write this book became calls to action I couldn't ignore, and I am grateful for that.

I am also fortunate to have a tribe of talented and dear friends who helped me make decisions about this book and refine its message and design. Rose Dixon and Eamonn Dickson, formidable scientists and professors at the UC Davis School of Medicine, thank you for spending hours workshopping my ideas and sharing your points of view. And Rose, thank you for being there with the right words of encouragement at the moments I needed them most.

Thank you to Karla Russek, MD, for being an early reader and believer, and for providing extensive feedback. Rhiannon Goodchild Mayor, thank you for your willingness to answer every phone call and weigh in with opinions, support, and positive energy. Christina Heath, thank you for the same, and for your help with the kids when deadlines ran late. And to Justin Heath, thank you for workshopping my ideas through the lens of one of the largest companies in the world.

I'm fortunate to be surrounded by these and many additional colleagues and friends who cheer loudly for one another's dreams. The support through every stage of this journey reminded me what community truly means, and I am grateful for every encouraging word, coffee, and reality check.

Finally, my family is my anchor, and none of what I do would be possible without them. My twin sister, Sara Dye, also an exceptional scientist and UC Davis professor, always offers an unwavering and energizing belief in me during the hardest stretches. This book was no exception. Her words, "If anyone can write this specific book on this specific topic, it's specifically you," became a mantra I returned to often.

I owe significant thanks to my parents, who have always enveloped me with support. My mom, Shirley Robinson, modeled excellence and passion as a devoted working mother at the highest levels, and was always there for me no matter what. She proved that purpose and love are not competing forces, but dual commitments that can enrich each other and create a life of extraordinary impact. In retirement, she pours that same unwavering dedication into her grandchildren (often at wild hours and with no notice) which is why I can have the career that I have and how I completed this book.

I am also grateful for my dad, Val Robinson, whose drive, determination, and entrepreneurial spirit showed me what is possible when you build something you believe in and constantly cheers me on as I build my own.

My husband, Jay, meets every one of my professional "really great ideas" with unwavering support, even when it adds significant chaos to our already full lives. This book was no exception. His belief in me has always outpaced my own, and the love and support in both words and action that he puts behind that belief is a gift that I have felt and appreciated every single day for nearly two decades.

To my daughter, Ella: thank you for the courage and healing, the resilience, the laughter, and The Hug that made me whole.

To my son, Jack: thank you for the steady presence, the snuggles, the joy, and the unforgettable jumbotron moment.

And to you both: thank you from the bottom of my heart for your patience during the many nights I said, "just a few more hours." I didn't step away from anything to write this book; I wove it into an already full schedule, and you navigated the whirlwind with remarkable generosity. When you asked me to bring a printed cover proof of it to show your friends at school, it moved me deeply. In that moment, I realized that you weren't just patient, kind, and guilt-assuaging through this process; you were proud of me, too. You are incredible souls and the reasons behind everything that matters most in my life.

Author Bio

Vanessa Errecarte, MA, MBA, is an award-winning lecturer and marketing consultant who created and teaches one of the nation's only for-credit MBA courses in personal branding at the UC Davis Graduate School of Management. She also teaches an array of other popular marketing courses and has been twice named Teacher of the Year. A Poets & Quants "Best & Brightest" MBA recognized her as a "favorite professor," and she considers it one of her life's greatest honors to be trusted by students as they chase their dreams.

For more than two decades, Vanessa has helped thousands of organizations and professionals clarify their value, stand out, and create meaningful impact. She is the founder of Marketing Simplified, a widely recognized consulting and training agency honored as Business of the Year, a frequent speaker at major industry events, and a contributor whose insights have appeared in the *Financial Times*. Dedicated to service, she lends her expertise to multiple boards and philanthropic efforts. Outside of work, she's happiest soaking up time with her family and friends—and earning the carbs she loves with her workout shoes.

Index

Note: Page numbers in italics indicate figures and tables.

Numerics
90-9-1 rule, 8

A
Aaker, David, 195
ABCs of Framework Creation, 114–16
   actionable, 114
   backup, 115
   core concept, 115
about page, websites, 101–2
advertisement, 199
AEIOUs, 70–1, 117, 145, 225
   authority, 65–6
   expertise, 66
   involvement, 66–7
   offer, 67
   outcomes, 69–70
   understanding, 67–8
AI tools, 131
analysis paralysis, 93
Anderson, Jennifer, 47–58, 66, 97, 148, 219
   counterintuitive approach, *49*
   educational content, 49
   meal plan, 50
   TRUTH framework, 52–6
Apple, 79, *79*, 126

architecture, brand websites, 93–104
   homepage, 93–4
   Opt-In, 96
audience, 37, 221

B
Babymoon Surrogacy, 61
batching calendar, 150, *150*
Bechky, Beth A., 154
behind-the-scenes posts, 152
Berger, Jonah, 63
BetterBites® picky eating program, 50
Beyond series, 178–9
   Beyond Arches, 178–9
   Beyond Canyonlands, 179
   Beyond Yosemite Valley, 178, 180
Bhattal, Armaan, 28, 186
biography
   Carrie's preview, *99*
   social media, 148–9
BioMat Transport, 60, 86
blog page, websites, 102
brand
   clarity, 20–1, *24,* 30
      accolades, 27
      attributes types, 26
      awards, 27
      credentials, 26
      extrinsic, 26

Index

brand (*continued*)
    intrinsic, 26
    lived experience, 26–7
    P/P self-interview for, 22–4
    qualifications, 26
    traditional certifications, 26
  naming/names, 78–9
    framework, 87–8
    logo, 83–4
    types of, 79–81
    WIP Up, 81–3
  plan, 207, 210, 213
    goals, 209, *209*
    structure, 207–8, *208*
  visibility, 12
  without customer, 35–6
Brown, Brené, 66–7
business websites, 106–7

C

call to action (CTA), 55, 136
Canva, for logo, 83–4
CARE framework, 120, 157
Cialdini, Robert, 65
clarity, brand, 20–1, *24,* 30, 111
  accolades, 27
  attributes types, 26
  awards, 27
  credentials, 26
  extrinsic, 26
  intrinsic, 26
  lived experience, 26–7
  P/P self-interview for, 22–4
  qualifications, 26
  traditional certifications, 26
coaching, type of, 98
Coca-Cola, 14
Coke Zero, 14
color, brand logo, 84–5
combination posts, 152
confidence, 111, 141
connection, 111
connotative, brand name, 80
consistency, 129, 135, 155, 182
contact page, websites, 102
content creation, 37
  brand statement, 27
  visibility boost, 13

cornerstone content, 129–30, *131,* 222
cost per acquisition (CPA), 199

D

Davis, Gerald F., 154
Delaney, Carter, 109–10
descriptive name, 79–80
design, brand logo, 83–4
digital ads, 199
digital footprint, 222
digital home, 91
direct messages (DMs), 37
Disney, 14
Drybar, 20–1
Dry Eye Guide, 17–18
Dunning, David, 223
Dunning–Kruger effect, 223, *223*

E

Elaboration Likelihood Model of Persuasion, 113
email, 136
  marketing, 103–4
engagement ratios, 180, 182, 183
EPIC Method, 7
  cultivating brand, 13
  definition, 11
  establishing brand, 11–12
  informing audience, 13
  packaging, 12–13
  road map, 15
  "Wait, what?" moments, 12, 20, 51
  see also brand
evidence-based strategy, 222
expertise, 51, 221

F

FaceTime approach, 35
face-to-camera videos, 160
Fauver, Tracy, 157, *163, 172,* 220
feedback, 6, 51, 183, 222
FIGS, 21
focal point, *171*
frameworks, 111–13
  ABCs of Framework Creation, 114–16
  AEIOUs, 117

CARE, 120
credibility, 113
   to leadership post, 117–18
   PITCH, 110
   Three Cs, 119
   Three Ws, 118
   TRUTH, 52, 55–6, 63, 116, 132, 154, 187
      how to act, 54–5
      real problem, 53
      tested reasoning, 54
      trope, 52–3
      understanding, 53–4
      website, 94

G

Garay, Leticia, 215–16
Garcia-Solano, Desiree, 59–65
growth and negative comments, 222
guest blogging and podcasting, 198

H

Hargadon, Andrew, 37, 38
Hasson, Heather, 21
Help a Reporter Out (HARO), 197
Here Comes the Sun (podcast), 126, 127
homepage, brand websites, 93–4
Hornick, Lisa, 17–19, 24, 28, 37, 43, 219
The Hug, 4–7, 15, 145, 225, 245

I

Ibarra, Marisol, 125–30, 220
ideal customers, 36, *42*
   audit your audience, 36–7
   customer call interview script, 38–9
   ideal customer avatar (ICA), 40–1, *41,* 45
   information vs transformation, 43
   interview reflection, 39
   as marketing tactic, 44
   mismatch, 43
   product, 41–2
   real audience, 44–5
impostor, 13–16
Influence, 65
influencers, 9
informational snippet, websites, 98, *99*
information vs transformation, 43

integration, brand name, 82
interviews
   vs self-interview, 25
   with trusted others, 25
intonation, 164–5
I Survived Bear Grylls, 34, 37

K

KevFitness Instagram, 34, *169–171*
Kids Eat In Color, 66, 148
   website header, *97*
Kruger, Justin, 223

L

large language models (LLMs), 131–2, 137, 196, 197, 224
leadership content, 134
   from long form to short form, 150
The Lean Startup, 179
Leung, Kevin, 33–6, 40, 53, 167, 219
   content, 167
lighting, video, 163–4
LinkedIn, 126
local media links, 196–7
local speaking opportunities, 195–6
logo, brand
   color, 84–5
   design, 83–4
   name with, 77–8
luggage company content, 181

M

Managing Innovation course, 38
map template, websites, *103*
marketing
   approaches, 201–2
   email, 103–4
   profession, 4–6
   and public relations plan, 194
   skills, 192
   strategies, 191–3
   text, 103–4
   theory, principle of, 92–3
Marketing Simplified, 5
McPartland, Shannon, 56–8, 203–6
media icons or scrolls, websites, 100

Index

memorization, 161
mistakes, 160
monetization, 182–3, 188
   checklist, 184
   incorporation, 184
   legal protection, 184–5
   sales tax requirements, 185
   tools for, 185–6
MVP approach, 178

N

naming/names, brand, 78–9
   connotative, 80
   descriptive name, 79–80
   framework, 87–8
   integration, 82
   logo, 83–4
   practicality, 82–3
   surname, 80–1
   types of, 79–81
   WIP Up, 81–3
   words, 81–2
nano-influencer network, 199
Nguyen, Christine, 211, 220–1

O

online-offline connection, 196
opt-in architecture, brand websites, 96, *98*

P

The Paradox of Choice, 93
performative support, 195
personal branding, 3, 48
   future of, 224–6
   service-first, 7–10
personal posts, 151–2
   redefining, 3–7
photos
   backgrounds, 172
   SPLASH, 168
      to avoid chaos, 169
      backgrounds, 172
      horizontal and vertical, 171
      left to right, 168
      points of interest and angles, 168
      segmentation, 168
      space, 170

Pink Grubz, 211
PITCH framework, 110
placement, face-to-camera video, 162
plan, brand, 207, 210, 213, 222
   goals, 209, *209*
   structure, 207–8, *208*
posts
   behind-the-scenes, 152
   be inquisitive with AI, 154
   combination, 152
   engaging, 152
   first sentence of, 153
   fun/pop culture, 153
   headlines, 153
   LinkedIn, 152
   observe others, 154
   opt-ins, 153
   personal, 151–2
   subject lines, 153
   types of, 151
practicality, brand name, 82–3
Prince, Carrie, 89–91, 137, 220
   brand, 137
   coaching website, *94, 95,*
      95–6, *99*
   leadership coaching, 97
   product, 41–2
   promotion, 10
prompts, story lead-ins, 227–9
pull marketing, 7, 225

R

Ramirez, Eddie, 75–8, 84, *84*
readiness myth, 217–18
rebranding, 78–9
redundancy, 129
Reis, Eric, 179
relatability, 63, 70
   emotion, 63
Reticular Activating System (RAS),
   51–2
reverse branding, 206
   benchmarks, 211
   five-year plans uncover holes, 211
   power of, 211
ripple effect, 217
Rose, Todd, 8
rule of thirds, 162–3, *163, 169*

S

Sabor y Soul, 77, *84*
   logo, *84*
Schwartz, Barry, 93, 170
script, 161–2, 221
scroll-stopping approach, 48
search engine optimization (SEO), 133, 160
self-interview, P/P for brand clarity, 22–4
self-promotion, 9
service-first personal branding, 7, *10*, 177
   AEIOUs, 70–1, 117, 145, 225
   clarity, 30
   ideal customers, 36
   knowledge sharing, 10
   monetize, 182–3
   MVP approach, 178
   P/P self-interview for brand clarity, 22–4, 30–1
   retreat, 21
   ripple effect, 29
   serving audience, 36
   statement, 27
   thought leadership, 10
   value of, 8–10
   visibility, 9–10, 15
   without customer, 35–6
service-first visibility, 194–5
   guest blogging and podcasting, 198
   local media links, 196–7
   local speaking opportunities, 195–6
   online-offline connection, 196
   source of sources, 197–8
Shankman, Peter, 197
Shopify, 104
simplicity, 128
sneak peeks, websites, 98–9, *100*
social currency, 63
social media, 4
   advocacy, 4
   baseline, 133–5
   biography, 148–9
   blog-style posts, 67
   cornerstone content, 147–8
   daily update, 19
   Ella's story, 3–7, *141*, 143–4
   influencer, 10
   involvement story, 145–7
   long-form content, 145–9
   thought leadership, 10
software, websites, 104–5
source of sources, 197–8
SPLASH, photos, 168
   to avoid chaos, 169
   backgrounds, 172
   horizontal and vertical, 171
   left to right, 168
   points of interest and angles, 168
   segmentation, 168
   space, 170
SPLIT method, 161–5, 173
Spotify, 126
Stanton, Taylor, 177, 220
Stop Overthinking, Start Executing concept, 110
surname, brand name, 80–1
Survivor, 33–5, 168, 219

T

text, 136
   marketing, 103–4
texting, 136
Thao, Maikhou, 200
Three Ws framework, 151
tripod, face-to-camera videos, 165
TRUTH framework, 52, 55–6, 63, 132, 154, 187
   how to act, 54–5
   real problem, 53
   tested reasoning, 54
   trope, 52–3
   understanding, 53–4
   website, 94

U

URL, 105

V

validation, 186
video
   SPLIT method, 173
   story lead-in, 173
   tips
      cut tool, 166
      deleting, 166
      editing tools, 165

video (*continued*)
  intonation, 164–5
  lighting, 163–4
  memorization, 161
  placement, 162
  practice, 166
  script, 161–2
  subtitles, 166
  tripod, 165
visibility
  boost, 13
  and controversy, 222
  ripple effect, 10
  service-first, 194–5
    guest blogging and podcasting, 198
    local media links, 196–7
    local speaking opportunities, 195–6
    online-offline connection, 196
    personal branding, 9–10
    source of sources, 197–8
vowels, 65–71

W
Webb, Alli, 20–1
websites, 92–3
  about page, 101–2
  architecture for brand, 93–104
    homepage, 93–4
    Opt-In, 96
  blog page, 102
  business, 106–7
  Carrie Prince Coaching website header, 95
  contact page, 102
  informational snippet, 98, *99*
  Kids Eat In Color website header, 97
  map template, *103*
  Marketing Simplified website header, 98
  media icons or scrolls, 100
  sneak peeks, 98–9, *100*
  software, choosing and integrating, 104–5
  TRUTH framework, 94
  URL, 105
  VABlog, 130–2
  You Can Date Better website header, 94
Wilson, Ryan, 106–7, 191, 198
WilsonTech Fleet Services, 193
WIP Up, 81–3
WordPress, 104
words, brand name, 81–2

Y
You Can Date Better website, 94
YouTube, 133